Commons Debates 1628

Volume I

The House of Commons, 1628

Commons Debates

1628

Volume I: Introduction and Reference Materials

Edited by
Robert C. Johnson, Mary Frear Keeler,
Maija Jansson Cole, and William B. Bidwell

The Yale Center for Parliamentary History

New Haven and London   Yale University Press

1977

Library of Congress catalog card number: 75–43321
International standard book number: 0–300–02033–3

Designed by John O. C. McCrillis
and set in Baskerville type.
Printed in the United States of America.

Published in Great Britain, Europe, Asia, and Africa by
Yale University Press, Ltd., London.
Distributed in Latin America by Kaiman & Polon,
Inc., New York City; in Australia and New Zealand by Book & Film
Services, Artarmon, N.S.W., Australia; in Japan by
Harper & Row, Publishers, Tokyo Office.

Permission to reproduce the frontispiece of the
House of Commons, 1628, has been granted by
the Society of Antiquarians, London.

The Yale Center for Parliamentary History

CONTENTS

Volume I

DIRECTORIAL
ACKNOWLEDGMENTS

The main roles of the Director of the Yale Center for Parliamentary History have been two: first, that of initiator of the Center and its main editorial effort to date, *Commons Debates 1628*, and, second, that of fund raiser for the Center and its editorial work. As initiator, he has enjoyed some success, of which the existence of the Center and the publication of these first volumes of *Commons Debates 1628* are the evidence; as money raiser, he alone knows the range of his failures and the depths of his ineptitude.

In his search for funds he has received and benefited from the wise advice of Professors John M. Blum, the late Frederick W. Hilles, George W. Pierson, Eugene D. Rostow, and John G. Simon, and of Mr. Lloyd Taft. Professors Blum and Rostow and Mr. Taft have intervened in behalf of the Yale Center with possible supporters.

At several times of especially acute need and fiscal disarray at the Center, it has received from the Yale Concilium on International and Area Studies and from the Yale University Library help toward paying for necessary student assistance and toward acquiring necessary books and microfilm. For their sympathetic response we owe our thanks to Joseph M. Goldsen, Director of the Concilium, and to Rutherford Rogers, University Librarian.

One of the few gratifying residues of the Director's quest for funding has been the meetings that it brought him to with Charles H. Taylor, Jr., Richard N. Cooper, and Hanna H. Gray, the truly notable people who have been successively Provosts of Yale University since 1964. At each such meeting the Director arrived with his hand open and extended, palm up. Occasionally he left with that palm as empty as when he entered the Provost's office, and a few times he left with

indispensable aid, especially the initial "seed money" grant to get the project started. Most important and so far not costly to the University, on four or five occasions he has received the promise of "backstopping", the assurance of a period of emergency help, should other resources fail to appear. Whatever the result of a particular sortie into the provostial domain, however, he has always had the enjoyable sense that he was dealing with sympathetic and thoughtful persons who would do what they could to help within the bounds of reason and the appropriate allocation of available resources.

The Director's first encounter after he joined the faculty in 1964 with Kingman Brewster, Jr., the President of Yale University, had to do with the former's hopes and proposal for reviving interest at Yale in the work on the preparation and publication of accounts of seventeenth-century parliaments, initiated years earlier by the late Professor Wallace Notestein. He will long remember with a mixture of gratification and rueful amusement Mr. Brewster's enthusiastic but in retrospect somewhat ambiguous response to the proposal, "You may be sure we are behind you".

Outside the University the Yale Center for Parliamentary History received help to support its editorial work on *Commons Debates 1628* from the American Council of Learned Societies, and from the American Philosophical Society, both in 1969–1970. The Director also enjoyed an attentive ear to his tales of woe and kindly advice from the former President of the Council, Frederick Burkhardt. To both organizations he is most grateful.

From the start, the most generous and steady support for the work of the Center has come from the National Endowment for the Humanities. In my relations with the Endowment it has been a particular pleasure and good fortune that my dealings have been with Dr. William R. Emerson, the first Director, Division of Research and Publication and his successor, Dr. Simone Reagor. They have been consistently helpful, sensible, and considerate. The current Chairman of the National Endowment, Dr. Ronald Berman, has been equally so, particularly in providing aid in the occasional crises that the editorial work of the Center has encountered. With such humane and intelligent people in these crucial positions at the National Endowment for the Humanities, the public and the scholarly community are both superbly served. Of the debts of the Yale Center for Parliamentary History to the National Endowment the deepest and most abiding, however, is to my old friend Dr. Barnaby C. G. Keeney, its first Chairman. With the perception of quality that is characteristic of him, and the capacity to do two things at once, one well and one badly, that is also characteristic of him, Dr. Keeney was able to grasp the scholarly merits of the editorial project I outlined to him and at the same time to go down to devastating defeat at the hands of a subordinate in a game of bottle pool. We will never see another like him.

To find funding for scholarly work in the humanities is difficult; to find it for the publication of such work, once completed, is nigh on to impossible. To people and institutions that lend a helping hand in such circumstances a special debt is owing. The Center is deeply grateful to the Yale University Press for its generous support toward the publication of the first three volumes of *Commons Debates 1628*. I am personally obliged to Helen Taft Manning for her contribution in honor of the late Wallace Notestein and to Robert Bergstein of Cincinnati for his gift made out of friendship to me. Finally, a most generous grant from the Snow Memorial Trust provided the Center with the means to proceed with the publication of *Commons Debates 1628*.

As Director, it has been my good fortune to work with many scholars on the Editorial Board and Advisory Council of the Yale Center for Parliamentary History who have given time, thought, and experience to the editorial task now approaching completion. My special gratitude goes to the editorial staff of *Commons Debates 1628*—to Elizabeth Foster, who brought her long experience to getting the work started; to Robert C. Johnson, who devoted many years to the Executive Editorship, several involving great personal hardship and difficulty; to Mary Keeler, who took over the Executive Editorship at a crucial time and is now seeing the work to its completion; to William Bidwell, who joined the staff at a hard time and saw it turn to a better one; and most especially to Maija Cole, who has worked on the project almost from the very beginning, and whose equanimity, balance, and good cheer in good times and bad have been more helpful than I can adequately express.

Finally, the editorial staff and the Director of the Yale Center for Parliamentary History wish to pay their debt of homage to the man who inspired their whole long effort, the late Wallace Notestein, by dedicating these volumes to him.

J. H. Hexter
Yale University
17 April 1976

EDITORIAL
ACKNOWLEDGMENTS

Since its beginning in 1966, a number of scholars from both sides of the Atlantic have given scholarly aid to the Yale Center for Parliamentary History in its project for publishing all known independent accounts of the parliament of 1628. I am particularly grateful to Dr. Elizabeth R. Foster for organizing the project, ordering microfilms of many of the diaries, and setting up our files. I am equally grateful to Miss Norah M. Fuidge and John W. P. Ferris, both of the History of Parliament Trust, in London, who transcribed many of the more difficult parliamentary diaries; their knowledge of early seventeenth-century handwriting saved us from making numerous errors of transcription. Patrick B. Miller, Peter W. Hasler, Daniel P. Gallagher, and Otto Chu have painstakingly assisted in collating the thirteen texts of the Proceedings and Debates. Robert Zaller participated in the early stages of the project and transcribed one text of the Proceedings and Debates. Our next-door neighbor in Sterling Memorial Library, Dr. James P. Reilly, Director of the Leonine Commission, has frequently assisted us with some of the Latin in the manuscripts and has given us some very valuable advice in regard to certain editorial problems. Dr. Carroll P. Cole has been of great help in identifying a number of allusions to the classics.

I am also very grateful to Professor Coburn V. Graves of Kent State University, who has been indispensable in working on the Latin in the text and has also provided the translations; to Professor Samuel E. Thorne, of Harvard University, for assisting with some passages in Law French; to Professor John K. Gruenfelder, of the University of Wyoming, who has provided us with transcripts of numerous letters relating to the elections of 1628, which will be published in the Appendix volume; and to Professor Robert E. Ruigh, of the University of Missouri, who, in his extensive search for diaries of the parliament of 1624, has given us valuable leads on manuscripts relating to the parliament of 1628. Dr. Charles M. Gray of Yale University has given helpful advice about many legal citations. We are grateful to Professor David S. Berkowitz of Brandeis University for helpful suggestions about editorial procedures; and to Professor Vernon F. Snow for advice about additional manuscript materials relating to the parliament of 1628 and to other Stuart parliaments for the Yale Center for Parliamentary History.

A number of suggestions made by Professor G. R. Elton, of Clare College, Cambridge University, have been helpful.

We express our thanks particularly to Mr. Edward Tripp, Executive Editor of the Yale University Press, for his patience, his helpful suggestions, and his encouragement, and to Mr. Charles Grench, whose advice about details in seeing the volumes through the press has been invaluable. We have also been greatly assisted by Mrs. Dorie Baker and Mrs. Maureen Bushkovitch, copy editors of the Yale University Press, in preparing the text of the volumes for publication, and by Mrs. Katharine Meech and Richard Philibert, our typists.

I wish to express the deepest gratitude to the editorial staff—to Mary Frear Keeler who came on the staff in 1974, Mr. William B. Bidwell, who joined it in 1972, and Mrs. Maija J. Cole, who has been on it from the very beginning. In August 1974, when problems with my health made it impossible for me to finish the task, Dr. Keeler succeeded me as Executive Editor of *Commons Debates 1628*. Within a few months she performed the remarkable feat of finding her way about in a project almost a decade old and far along in its way to completion. Her erudition, industry, unfailing good-nature and aplomb have been invaluable assets in the editorial work during its last crucial stages. William Bidwell joined the staff when for the first time in several years we had a budget adequate to provide the staffing necessary for efficient operation. His meticulous attention to some of the more demanding editorial tasks has greatly contributed to this work. Finally, and above all, I wish to express my gratitude to Mrs. Maija Jansson Cole, who has been with the project since its beginning and without whose dedicated work, especially while I was teaching full time at Temple University, these volumes could not have been completed.

Most of the Center's work has been done at Yale University and we are grateful for the courteous assistance we have received from the staffs of the Sterling Memorial Library, the Yale Law Library, and the Beinecke Rare Book and Manuscript Library. We are especially indebted to Mr. Arthur H. Charpentier, Librarian of the Law Library, who has given us easy access to a large number of law books, some of them dating back to the sixteenth century; to Mr. James M. Osborn, of Yale University, for allowing us to examine his valuable collection of manuscripts relating to seventeenth-century parliamentary history; and to Mr. Stephen R. Parks, Curator of the Osborn Collection.

In our researches in England, we have received the same courteous treatment and helpful assistance. We are especially grateful to the staffs of the British Museum, the Public Record Office, the Bodleian Library, the Cambridge University Library, the Library of Trinity College, Dublin, the Sheffield City Library, the libraries of the Inner Temple and Lincoln's Inn, and the Institute of Historical Research in London. Mr. Maurice F. Bond, Clerk of the Records in the House of Lords, and H. S. Cobb, Senior Assistant Clerk of the Records in the House of Lords, have been of great help to us, as have Neville Williams, Deputy Keeper of the Public Record Office, and Miss Margaret Cash, Archivist of the Hampshire Record Office.

The meetings of the Editorial Board and the Advisory Council have been very helpful, especially during the initial stages of the project when editorial policies were being worked out. I have also profited greatly from conversations with my old friend, the late Professor David H. Willson, who first introduced me to the study of early seventeenth-century parliamentary history.

I am very grateful to Temple University for granting me three leaves of absence, in addition to convenient (and in some years reduced) teaching schedules to do editorial work.

The editors wish to acknowledge and thank the following persons and libraries who have kindly granted permission for the publication of their manuscripts in this work: Maurice F. Bond, Record Office, House of Lords, for permission to print the Journal of the House of Commons, 1628, extracts from the House of Lords MS. Minute Book for March to October 1628, quotations from Braye MSS. 89 and certain petitions from the Main Papers; the Marquess of Downshire for permission to use the Trumbull Add. MS. 50; Earl Fitzwilliam, his trustees, and Mr. John Bebbington, City Librarian, Sheffield City Libraries, for permission to use MSS. Treatise 10 in the Wentworth Woodhouse Muniments; the Massachusetts Historical Society for permission to use a journal of proceedings, 1628; the Board of Cornell University Library for permission to use MS. H112, a journal of proceedings, 1628; the Bodleian Library, Department of Western Manuscripts, for permission to use MS. Eng. hist. c. 202–203, MS. Eng. hist. c. 330, and Rawlinson MS. A. 78; Exeter College, of Oxford University, for permission to use Exeter College MS. 1 & 2, a journal of proceedings, 1628; the British Museum for permission to use three journals: British Museum Add. MS. 27,878; Add. 36,825; and Harleian MS. 4771; also, for permission to print extracts from Harleian MSS. 6799, 6800, and 6803. Permission has been granted by W. W. S. Breem, Librarian, to use the Petyt MSS. 537/23,27 in the Inner Temple Library, and by the Duchy of Cornwall Record Office to use their journal of the proceedings in 1628. The East India Company petition is printed by permission of the Folger Shakespeare Library, Washington, D.C.

Permission to publish individual diaries has been granted by: Mr. F. H. M. FitzRoy Newdegate, for the diary of John Newdegate now on deposit in the Warwickshire Record Office; the Board of Trinity College, Dublin, for permission to publish the diary of Sir Richard Grosvenor; the British Museum, for permission to publish the Stowe MS. 366, Harleian MSS. 2313, 5324, and 1601; the Public Record Office, London, for permission to publish the diary of Sir Edward Nicholas; the Huntingdon and Peterborough County Council for permission to publish MS. D.D.M. 58, the notes of Sir Nathaniel Rich. Also, permission has been granted by the Public Record Office to print several individual state papers. For this we are most grateful to them.

We would also like to thank the Worshipful Company of Goldsmiths for permission to quote material from the minutes of the Goldsmiths' Company; the Brewers' Company, for permission to quote from their archives in the Guildhall Library; and the Vintners' Company.

The Selden Society has graciously granted permission to reprint in Legal Citations the excerpt from Bildeston's case.

We are grateful for permissions granted by the owners of the prints that are reproduced in these volumes. The owners' names are listed on the copyright page of each volume.

Robert C. Johnson
Temple University

I wish to add to my predecessor's comments my own note of appreciation to all who have assisted me after I joined the undertaking of editing *Commons Debates 1628*. Without the careful work of Maija J. Cole and William B. Bidwell, their devotion to the project, and their guidance into the intricacies of the editorial procedure, the work could not have been done. The staff of the Yale University Press have been most helpful at many points. And particularly I am indebted to Professor J. H. Hexter. His tireless efforts in securing financial support for the project from the beginning are only a part. He has taken a keen interest also in editorial decisions, has given (and taken!) generously of time, and from his deep knowledge of the period has made dozens of helpful suggestions. All of the staff are grateful to him for his constant and enthusiastic support.

Mary Frear Keeler
Yale University
29 April 1976

Commons Debates 1628

Volume I

INTRODUCTION

The Introduction to *Commons Debates 1628* will concern itself, first, with an account of the manuscripts recording the proceedings in and of the House of Commons from 17 March 1628, when Charles I opened parliament, to 26 June 1628, when he prorogued it; and, second, with the principles, practices, and procedures we[1] have followed in editing those manuscripts.

We have given the whole work the title *Commons Debates 1628*, because overwhelmingly the sources published in these volumes are a record of proceedings and debates in the House of Commons. The hitherto unpublished records on the proceedings of the House of Lords in 1628 are not extensive (see below, Section I, A, 1), nor are the unpublished records of the actions of the King in relation to the parliament. Such sources on proceedings of the King and the Lords as our search has uncovered we will print as part of the general appendix in Volume V of *Commons Debates 1628*. To have designated these volumes by some other title, however, would have given bad guidance as to what their contents actually are.

The records that have been used in this edition are described below. The order, which has been followed also in the daily arrangement of edited texts, is as follows: (A) official sources; (B) narratives (compiled accounts); (C) diaries, or notes by members with the fullest diary first, followed by the others according to degree of completeness;[2]

(D) collections of speeches; (E) correspondence.

I. MANUSCRIPT SOURCES FOR COMMONS DEBATES 1628

A. Official Sources

1. Manuscripts relating to the House of Lords.

Besides the printed *Journals of the House of Lords*, which include reports of three major conferences between the two Houses (on 7, 16, and 17 April), and the *Notes of the Debates of the House of Lords, officially taken by Robert Bowyer and Henry Elsing, Clerks of the Parliaments, A.D. 1621, 1625, and 1628*, ed. by Frances Helen Relf (Royal Historical Society, 1929), the following manuscript records of the Upper House are related to the proceedings of the Commons: (a) the Minute Book of the House of Lords (M.M. House of Lords Record Office MS.);[3] and (b) several petitions in the Main Papers in H.L.R.O.[4] Excerpts from a narrative concerning the petition of right, compiled by Henry Elsynge (Carte MS. 200, ff. 2–50v), are printed in the Appendix. Another document among the House of Lords records, a commonplace book that contains some notes regarding the parliament of 1628,[5] has been examined but, because the notes appear to have been made from separates and resemble closely the materials in the Proceedings and Debates, we have not included it in this edition of the debates. Also examined, but found to be of slight value for our purpose, is a diary of proceedings in the Upper House in 1628 (mainly on the legal arguments relating to the liberty of the subject), which is among the Ellesmere Manuscripts (nos. 7785, 86, 87, 88) at the Huntington

---

1. Here and hereafter in this Introduction, the "we" is by intention ambiguously editorial and/or collective. It represents primarily the Executive Editor, occasionally the collective judgment of the Editorial Staff or the Editorial and Advisory Boards.

2. The only exception is the Lowther diary (see below, Section I, B, 7), which has been placed last because it has notes only for the closing weeks of the session, 4–26 June.

3. See Maurice F. Bond, *Guide to the Records of Parliament* (London, 1971), pp. 34–35. Some use has been made of the Minute Book for editing portions of the *Commons Debates 1628*, as in the Selden/Suffolk business (14 April).

4. Various petitions we have printed have come from this source, e.g., the petition of John Greate (17 April).

5. See Bond, *Guide to the Records of Parliament*, p. 279.

Library. On the Braye MSS. 89, H.L.R.O., see below (Section I, D).

2. *MS. Journal of the House of Commons.*

The manuscript Journal for 1628 is in the House of Lords Record Office, MS. 18. Because much has been written previously about the Journals of the House of Commons of the early Stuart period,[6] little needs to be added here. Like most of the journals for the period 1604–1629, the Journal for 1628 is a very incomplete record of what was done or said in the Lower House. It is, as Professor Wallace Notestein described it, a "Book of Notes" or "Minute Book", as opposed to a much more complete account, which the "Clerk's Book" was intended to be.[7] It consists of the notes hurriedly jotted down by the Clerk of the House of Commons or his assistants while the House was in session. Sentences are often unfinished, the names of committee members are frequently given inaccurately, and numerous words, sentences, or even whole paragraphs are crossed out. Most of the Journal is in one hand, although on some days (notably 3 April, 17 April, 24 April, 4 May, 10 and 28 May) the handwriting is in that of another person, the Clerk's son.

The members of parliament had taken the position that the Clerk should not record the speeches given in the House. They objected when the Lords requested that the Clerk take the Journal of the parliament of 1621 to a conference of the two Houses on 17 April. The Lords wished to see the record of a speech delivered by a "learned member" of the Commons (i.e., Sir Edward Coke) concerning a bill "to explain the statute of Magna Carta". In the face of the Lords' request, Sir Edward Coke declared that "The Clerk's office is not to take our sayings, but to take the orders of the House only"; and the Commons instructed Secretary Coke to inform the Lords "that the entry of the Clerk of particular men's speeches was without warrant at all times . . .".[8] Thereupon the House, turning to a procedure developed in earlier Stuart parliaments (from 1607), appointed a committee of eight members to meet weekly "to survey the Clerk's book; and report to the House as they shall see cause, but to make no alteration without warrant of the House".[9]

The Clerk of the House of Commons in 1628 was John Wright, who served in that office from 1612 to 1633.[10] As a note-taker he appears inferior to several of the diarists, even when recording only the official business of the House. His handwriting was very poor and at times almost illegible, particularly when he jotted down names of committee members. He made occasional errors, such as his entries on 22 and 28 March in which

6. See Wallace Notestein and Frances Helen Relf, eds., *Commons Debates for 1629* (Minneapolis, 1921), pp. xi–xiv; Elizabeth R. Foster, ed., *Proceedings in Parliament 1610* (2 vols., New Haven, 1966), I, xxxiv–xliii; and Sheila Lambert, "The Clerks and Records of the House of Commons, 1600–1640", *Bulletin of the Institute of Historical Research*, XLIII (1970), 215–231.

7. Notestein and Relf, *Commons Debates for 1629*, p. xiii.

8. See Vol. II, pp. 509, 512.

9. A committee was named in 1607 to peruse certain entries in the Clerk's "Journal Book", and was revived in 1610, with instructions to work with the Committee of Privileges (*C.J.*, I, 385, 392; and Foster, *Proceedings in Parliament 1610*, II, 33). The Clerk's Book was examined at least once before the dissolution of the parliament of 1614, and during the parliament of 1621 a Committee on Entries was active also. Such examina-

tions occurred likewise in the parliaments of 1624 and 1626; that of 1625 ended before its organization had been completed. *C.J.*, I, 466, 683, 830; *Commons Debates 1621*, II, 55n73, 545; V, 142, 447.

10. Bond, *Guide to the Records of Parliament*, p. 305. Wright was frequently out of favor with the Court, and after the adjournment of the parliament of 1621 he was arrested—perhaps, as Notestein suggests, for giving out documents. On 17 March 1628 Sir James Bagg wrote to Buckingham: "Wright, the Clerk of Parliament, of all men since my being of that House, hath done worst service to his Majesty. . . . Confer with some of your servants about him, he is the most usefullest man of the House". S.P. 16/96:36. In Notestein and Relf, *Commons Debates for 1629*, p. xxv, the date of the letter is wrongly given as 1629. The letter is printed in the Appendix.

he confused Newport, Cornwall, with Newport Medina, which is on the Isle of Wight. He wrote "Sir Thomas Gleane" on a committee list of 1 April, when Sir Peter Gleane was meant;[11] and inserted on 17 May the name of "Mr. Marsh", although there was no such man in the House.[12] Wright was not the only Clerk to make such errors, however; and it should be recalled that in a body of almost five hundred members, where nominations for committees were shouted out, mistakes of this kind could easily occur.

When the printed *Commons Journal* was being prepared, the person who transcribed the MS. Journal of 1628 made, on the whole, an accurate transcription. A few small errors crept in, such as his reading, on 15 April, of "re-estating" as "re-establishing"[13] certain properties of William Morgan, or occasional misreading of a "Mr." as a "Sir". He sometimes listed members of committees whose names had been deleted in the manuscript. One thing the transcriber did not do was reproduce various passages of the Journal that are crossed out in the manuscript. These deletions are of some importance, however, because they show at times actions of the House that were later revoked or changed. An important example is that of the four resolutions that had been passed in the committee of the whole House on 1 April, three concerning the liberty of the subject, and a fourth concerning the propriety of goods. On 3 April all four were duly reported to the House, and the first three were formally adopted. In the case of the fourth, as the deleted entry shows, the House first approved the draft of the resolution regarding goods but then returned it to the committee for a revision in wording. As a result, the wording was sharpened considerably, with attention being called especially to forced loans, and

the House then adopted the more strongly worded resolution.[14] Although crossed-out passages have not been preserved in the printed *Journal*, we have included from the MS. Journal all of those that, as in the example cited, provide additional information on the proceedings of the House.

We decided to reprint the Commons Journal for 1628 for two reasons: first, to provide an annotated and, so far as is possible, an accurate text; and second, to make available the Clerk's account of the proceedings, including the lists of committee members and the records of the reading of bills, to those scholars who may not have easy access to the printed *Journals*. A complete and wholly accurate text is impossible to achieve. Even by the middle of the eighteenth century, when the Journal was being transcribed for publication, the manuscript had deteriorated, and several pages were frayed and torn at the corners and sides. Where the words lost were obvious, such as "the" or "for", the eighteenth-century transcriber inserted these words in brackets, and in the case of longer words or names, he used asterisks in place of the missing words to indicate that the manuscript was torn. We have kept words inserted by the transcriber, indicating them by italics. At times we have been able to supply a missing word from other sources. We have been able, for example, to enter *Lostwithiel* in the record of 19 March, supplying from our List of Members the name of the borough for which Sir Robert Carr was returned.[15] In the important debate on 14 April we have inserted Sir Edward Coke's name where the speaker was not identified in the Journal, but was identified in another of the accounts of that day's proceedings.[16] Such insertions as are based on other sources we have enclosed in brackets.[17]

11. See Vol. II, p. 227.
12. See n. 9, 17 May.
13. See n. 1, 15 April.
14. The crossed-out passage in the MS. Journal shows the weaker wording of the resolution before the change. The alteration in wording is noted by New-

degate and Harleian MS. 1601, but not in the Proceedings and Debates or Stowe MS. 366. See n. 18, 1 April, and also Vol. II, p. 276.
15. See Vol. II, p. 12, and below, p. 53.
16. See Vol. II, pp. 445, 448.
17. Also enclosed in brackets are insertions taken

We have printed names of committee members in columns, as they appear in the manuscript.

B. Narratives (Compiled Accounts)

Among the manuscripts relating to the parliament of 1628 are several collections of materials, arranged in chronological order, to which we have given the general term "narratives". In contrast to the official records, they include many of the speeches of individual members. The arrangement of the materials, many of which were probably circulating as "separates", i.e., separate copies of speeches, bills, etc. (see below, pp. 9–11, 33), suggests that the purpose of their compilers was to present an ordered narrative of the proceedings of the House of Commons. For a fuller description of this type of document, see below (Section I, B, 2).

1. *British Museum, Harleian MS. 6799, ff. 288–336.*

This is part of a collection of papers that, along with Harleian MS. 6800, once belonged to the Alfords, a family associated with several parliaments of the seventeenth century, including that of 1628. The nature of the collected materials, among which are separates of the major speeches, as well as other parliamentary documents of the 1628 session, suggests a possible intent to compile a full account of the proceedings.[18]

The portion of Harleian MS. 6799 that has been arranged in journal form, however, is incomplete, covering only the period from 20 March through 22 March. In spite of its being just the beginning of a narrative, it contains for the dates covered a number of speeches and briefs of bills that are not included in the other compilations.[19] Since it relates only to the early part of the session, it is placed in this edition before the Proceedings and Debates, which covers the whole session.

2. *Proceedings and Debates.*

This is a composite text assembled and named collectively by the editors of *Commons Debates 1628*.[20] It was produced by collating thirteen manuscript copies of a compiled narrative of proceedings in the House of Commons during the first session of Charles I's third parliament.[21] There are probably several more copies of the Proceedings and Debates for 1628 than the thirteen we collated[22] and the two we rejected, one because it was a late copy, and the other

---

from marginal notes on the MS. Journal. We have included only notes that are in the Clerk's hand.

18. Some examples of the methods of compilation of this incomplete journal (Harl. MS. 6799) can be given. On the first day, 20 March, when the committee to deal with elections and privileges was chosen (f. 288), there is the notation, "Here enter the names of the committee, etc., with the order thereupon made,". However, the list of the committee members, with the order, appears separately on f. 287, indicating that it was received as a separate document. Again, the letters mentioned on 20 March by William Coryton (f. 288–288v), though read in the House, were not inserted; nor was the petition concerning the new importation of wines that was read on 22 March (f. 335), although words "which is as followeth" were written at that point. In the case of the petition to the King for a general fast on 21 March, space was left in the MS. for the petition to be inserted (f. 290v), but the text of the petition is given on ff. 283–284.

19. On the other materials in Harl. MSS. 6799–

6800, see below, Section I, D.

20. The method of preparing the composite text is described below in Sections II, A and II, B.

21. In his Introduction to *Commons Debates for 1629* (p. xliii n 3), Professor Wallace Notestein cited several of these manuscripts listed below (MSS. 3, 12, 13). He mentioned also Petyt MS. 537/26 (an imperfect one; cf. MS. 11, below), and one belonging to the Marquis of Bute (see H.M.C., *Third Report, App.*, p. 205). In *Proceedings and Debates of the British Parliaments Respecting North America* (5 vols., Washington, D.C., 1924), I, 79–96, Leo Francis Stock used MSS. 1, 3, 6, 7, 12, and 13 listed below. The manuscript Stock refers to as belonging to Lord Lucas is now in the Bodleian Library (see MS. 6, below).

22. In his search for manuscript copies of the True Relation, the "compiled narrative" for the session of 1629, Professor Notestein found forty-eight. Another for 1629, which is not included in his list, is Hunter MS. 52 in the Chapter Library at Durham, described by Edward Hughes in *E.H.R.*, LXXIV (1959), 672–679.

because of major defects.[23] The number and importance of the variations among the copies actually used were insufficient to warrant a more intensive search for additional ones. For convenience in referring to them hereafter the manuscripts are here numbered from 1 to 13.

MS. 1. Trumbull Add. MS. 50 [Berkshire Record Office, Marquess of Downshire MSS.] lacks a title page, but has a bookplate reading: "*Virtute et industria* Wm. Trumbull, Esq.". It consists of ff. 1–231v, written in one hand for 1628 (17 March–26 June), beginning with the sentence: "The Parliament began on Monday . . .".

A second volume, written in a different hand and dealing with the session of 1629 has on f. 1 (20 January) the title: "A true relation of every day's proceedings in Parliament since the beginning thereof being Tuesday the 20th of January 1628". Inside the front cover of the second volume is an inscription: "Arth. Langford his booke, The first of May 1629", and underneath, as if it were the signature of the copyist, is the name, "John Slaughter".[24]

MS. 2. Wentworth/Sheffield [Sheffield City Libraries, Sheffield, Wentworth Woodhouse MSS.] lacks a title page, but f. 1 opens with the same sentence as in Trumbull Add. MS. 50. It consists of ff. 1–286, in a single hand (17 March–26 June). The hand somewhat resembles that in Trumbull MS. 50 but there are differences in the formation of various letters, especially capital *A* and *I*.

Another manuscript narrative of the 1628 proceedings is in the same collection. It appears to be a copy and in a later hand. This second manuscript is bound in leather and has neither markings on the outside binding nor a name or bookplate on the inside. This manuscript, because of the evidence that it was a late copy, was rejected from the collating procedures by the editors.

MS. 3. Massachusetts Historical Society MS. (unnumbered) [Library of the Society] has ff. 3–283. It begins with the Lord Keeper's speech (17 March) and continues through 26 June but has occasional folios torn out and/or spoiled by damp. The original holder of this manuscript is unknown; it was purchased in November 1790 by Thomas Wallcut from the library of the late D. Byles.

MS. 4. Cornell University Library MS. H112 [Cornell University, Ithaca, New York] has 554 folios and is written in one hand. Bound in seventeenth-century morocco binding, with an illuminated title page, the title reads: "A journal of the proceedings in the Parliament holden at Westminster in the Third and Fourth years of the reign of our Sovereign Lord King Charles—containing two sessions, The First beginning the XVIIth of March, and ending the XXVIth of June then next following *An° Dm̄i.* 1628. The Second beginning the XXth of January in the same year and ending the Xth of March following. *Anno Domini* 1628".

On the inside cover, beneath a coat of arms with the motto, *Dieu et mon Droit,* is written: "The most high and mighty Monarch Charles the Second by the Grace of God King of Great Britain, France, and Ireland, Defender of the faith, etc.". The name R. Kruing (?) appears at the top of the page. A portrait of Charles I is the frontispiece. On

---

Written in a contemporary hand on the flyleaf is the following: "August the 10th, 1629, John Heath *empt Londino a* W. Walbanck". Walbanck was a London printer, but Heath has not been identified. There may be other True Relations.

23. One manuscript in the Wentworth/Sheffield collection (see below, under MS. 2) was rejected because its hand indicated that it must have been copied, probably in the eighteenth century. We rejected also Petyt MS. 537/26 (see below, under MS. 11) because

it is filled with copyists' errors, with many words and lines missing.

24. These two manuscripts are not mentioned specifically in the introduction to H.M.C., *Manuscripts of the Marquess of Downshire,* I, vi; but they are noted, as of the library of William Trumbull the Elder, in *British Museum Project: A Checklist of the Microfilms Prepared in England and Wales for the American Council of Learned Societies 1941–1945* (Washington, 1955), p. 49.

one page are the words: "This is my nephew John Davis's".

MS. 5. Bodleian MS. Eng. hist. c. 202–203 [Bodleian Library, Oxford University]. Two volumes, including proceedings for both sessions. Volume I, which lacks a title page, contains ff. 2–482v [to Thursday, 29 May], written in one hand. Volume II continues to the end of the first session on ff. 1–309v, partly in the same hand as Volume I, but partly in another, possibly two other hands. Volume II continues after f. 309v, with the proceedings of the 1629 session, for which the following title is inserted: "The Second Session of Parliament beginning the XXth of January in the fourth year of the reign of our sovereign King Charles and ended the tenth of March following. *Anno Dmī.* 1628". On the next page, on which the record of the proceedings begins, is a heading that reads: "A true relation of all the proceedings in Parliament the last sessions beginning the 20th of January until the dissolution thereof".

Volume I contains at the beginning, in a different hand, descriptions of the lives of some of the members with page references to Whitelock's *Memorials*, which was first published in 1682.

MS. 6. Bodleian MS. Eng. hist. c. 330 [Bodleian Library, Oxford University] lacks a title page. A brief table is on ff. i–iii; it is the beginning of an index, under such headings as "Aids", "Billeting", "Confinement", etc. This is in a different hand. The proceedings, beginning with a statement that the King "made a speech" (but without copying the speech), are on ff. 1–293, done in one hand, with the exception of an occasional day done in a second hand. It has no report of the second session.

MS. 7. Exeter College MS. 1 and 2 [Exeter College, Oxford University] lacks a title page; ff. 1–702v, written in one hand, beginning with the King's speech. Only the first session is reported. At the end is written: "For his excellency Robert Earl of Essex Lord

General of the forces raised for the defence of the parliament at the army". The statement is repeated below, with variations in wording and in handwriting. There are also the names of several unidentified persons, such as Peter Evens, Richard Vaughan, John Swan, and Marie French. Cf. MS. 10, below.

MS. 8. B.M., Add. MS. 27,878 [British Museum]. The manuscript is in one hand and has 560 folios. The title page, on which has been set an engraved border (similar to that of MS. 4, above), has the title: "A Journal of the Proceedings in the Parliament holden at Westminster in the iiid and iiiith years of the reign of our Sovereign Lord King Charles. Containing two Sessions. The First beginning the xviith day of March *Ano Domini* 1627 and ending the xxvjth of June *Ano Domini* 1628. The Second Beginning the xxth of January *Anno Domini*, 1628, and ending the xth of March following". It contains, for the 1628 session, ff. 3–560 in one hand.

There is a separate title page to indicate the start of the proceedings for the second session, and its dates. On this manuscript there are frequent marginal notes in a hand different from that of the text, which the editors have not been able to identify. The notes, similar to ones that Sir Simonds D'Ewes made on his compiled account for 1624 (see below, n. 97), suggest that whoever made them was familiar with parliamentary procedure and was interested in the issues of 1628.

MS. 9. B.M., Add. MS. 36,825 [British Museum] lacks a title page. Folios 3–660, in one hand, give proceedings of the 1628 session only. It begins with the King's speech of 17 March, under the simple heading: "The Parliament began on Monday *decimo septimo Marcii iiio Caroli Regis Anno Domini MDCXXVII*.

A partial index precedes the account of the debates.

MS. 10. Duchy of Cornwall Record Office MS. (unnumbered) [Buckingham Gate, London] has no title page; ff. 1–313v are in one hand, beginning with the heading, "The Parliament began on Monday..." [17 March], and the King's speech, and continuing through the session.

The manuscript contains a narrative account of the parliament of 1621, ff. 320–466 (a copy of the Pym diary, which is printed in *Commons Debates 1621*), but has nothing on the 1629 session.

At the end of the volume is written, "*Finis per me T. F.*". Also, "July *1ᵐ—4ᵗᵒ Anno tentationis* 1651". Underneath this inscription is the name of Thomas Fletcher, which may indicate that he was the transcriber. "Sir Gilbert Gerard, Baronet", and some names of unidentified persons are written on several of the later pages; "William Gerard", and other unidentified names are scribbled on the inside front cover. Two, "Peter Evens" and "John Swan", are also on the Exeter College MS. (MS. 7, above).

The text so closely resembles that of MS. 7 (e.g., omissions, etc., on 28 May) that one might have been a copy of the other. Cf. MS. 13.

MS. 11. Petyt MSS. 537/23,27 [Inner Temple Library], two volumes, with the first volume lacking a title page and including the dates of 17 March–28 May, ff. 1–355, and the second volume (537/27) including 29 May (misdated 28 May)–26 June, ff. 1–166; the arguments of the conferences (April), ff. 167–263; and the proceedings of the second session (20 Jan.–10 March 1629), ff. 265–337. Two hands are used for the manuscript, with no identifying marks.

Petyt MS. 537/26 [Inner Temple Library] is another narrative account of the 1628 parliament that the editors chose not to use because of the number of copyists' errors and omissions it contains.

MS. 12. B.M., Harleian MS. 4771 [British Museum]. The title page reads: "A diary of Proceedings in the Parliament which began

on Monday the 17ᵗʰ of March 3 *Car. Anno Dom.* 1627". Incomplete, it has ff. 2–201 running through 27 May. The book plate of John [Holles] Duke of Newcastle, Marquis and Earl of Clare, and the name of the Cavendish residence "Welbeck" written on an early page, identify it as a part of the Cavendish-Holles library at Welbeck Abbey in Nottinghamshire, which was transferred in 1718 to the library of Robert and Edward Harley [C. E. Wright, *Fontes Harleiana* (London, 1972), p. 193; and *Diary of Humfrey Wanley*, ed. by C. E. Wright and Ruth C. Wright (London, 1966), pp. xl–xlii]. This is the MS. often cited in the notes of S. R. Gardiner's *History of England*.

MS. 13. Bodleian Rawlinson MS. A. 78 [Bodleian Library, Oxford University] lacks a title page and is incomplete [17 March into 4 April], ff. 174–196v (folios numbered 1–22v in another hand). There is a brief table, the beginning of a subject index, on f. 174. At the end of the table is a note: "only to f. 58(?) of the large book is here transcribed". A note on f. 174v reads: "Begun in October 1661 per me J.S. Copied out of Sir G. Gerard's large folio book of the proceedings of the parliament in *3º Caroli*".

At the bottom of the last page is written: "This that is writt here reacheth to f. 5(?) in the greate booke".

The reference to Sir Gilbert Gerard's book suggests that this is a copy of MS. 10 (Duchy of Cornwall MS.). The Rawlinson A. 78 reaches to f. 58v of the Cornwall MS.

The editors have not tried to discover "families" among the manuscripts of Proceedings and Debates. It is easy, however, to distinguish two groups among them. The divergence between the groups is marked most clearly by two versions of several speeches so widely variant that we have had to print parallel texts in these volumes.[25] The first group comprises MSS. 1–3 in the

25. See in Volume II the Lord Keeper's speech, 17 March; the Lord Keeper's speech, 19 March; the Speaker's speech, 19 March; Sir Benjamin Rudyard's speech, 22 March; and in Volume III, Sir Henry Marten's speech, 23 May.

above list; the second, MSS. 4–13. There is nothing about any surviving manuscript to suggest that it was the original. Indeed, the "fair copy" appearance of each indicates that it could not have been the original but that it was produced by a secretary or a professional copyist. Two of the manuscripts listed above, MSS. 12 and 13, are incomplete. The rest extend from the opening of parliament, on 17 March, through the day of its prorogation, 26 June.

None of the manuscripts of Proceedings and Debates can be dated exactly. Some appear to have been copied some time during the Long Parliament,[26] and others to date from the Interregnum and the Restoration[27] or even later.[28] Possibly, but not certainly, several may have come from the period between 1629 and 1640.[29] All, at any rate, are in the hands of copyists.

Proceedings and Debates is a narrative of the major actions of the House of Commons, and of all the 1628 accounts it provides the fullest versions of the major speeches.[30] Each of the manuscripts that is complete (to the end of the session) also contains at the end the speeches at the important conference with the Lords of 7 April.[31] Comparison with the other accounts of 1628, and particularly with the other compiled account to which it has the strongest resemblance, Stowe MS. 366, shows that the other accounts, including the Stowe MS., often report a greater number of speakers, but record their remarks less completely.[32] With respect to the nonspeech material, and again comparing the Proceedings and Debates with Stowe MS. 366, it can be said with confidence that these two narratives are the clearest, most cogent, and most coherent accounts of the debates in the House of Commons of 1628 that exist. They do not often miss major points. They rarely slip up on the sequence of speakers whose remarks they report. And usually these reports are much better constructed and more orderly than any speaker's *ex tempore* discourse is. The narrative portions of both Proceedings and Debates and Stowe MS. 366 are, in short, the work of men who were in the House of Commons taking notes as the events they recorded took place. Both accounts are also the work of men who not long after the events,[33] sometimes not much more than a week after,[34] went through their notes and then wrote or dic-

26. MS. 7 and possibly MS. 10. Interest in the debates of 1628 regarding the liberty of the subject may have stimulated the production of more copies at this time. It was in 1642 that the pamphlet containing the arguments from the great conferences of April 1628—probably taken from separates—was printed.

27. From the Interregnum, possibly MS. 10; from the Restoration, MS. 13.

28. Later ones are the second of the Wentworth/Sheffield MSS. (described above with MS. 2); and one copied in 1732–1733 (H.M.C., *MSS. of the Duke of Buccleugh and Queensbury*, III, 327–328), which has not been used for this edition.

29. MSS. 1–3, which compose the first group among the thirteen we have used, may be earlier than those in the second group; they contain fewer signs of editorial change. The bookplate of Sir William Trumbull on MS. 1 (Trumbull Add. MS. 50) might suggest that the copy had been owned by Sir William Trumbull, Clerk of the Council, who died in 1635 (*D.N.B.*). However, since the bookplate is that of William Trumbull IV (eighteenth century), there is no way to prove that the manuscript came into the family's possession during the lifetime of the first Sir William.

30. For the consideration of speeches based on "separates", see below, pp. 9–11.

31. Those manuscripts have been used, in addition to the records given in a pamphlet printed in 1642, for editing the accounts of the April conferences.

32. For comparisons between the Proceedings and Debates and Stowe MS. 366 on this point, see below, p. 13, and also Section I, B, 3.

33. Probably daily in the case of the Stowe MS.

34. Evidence in the Proceedings and Debates manuscripts suggests that the intervals may sometimes have been about a week. For example, although the Clegate case was discussed in the committee for grievances on Friday, 25 April, and the House did not vote on the committee's report until Friday, 2 May (see Vol. III, pp. 76–78, 208), all of the Proceedings and Debates manuscripts record under date of 25 April both the committee debate and the subsequent report and vote in the House. Another example relates to a word in the Petition of Right. In the draft of the petition that MSS. 1–12 include under date of 9 May, a passage relating to taxation reads: "by means whereof your people . . . lend". The word *means* did not come into the petition, as a substitute for the word *pretext*,

tated their narrative of the proceedings. The two narratives sometimes report speeches differently from one another, but they rarely contradict one another about what a speaker said. They are complementary rather than conflicting accounts. Only men present at the debate could have set down the mass of informative notes that underpin the narratives, and only men present, relying at times on sharp personal memories, could have produced from such notes narratives that coincide so closely with *all* other records—Commons Journals and diaries alike—of the events they describe.

Another example of a compiled narrative,[35] remarkable because of the number of extant copies,[36] is the True Relation, a major account of the 1629 session of the same parliament. We believe there are important differences between the Proceedings and Debates of 1628 and the 1629 record, however, and that the way in which the two accounts were produced differed also. In their Introduction to *Commons Debates for 1629*, Wallace Notestein and Frances Relf provided what is still the most complete description of the material that went into accounts of proceedings in the House of Commons under Elizabeth and the early Stuarts. In it they suggest that Proceedings and Debates of 1628

is the counterpart of the True Relation 1629.[37] Because their comprehensive Introduction is still the fullest account of these matters, and the most authoritative, we need to pause here to provide the grounds for rejecting their hypothesis as to the relationship between the accounts of 1628 and 1629.

The value to be placed upon a historical source is related of course to the nature of its origin. In the view of Notestein and Relf, the 1629 account, and by implication the 1628 narrative, was a document "made up . . . of news-letters . . . issued as separates [i.e., separately] . . . combined by different compilers who were ignorant of the actual occurrences".[38] To make clear to the reader what a low estimate of the historical value of Proceedings and Debates this quotation implies, we will need to present more fully the Notestein and Relf account of "separates" and "news-letters"—which they describe as the constituent elements of the two compiled narratives of 1628 and 1629—of how they came into being, and how they were assembled into Proceedings and Debates and the True Relation.

A separate is "a parliamentary document . . . to be found in a single manuscript".[39] Its defining trait is that it is "complete in itself, not a fragment of a larger whole".[40]

---

however, until after the debate on 13 May, when the Commons agreed to accept it as a proposal from the House of Lords. (See Vol. III, p. 339 and n. 28; pp. 389–390, 395.) A further example is that of the discussions about Roger Maynwaring in June. Most of the record is given in the Proceedings and Debates MSS. under date of 14 June, although much of the debate occurred on 4 June, and Maynwaring's submission was not made until the 21st. An example of a note that must have been added after the parliament ended is the comment (19 April) on a substitute bill for Bromfield and Yale that passed on 25 June. See Vol. II, p. 565.

35. Compiled narratives for other Stuart parliaments can be cited also. The editors of *Commons Debates 1621*, Notestein, Relf, and Simpson, have described an elder sibling (Petyt 537/15) of the narrative component of Proceedings and Debates, which provided the basis of the compilation that they entitled "X", The Anonymous Journal (*Commons Debates 1621*, I, 5–16). Sir Simonds D'Ewes, though not himself a member of the parliament of 1624, was able to assemble a com-

piled narrative of that parliament, Harl. MS. 159 (as described to the editors by Robert E. Ruigh). Indeed, the well-known *Journal of Sir Simonds D'Ewes* of the Long Parliament, the first part of which was edited by Professor Notestein, is also a compiled account. The smooth narrative D'Ewes and his secretary produced was based on rough diary notes that have survived.

36. Five copies of the MS. "X" of 1621 were found (*Commons Debates 1621*, I, 6). For 1629, Notestein and Relf examined forty-eight copies; see also n. 22, above.

37. The hypothesis set forth in the Introduction to *Commons Debates for 1629* was endorsed by Professor Relf when she used one of the 1628 manuscripts (MS. 3 in our list above) as a source for her book, *The Petition of Right* (Minneapolis, 1917), p. 69.

38. *Commons Debates for 1629*, p. xix.

39. Ibid., p. xx.

40. Such a document "might be a declaration, a message . . . a protestation . . . the speech of a member" (*Commons Debates for 1629*, p. xx). For the

Some separates were prepared by individual members,[41] but by 1628 many of them "did not originate with the speakers themselves".[42] Instead, outsiders—scriveners and stationers —got copies of speeches of members, or made copies of those copies, or of versions picked up in tavern gossip, and peddled them to any customer they could find. So "separates are not a reliable source of information. . . . They are much more apt to be faulty than correct. . . .[43] They are speeches gathered by ignorant, careless, and often unscrupulous scriveners in roundabout ways and hastily put together for immediate circulation".[44]

A parliamentary newsletter, according to the description by Notestein and Relf, was "a daily or weekly narrative of parliament . . . sent out in many manuscript copies".[45] Although the general newsletter was of earlier vintage, they state that the parliamentary variety dates from 1628, when "two quite separate and distinct series of such letters" appeared.[46] One of these series, they suggest, seems to have been carried over to provide the basis for the True Relation of 1629;[47] and they suggest also that a set of newsletters for the Short Parliament and the *Diurnal Occurrences* for the Long Parliament may have come from the same hand or hands.[48] The hands, the argument continues, were those of the stationers and scriveners, the same unreliable men who wrote the separates. And the source was the same, too, "the conversation or notes of private members".[49]

Finally, the same hack journalists who produced separates and newsletters put them together into a consecutive account with such care and accuracy as we would expect from such men—*et, voilà* the "Parliamentary compilation",[50] that is, the True Relation, its antecedent, Proceedings and Debates,[51] and the succeeding like enterprise of the Short Parliament.[52]

Does this learned, complex, and shrewd reconstruction fit the True Relation? We do not know, and it does not matter to us. Does it fit Proceedings and Debates? This does matter, and in one respect the answer is, yes. That narrative is like, if not exactly like, what Notestein and Relf call a "Parliamentary compilation". That is, it has been put together by splicing manuscripts of speeches into a day-by-day narrative of the proceedings in the House. The point we wish to make here, however, is that *in all other consequential respects Proceedings and Debates diverges from the True Relation as Notestein and Relf describe it, and each point of divergence enhances the value of Proceedings and Debates as an account of the parliament of 1628.*

First, with respect to separates. Many that turn up as "true" separates—that is, as individual manuscripts, or in retranscribed collections such as Harleian MS. 6800, or in printed collections like Fuller's *Ephemeris Parliamentaria*—also appear in Proceedings and Debates. Such, for example, is Cresheld's speech of 27 March, which also appears in Fuller's collection.[53] Let us briefly consider this speech. The most striking thing about it is its length; it is about 3,500 words long. That is a *very* long speech, or rather a very long report of a speech.[54] As reported, it is also a very eloquent and closely argued speech, patently not an improvised affair. The occasional Latin quotation in the Pro-

---

parliaments of the 1620s, separates survive in great number and in numerous copies.

41. *Commons Debates for 1629*, p. xxx.
42. Ibid., p. xxix.
43. Ibid., p. xxxix.
44. Ibid., p. xli.
45. Ibid., p. xlii.
46. Ibid., p. xliii.
47. Ibid.
48. Ibid., p. xlv.

49. Ibid., p. liii.
50. Ibid., p. lvi.
51. Ibid., p. lviii.
52. Ibid.
53. Fuller, *Ephemeris Parliamentaria*, pp. 21–27.
54. Few other speeches of such length by private members appear in any of the accounts of proceedings in Commons in 1628. Versions of this speech in other accounts of the day are much shorter.

ceedings and Debates version is accurate and grammatical.[55] It is hard to believe that the separate of Cresheld's learned speech that appears both in the Proceedings and Debates[56] and in Fuller's book came into being the way Notestein and Relf decided that most separates did.

It should be pointed out that earlier in their discussion they had approvingly quoted Fuller's preface to his *Ephemeris Parliamentaria*, which presents a different view of the matter:

Some gentlemen, speakers in the parliament, imparted their speeches to their intimate friends; the transcripts thereof were multiplied amongst others (the pen being very procreative of issue of this nature).[57]

Of course surviving separates originated both ways, sometimes perhaps the lovingly polished work of the original author, as in the Cresheld speech, sometimes the haphazardly pieced-together production of commercial news gatherers.

Of the latter sort, which may be described as the degenerate type of separate, two examples may be cited. One is the much abbreviated report of Sir John Eliot's "passionate" speech of 22 March, which appears in the Braye Manuscripts (*H.L.R.O.*).[58] Another is a separate in Fuller's collection, which

consists of a cluster of speeches made on 2 April about the King's propositions on supply. It is actually a set of brief summaries of fifteen speeches.[59] It omits seven others that are reported in the Proceedings and Debates,[60] and the versions of those it reports are in every instance much abbreviated, as compared with the versions in the Proceedings and Debates. Clearly this sort of separate is in substance a different thing from the Cresheld speech of 27 March.[61]

For our purposes the crucial point is that *with few exceptions the separates that found their way into Proceedings and Debates are of the better sort.* In most respects and time after time they are the amplest and clearest versions we have of the speeches they report.[62]

Next we must turn our attention to the parliamentary newsletters, the second of the two elements from which Notestein and Relf believed compiled narratives like Proceedings and Debates were put together. According to them, Stowe MS. 366 was just such a newsletter. In support of this view is the physical appearance of the manuscript.[63] In the features that suggest periodic issue the manuscript conforms to the traits Notestein and Relf ascribe to a parliamentary newsletter;[64] it does, too, in containing no evidence as to its own authorship, and in

---

55. Although Richard Cresheld described himself overmodestly at the start of the speech, he was a Lincoln Inn's lawyer of some repute (he became a bencher in 1633), and had served as M.P. in 1624 and 1625. See Keeler, *L.P.*, p. 146; Foss, *Judges of England*, VI, 287–288.

56. For some unexplained reason the report in the Proceedings and Debates of the speech delivered on the same day by the eminent scholar, John Selden, is given in about half as much space (133 lines as contrasted with 263 for Cresheld). Yet, to judge by other accounts, Selden's speech was probably even longer than Cresheld's. Selden, 76 lines in Stowe MS. 366, 80 lines in Harl. MS. 2313; and Cresheld, 64 lines in Stowe MS. 366, 58 lines in Harl. MS. 2313.

57. *Commons Debates for 1629*, p. xxviii, quoting Fuller, Preface, 5v.

58. H.L.R.O. Braye MSS. 89, f. 27v, cited in n. 15, 22 March (Vol. II), which summarizes in nineteen words the grievances that Eliot "did passionately and

rhetorically set forth". A much longer report of Eliot's remarks is given in the Proceedings and Debates for that date.

59. Fuller, *Ephemeris Parliamentaria*, pp. 138–140.

60. Speeches of Perrott, Rich, Edmondes, Coryton, Giles, and the second and third speeches of Sir John Coke.

61. The origin of such a separate must be different also, although possibly it was derived from longer versions of the several speeches it includes.

62. Two differences between the versions of the Cresheld speech in Proceedings and Debates and in Stowe MS. 366 can be noted. While the version in Stowe is less than a fourth as long as the other, it contains many more exact citations to legal precedents; fewer specific references appear in the Proceedings and Debates version, even though the legal points are made.

63. For the description of Stowe MS. 366, see below, Section I, B, 3.

64. *Commons Debates for 1629*, p. lii.

offering an account only of the doings of parliament.

Fortunately for its value as a source it fails every other test that they use to identify the genre: (1) Stowe MS. 366 is much fuller than "a brief summary of events at Westminster";[65] (2) it cannot be described as giving "no information that was not of general interest";[66] and (3) while it is difficult to prove a negative, there is no evidence whatsoever that Stowe MS. 366 was "sent out in many manuscript copies".[67]

Since the Stowe MS. 366 is the only known manuscript account for either of the parliamentary sessions of 1628 and 1629 that bears the physical stigmata of a "parliamentary newsletter",[68] it appears that such a type of source for the parliament of 1628–1629 is very rare, if indeed it existed at all.[69]

Returning now to Proceedings and Debates of 1628, there is no reason at all to suppose that what is left after subtracting the "separates" is such a "newsletter" base, least of all to regard that base as a careless account put together out of gossip by hacks. The basis (or bases) of the True Relation for 1629 looks like and may indeed be something of the sort. There is no question, however, in the case of the Proceedings and Debates, of an unknown number of unskilled hands patching together inaccurate information about a sequence of occurrences in the House that they had not witnessed. The profound difference between

the Proceedings and Debates and the True Relation in this respect becomes evident if one examines the major deviations of the manuscripts of the True Relation from each other. One finds whole speeches or series of speeches in a day's proceedings placed in divergent order; whole speeches put in on the wrong day; or two totally different accounts of the proceedings for several days in a row. Such gross variations are so frequent that scarcely a day passes without a half-dozen such variations cropping up among a half-dozen to twenty manuscripts.[70] *To such disarray there is nothing comparable in the narrative base of Proceedings and Debates.*

Among the various copies of Proceedings and Debates, speeches are rarely placed in different sequences or omitted. By comparison with other accounts, however, we find that on a few occasions the account in Proceedings and Debates merged into a single day's proceedings matters about which debates occurred on different days. For example, grouped in this account under the date of 25 April, are two discussions regarding Nicholas Clegate that occurred a week apart, one in committee and one in regular session. Similarly, several speeches and notes of action regarding Roger Maynwaring, which occurred on different dates in June, are grouped in the Proceedings and Debates under the date of 14 June.[71] Even this chronological mixing, however, is not random or arbitrary:

---

65. Ibid.

66. Ibid. Hardly of "general interest" are items appearing in the Stowe MS. 366 report for 19 May 1628 concerning the naturalization of James Freese or a committee report on a proposal to change a word in a statute of 1624 (see Vol. III, p. 469).

67. *Commons Debates for 1629*, p. xliii. Stowe MS. 366, although the record for each day was folded and dated, has no address of a recipient, such as appears on the outside of the usual newsletter. Besides the Stowe MS. 366, only one other copy is known to exist (Stowe MS. 367), and this one bears no marks to suggest periodic distribution. See below, Section I, B, 3, and n. 119.

68. None of the manuscripts of the Proceedings and Debates for 1628 or of the True Relation of 1629 meets the physical description.

69. We have not discovered other examples of "par-

liamentary newsletters" sent out in a regular series for the entire session. Some letters regarding parliamentary affairs were sent by members themselves, such as those from Christopher Lewkenor to the Duke of Northumberland, and those that were sent out by Thomas Alured to different persons (see below, Section I, E, Contemporary Correspondence); but we have no evidence that they had wide circulation or that they covered all of the dates of the session, as does the Proceedings and Debates or Stowe MS. 366.

70. Merely to list "variations in order and omissions in the copies of the True Relation" for the twenty-five days that the Commons actually carried on business, the editors of *Commons Debates for 1629* needed sixteen pages of appendixes.

71. On these Clegate and Maynwaring discussions, see above, n. 34.

chronological order is indeed disrupted, but only in favor of topical order.

Nor is this apparent difference in orderliness between Proceedings and Debates and the True Relation merely a result of the difference in the numbers of manuscripts. The quantitative difference in the number and scope of errors is a symptom of a fundamental qualitative difference between the two narratives. It is a difference between a narrative or narratives compiled by several outsiders with varying and uncertain access to knowledge of what happened in the House and a narrative that bears no marks whatsoever of such lack of information.[72] The person (or persons) who ultimately put Proceedings and Debates together knew what he was about and did his work of compiling neatly and knowledgeably. It well may be that "the True Relation is a compilation made up from different sources and put together by different persons". In the case of Proceedings and Debates it seems beyond doubt that all the manuscripts ultimately derive from a single, initial, well-organized compilation.

Given our purpose—to dissociate Proceedings and Debates for 1628 from the True Relation of 1629, to demonstrate the differences between the two—we might close our discussion here. Having acknowledged the structural similarity between them (both are parliamentary compilations), we have taken note of their substantive differences—the True Relation, incompetent and confused; Proceedings and Debates ordinarily reliable because it was put together by competent and experienced hands out of sound material. But we feel obliged to speculate further.

When we ask ourselves whose those hands were, or to what sort of man or men they belonged—if not the unreliable stationers and scriveners—we can speak with somewhat less assurance, but also with some confidence. We have seen that in the compiled narrative separates must have been inserted into the daily record of the debates. We know that whoever was responsible for assembling Proceedings and Debates was careful and painstaking about where he inserted them. Considering the length of the account and the way that the insertion of separates into a pre-existing journal increases opportunities for confusion and mistakes, the number of common editorial errors chargeable to the compiler is very low.

The compiler must also have been one who not only understood parliamentary procedure, but who had access to separates, speeches, drafts of bills, and other items of parliamentary business that needed to be inserted into his account. And he was probably able to follow closely reasoned legal arguments well. In the case of the Cresheld speech of 27 March, he eliminated a good many of the specific citations to precedents, unless Cresheld himself did so in polishing the speech for distribution.[73] The version of Selden's speech of the same day, although reported by all the other note takers—the journal writer of Stowe MS. 366, the diarists Newdegate, Harleian MSS. 2313 and 1601—is presented more clearly and with more accurate citation of precedents than in those accounts. It is probable that the Proceedings and Debates copy was supplied by Selden himself for the record.[74] Two days later, on 29 March, came a debate that is filled with legal precedents cited by a cluster of lawyers. The number of surviving separates for these speeches is small: one each for the speeches of the Solicitor[75] and Hakewill,[76] and one for the second and less important speech by Sir

72. The errors in Proceedings and Debates are usually copyists' errors, rather than compilers' errors.

73. There are numerous separates of Cresheld's speech. See also n. 62, above.

74. The copy of Selden's speech among his papers (John Selden, *Opera Omnia* [3 vols., London, 1726], III, cols. 1954–1956) agrees with the version in the Proceedings and Debates. The only other copy we have found, doubtless taken from the *Opera Omnia*, is printed in Howell, *S.T.*, III, 78–79.

75. Howell, *S.T.*, III, 80–81.

76. Ibid., III, 76. The Hakewill speech appears also in Rushworth, *Hist. Collections*, p. 511. In both cases its date is given as 27 March.

Edward Coke.[77] For the much longer speech of Sir Edward Coke on that day, and for Sherfield and Saunders,[78] there are no separates. Yet the reports of these speeches in Proceedings and Debates are sound.

In the absence of any direct evidence, we cannot hope to identify with confidence the person or persons responsible for producing Proceedings and Debates. What we can do, however, and what may help others in considering the problem of how Proceedings and Debates came to be, is to use the information we have about the House of Commons, about its officers and procedures, and about some of its members in 1628, as the basis for a suggestion on this point. In so doing, we do not propose our hypothesis as a general alternative to the reconstruction in *Commons Debates for 1629*. That description may indeed serve for the True Relation. The hypothesis we outline below is offered as a different explanation for 1628, one that may be of convenience to other investigators. We begin with a list of established facts.

Among the items of information about the House of Commons and its records the following can be stated as verifiable facts.

(1) Accounts of the House of Commons, 1628.

(a) The Journal of the House of Commons, compared with four other accounts—the two narratives, Proceedings and Debates and Stowe MS. 366, and the diaries of Grosvenor and Newdegate—is a very slight thing, on many days only a few paragraphs, in contrast with several pages in the other accounts.[79]

(b) The proceedings of the House when it sits as the committee of the whole House are never recorded in the Journal, but debates in that committee are included in the Proceedings and Debates and other accounts.

(c) Versions of important speeches by lawyers of

which no separates have ever been found appear in the Proceedings and Debates.[80] Some of these are almost certainly too short and compact, too filled with legal citations, to be verbatim transcriptions. They are too accurate to have been based on notes taken while the speeches were being made.

(d) Accounts of some business of the House (e.g., messages), which in earlier parliaments were included in the Journal, appear only sporadically and irregularly in the Journal in 1628, but are included in the Proceedings and Debates.[81]

(e) When the Commons Journal and Proceedings and Debates report identical happenings in the House, they do not do so in indentical words.

(2) The Journal of the House of Commons.

(a) By 1628 the Commons Journal contains little that was not noted in one or more of the other accounts of proceedings in the House except for lists of members of committees.

(b) It had not always been thus. From the accession of James I through 1626 the Commons Journal had in fact been two parallel documents: first, a set of rough scribbled notes, taken while the House was in session, that briefly described the actions of the House, some of the debates, and the names of some who spoke; second, a more complete and coherent version, drawn from the previous notes, which included debate, but omitted the names of the debaters.

(c) For some sessions of the parliaments between 1603 and 1629 both accounts survive,[82] for most, only the rough notes. In the latter instances, no one knows what became of the amplified transcription, evidently intended as the official record, if indeed such a transcription was completed.

(d) By the 1640s the Journal achieves the form that it has retained ever since, a record of the business done by the House—its actions—but no record of its discussions.[83] The Journal

77. Howell, *S.T.*, III, 81.

78. See below, Vol. II, pp. 190–192, 188–189, and 189–190.

79. E.g., 29 March, 2 April, 15 April, 18 April, 3 May, 6 May.

80. See the speeches of Sir Edward Coke, Sherfield, and Saunders of 29 March.

81. For example, on 4, 7, 12, 15, and 22 April, Proceedings and Debates gives the contents of messages

reported in the House, which the Commons Journal merely mentions. On 3 and 25 April both the Journal and the Proceedings and Debates describe the contents of messages.

82. For the first session of James I's first parliament, for example, both versions survived and were printed in the *Journals of the House of Commons*, I, 139–256, 933–1002.

83. On the 1628 order against the recording of

never records any transaction of the House sitting as a committee of the whole House except when the committee's recommendations or resolutions are brought before the House for official approval.

(3) The Clerk of the House of Commons.

(a) The Clerk seems always to have been present unless the House stood adjourned, to be available for service that might be demanded of him without advanced notice.

(b) Responsibility for "keeping the Journal" lay with the Clerk of the House of Commons. Although no complete explicit rules had ever been laid down by the House as to what he should keep in the Journal, his "book" had been examined regularly by committees appointed by the House since the reign of James I.[84] He might use his assistants in keeping the record, as a different hand in the rough notes sometimes shows.

(c) The Clerk was responsible for having available to the House all the documents that came to the House from the Lords, the crown, or private petitioners, or that were generated by discussions during the session by the House itself.

(d) The Clerk and his staff had other and remunerative tasks. At a per-line rate they supplied members on request with copies of documents appropriate to their needs— orders and resolutions of the House, bills in various stages of consideration, copies of petitions, and so on. Since the Clerk took a percentage of payments on all documents, it appears that it was to his interest to hire, at line rates, an adequate number of copyists.

(e) The Clerk did not take notes *for the Journal* on debates in the committee of the whole House.[85]

(f) Although the Clerk was a crown appointee, and feed by the crown, he held office for life.

(4) John Wright, Clerk of the House of Commons.

(a) John Wright became Clerk of the House of Commons in 1612 and held the office until his death in 1633. He had thus been Clerk during all the parliaments of the 1620s.

(b) It was Wright who was responsible for the abundant record of the parliament of 1621 that appears in the printed *Journal of the House of Commons*.[86] He was responsible also for the record with reduced accounts of debates in succeeding sessions, and for the record, lacking debate, for the Journal of 1628.

(c) In 1621 a diarist noted that "one week after the parliament was adjourned, the Earl of Southampton, Sir Edward Coke, Sir Edwyn Sand[y]s, and Wright, the Clerk of the parliament House, were committed . . . for what cause is not known".[87]

(d) In 1628 (17 March), just before the parliament sat, Buckingham's henchman, Sir James Bagg, wrote to his patron: "Wright, the Clerk of the parliament of all men sithence my being of that house hath done worst service to his Majesty".[88]

(e) On 23 March 1621 the diary of John Smyth of Nibley mentions "two books kept by the Clerk, the one of business of the House, the other of the committees of the whole House".[89]

(f) The "Book of Committees" for 1621 records only proceedings in the committees of the whole House for 19 February to 2 March.[90] Notestein, Relf, and Simpson identify it as possibly the work of the Clerk's son and deputy.[91]

(g) John Wright's son assisted his father during the parliaments of the 1620s. He kept the Journal for a brief interval in 1621 when his father was ill,[92] kept some Journal notes and also notes of the committee of the whole House in 1625,[93] and in 1628 wrote the Journal notes on several days.[94]

---

speeches in the Journal see above, Section I, A, 2.

84. See above, n. 9.

85. According to a manuscript about procedure relating to the first parliament of James I, when the House went into the committee of the whole House, the Clerk's chair was used by the man who presided at the committee. Both the Speaker and the Clerk were present, but not in their usual places. Cotton MSS., Titus F. IV, f. 121v, cited in Notestein, *The House of Commons 1604–1610*, p. 464.

86. *Commons Debates 1621*, I, 101–102.

87. *Diary of Walter Yonge, Esq.*, Camden Society, 41 (1848), p. 41. The other persons named had been active

in the "opposition" in that parliament.

88. S.P. 16/96:36. Cf. above, n. 10.

89. *Commons Debates 1621*, V, 318.

90. Ibid., VI, 249–278.

91. Ibid., I, 96–97.

92. Ibid.

93. See M. F. Bond's Introduction, *The MSS. of the House of Lords*, n.s., XI, *Addenda 1514–1714*, pp. xi–xiii. The committee book, 23 June–8 August 1625 (H.L.R.O. MS. 3410), is also printed in *Addenda 1514–1714*, pp. 204–207.

94. The second hand in the manuscript Commons Journal for 1628 has been identified for us by M. F.

(5) The Committee of the Whole House.

    (a) When the House of Commons wished to discuss some matter free of the formal rules and restrictions on debate that applied during regular sessions and free of the presence in the chair of the Speaker, who was the King's nominee, it went into sessions of the committee of the whole House.

    (b) For formal business, such as receiving messages or resolving on answers to them, however, the regular session of the House was required, with the Speaker in his chair and someone in the Clerk's place to record the delivery of the message and the response to it.

    (c) In 1628, up to late May, the House of Commons spent a great deal of its time and conducted nearly all of its main debates while sitting as the committee of the whole House.[95]

(6) Accounts of Proceedings, 1621–1629 (narratives and diaries).

    (a) All unofficial accounts of the proceedings in the Commons in the parliaments of the 1620s fall short when tested by absolute standards such as fidelity, accuracy, copiousness, completeness, clarity, and freedom from error.

    (b) "X", the anonymous journal of 1621, is by the above criteria superior to all previous private accounts.

    (c) By *one or another* of the six criteria listed above, one diary or another of the 1620s is occasionally or even constantly superior to the Proceedings and Debates for 1628;[96] but, when all six criteria are considered, none of them matches it. Proceedings and Debates, by "weighted averages", is the best of all accounts of the parliaments of the 1620s.

    (d) The True Relation for 1629, when tested by the same criteria, is among the least satisfactory of the accounts of the period.

    (e) The number of surviving accounts of proceedings for the parliaments of the 1620s varies. The largest number exist for the parliaments of 1621 and 1624, very few for

1625 and 1626.[97] For the parliament of 1628–1629, in addition to several diaries, there are numerous copies of a single account for each of the sessions.[98]

(7) Members of the House of Commons in 1628.

    (a) The parliament of 1628 included an extraordinary array of legal talent, not only men with some knowledge of the law, but legal scholars and men of eminence in the courts, and, most distinguished of all, the venerable Sir Edward Coke.

    (b) The House of Commons that assembled in 1628 had leaders, men who were identified as such by the members. Most of the leaders had sat in four previous parliaments, especially in those of the 1620s, and all but one had sat three times before. Hakewill, the great lawyer, although he had not been a member since the parliament of 1621, had served in 1601, 1604–10, and 1614. John Selden, who had been an M.P. in 1624 and 1625, had worked with the parliamentary leaders of 1621 without being a member himself. He had served just before the 1628 session as counsel for Sir Edmund Hampden in the Darnel case and was internationally known as a scholar.

    (c) The leaders spoke often of their awareness that they were living in a historic moment, and of their concern that what they accomplished, and the legal arguments on which they stood, should be made a matter of record.

    (d) Of the twenty most eminent members of the House in 1628, all but two took part also in the proceedings of 1629.

    (e) The two men missing from the group in 1629 were Sir Edward Coke, whose absence was allowed at the beginning of the session,[99] and Sir Thomas Wentworth, who had been raised to the peerage on 22 July 1628.

Additional verifiable facts might be assembled, but with those that have been listed in the simplest form above, we can begin our

---

Bond as that of John Wright's son. For the dates, see below, n. 111.

95. The various accounts of the proceedings of 1628—Journal, narratives, and diaries—make this abundantly clear.

96. E.g., the Barrington diary for 1621 is more copious than Proceedings and Debates.

97. For 1621 see *Commons Debates 1621*. For 1624 fourteen unpublished private accounts are known, of

which one is a compilation by Sir Simonds D'Ewes (Harl. MS. 159). For 1625 and 1626, the numbers are two and four, respectively. These figures are based on the summary by R. C. Johnson, in *Bulletin of the Institute of Historical Research*, XLIV (1971), 293–300.

98. I.e., the Proceedings and Debates for 1628 and the True Relation for 1629.

99. *C.J.*, I, 921. He was now seventy-seven years old.

revised suggestion about how Proceedings and Debates of 1628 came into existence, and how it ended.

When the leaders of the Commons of 1628 assembled, they knew what things they wanted done, and more important were in agreement about the order in which they wanted them done. First, they believed it necessary to get on record the most pressing grievances: that the King's government had taken the property of the subjects against the law, had imprisoned those who had protested, and had denied the protesters due process of law.

To state the grievances, and to discuss them, was easy enough, but it was harder to be sure that a good record of the grievances and of the action of the House on them could be made and preserved. No one knew what the result of an application to the King for redress of the grievances of the subject would be, whether he would deny it or grant it, or whether what he granted would be sufficient to secure the fundamental liberties of Englishmen.

As to the record, that was an equivocal business too. If it was to be an official record, it must have the agreement of the Lords and the consent of the crown and be properly enrolled on the statute roll. But there were no grounds for assurance that this process could be carried through to the desired end. Anything less than that sort of record was equivocal. Merely inserting a document in the Journal of the House of Commons—even if it was painstakingly prepared—would not bind anyone. It did not even ensure the survival of the document, as the experiences with the apology of 1604 and the Protestation of 1621 had made clear.[100]

Among the leaders of the 1628 House of Commons were men experienced in matters of parliamentary records. At least four had kept diaries of their own in earlier parliaments, Erle, Pym, Rich, and Wentworth. Several had served on committees to examine the Clerk's book in previous parliaments and were so assigned again in 1628. Six of the eight designated for the task on 17 April were in the "leadership" group: Alford, Digges, E. Littleton, Noy, Rich, and Selden.[101] The six men appointed on 19 June to see that the correct entry was made in the Clerk's book concerning the King's cancellation of the commission and warrant for raising money by imposition were Sir Edward Coke, Eliot, Littleton, Phelips, Rich, and Selden.[102] Among the leaders who had kept parliamentary diaries before or had worked with the Clerk's book, only Rich appears to have kept notes for himself in 1628, and his are fragmentary and begin late in the session.[103]

If these men believed it important that a good account of their activities should be preserved, and if they were too busy to keep their own notes, it may not be unreasonable to assume that they knew that a reliable record was being kept in some other way, by someone whom they trusted. Possibly they knew of a careful diarist, whose notes might become the base for a filled-out record, using the materials that came to the Clerk officially. Or possibly they relied upon the records kept by the Clerk himself and his assistants.

It is worth looking more closely at the roles of John Wright, the Clerk, and his son, who was his deputy. Both men had had long experience at taking notes on the actions of the House and the debates that preceded those actions. The expansion of the record of debates in the Journal that took place after Wright succeeded to the post in 1612 was a

100. Somehow copies of the Apology of 1604 had survived, though not in the Journal, to be made use of in 1621; but James I proved in 1621 that no record simply in the Commons Journal was secure from the King when parliament was not in session.

101. *C.J.*, I, 885. The other two were Sir Thomas Hoby, an old "parliament man", and John Bankes, a lawyer. Besides these, the following also had been

named to perform this duty in previous parliaments: Sir Edward Coke and Sir John Eliot, *C.J.*, I, 520, 669, 718, 818. The men selected for the review of the Clerk's book were men of considerable experience in parliament.

102. *C.J.*, I, 915.

103. See below, Section I, C, 6.

sign of Wright's assiduity. Not only did he keep the record of debate and action in the regular sessions of the House, in which he "put down more speeches than anybody else";[104] he also kept a separate record of the transactions in the committees of the whole House.[105] His son served as his deputy when Wright briefly fell ill in 1621. During his father's absence, the son, doubtless following paternal example and instruction, took notes on the debates in the committee of the whole House.[106] His notes provide more names of those who spoke in the committee discussions than do any of the diaries of members.

We do not know what actions of the elder Wright led to his being in disfavor with the government after the parliament of 1621. His arrest at the end of the session, along with several of the opposition leaders, suggests that he had shown sympathy with them. Possibly he had resisted the seizure of the Journal, which must have occurred before King James's ripping-out ceremony.

The shrinking of the Journal of the House of Commons in 1624, which has been noted previously, is probably related to the events at the end of the session of 1621. The Clerk himself may have become more cautious about how much he would enter into the record. The members also, concerned about what and how much should be recorded, on

several occasions during this session, took care to examine the Clerk's book, "in what manner the Clerk hath used to take his notes, and make his Entries".[107] Again Wright's son was his father's assistant,[108] and again committee books seem to have been kept by them.[109] The reduced record in the Journal continued into the parliaments of 1625 and 1626, and committee books were kept by the Clerk at least for 1625.[110]

We do not know exactly how John Wright and his son dealt with the records of 1628, except that the son continued to be his father's deputy and wrote the record of the business of the House on several days.[111] If a parallel record for the committee of the whole House was being kept, as in the earlier parliaments of the 1620s,[112] one or possibly both of the Wrights must have been involved in that work. There is some evidence that this was so.[113] We know further, that whatever the occasion for the elder Wright's arrest in 1621 may have been, he was still held in distrust in court circles in 1628 as the man who had "done the worst service to his Majesty" in the last four parliaments. The inference is that, as Clerk, Wright had cooperated with the critics of the crown before, and might be expected to do so again.[114] We believe that the records of the session provide strong evidence of such cooperation.

In the first place, the limits placed upon

---

104. *Commons Debates 1621*, I, 101.

105. Ibid., V, 318.

106. Ibid., VI, 249. Why this son's committee book has survived among the official records of the parliament, and not the father's, we have no way of knowing.

107. *C.J.*, I, 673, 676, 683, 761. On the last occasion (10 April 1624), it was ordered that the book should be examined daily.

108. The House of Commons included the son in the fee allowances for the Clerk, 29 May 1624. *C.J.*, I, 798.

109. Among the papers of the Clerk that were taken to Secretary Windebank after Wright's death were listed three committee books of 18 *Jac.*, 22 *Jac.*, and 1623 (*sic*), as well as two committee books of 1 *Car.* Sheila Lambert, "The Clerk and the Records of the House of Commons", *Bulletin of the Institute of Historical Research*, XLIII (1970), 230.

110. See above, nn. 93 and 109.

111. The son recorded the proceedings of the House on 3, 17, 24 April, and 10 and 28 May; and he made occasional entries on at least the following dates: 8, 12, 19, 24, 27, 29, and 30 May, and 23 June. The "second hand" of the manuscript Journal is identified by Mr. Maurice Bond, Clerk of the Records, House of Lords. He has written to us that the son's hand in the Journal "suggests that they [the Wrights] were working together quite actively in 1628".

112. See above, nn. 93 and 109.

113. Among Wright's papers in 1633, according to the Lambert article mentioned in n. 109 above, were "three committee books for Religion, Grievances, and Courts of Justice, 4 *Car.*". What became of them is not known.

114. Bagg's letter to Buckingham, 17 March 1628. S.P. 16/96:36. In his letter Bagg suggested that the Clerk might be persuaded to do more for the King this

what the Clerk could enter in the Journal regarding actions in formal sessions of the House must have freed him for other kinds of activity. To note for the Journal decisions when the House was acting as a court of record, to list the names of members chosen for committees, and to keep notes at the start of the day about the readings of bills would not have required a great amount of his time. The flow across his desk of drafts of bills, copies of petitions and messages, and the orders for multiple copies of various matters, could have been handled by his hired assistants.[115]

Second, since so much of the time of the 1628 session was spent in the committee of the whole House, now on one subject and now on another, and the Clerk had to be on hand for any service that the members might require of him, it can be assumed that he was present while the committee did its work. Keeping notes on its debates in 1628, whether officially or unofficially, may have become a part of his role, as in the earlier sessions mentioned above.

Third, it is clear from the records that the leaders of the House, especially the lawyers, prepared their major speeches with care. They probably had either a copy or a precis of any such speech ready before the speech was actually delivered in the House or the committee.[116] Plans for the order of speeches, even those of less well known members on the days of the great committee debates on the subject's liberties, must have been made beforehand; Mr. Littleton, in the chair for most of those debates, was surely not recognizing members at random. It would have been reasonable for copies of those speeches to have

come into the hands of the Clerk, and for him to keep them together with his notes of the committee's decisions.[117]

In view of the provable facts that are at hand, and the inferences that can be drawn from the evidence provided by the records of the session of 1628, we believe it is reasonable to suggest: that the narrative we call Proceedings and Debates was compiled by persons inside the parliament, not from outside; that it is based on notes taken in committee as well as in the House in formal session—notes taken possibly by the Clerk himself, or certainly by one who knew procedures well; that the compilation of these notes with the related separates inserted was done also by persons who were in the House; and that either the Clerk, or persons working closely with him who had the confidence of the political leaders, did the job of compiling, working at intervals while the parliament was sitting, and completing it fairly soon after the session ended. The circulation at the time was probably not wide, for general circulation of a record in which speakers and their views were identified was contrary to the wishes of the members in 1628.

As to why, if such a method was used to compile a record in the session of 1628, it appears not to have been used to produce an equally valuable and coherent account for the session of 1629, several suggestions can be offered. First, with the completion of work on the Petition of Right, the leaders may have felt that the need for so complete a record had passed. Second, at least one strong leader who might have pressed for such a record—old Sir Edward Coke—seems not to have attended in the session of 1629.[118] Third, and

---

time if proper tactics were used. Cf. above, n. 10. For Bagg's letter, see the Appendix.

115. See above, p. 15.

116. Exceptions are the great arguments at the April conferences with the Lords, copies of which were ordered to be supplied afterward for the records of the House of Commons.

117. An interesting example comes from the speeches of Selden and Noy in the debate on martial law on 7 May, with Littleton in the chair. In Proceedings and

Debates the major speeches of those two eminent lawyers are filled with Latin and Law French—unlike the record of the comment afterward—but in Grosvenor's diary, which follows closely what Selden and Noy said, most of the report is in English. The only separate that we have found that contains these Selden and Noy speeches of this date is in the Braye MSS.; in it, too, appear the Latin and French wording.

118. He was absent at the start (C.J., I, 921), and was later called on to attend (Commons Debates for 1629,

possibly the strongest of the suggestions, another of the leaders of 1628, Thomas Wentworth, had by the 1629 session joined the ranks of the King's supporters, and methods with which he must have been acquainted in 1628 could no longer be used with safety.

In writing at such length about the possible origin of the original version of the 1628 Proceedings and Debates, we are aware that absolute proof of the theory we have developed is lacking. We have offered it as an alternative to the Notestein and Relf explanation based on the True Relation for 1629 that we think is not applicable to the proceedings and Debates for 1628. Other scholars, after they have examined the evidence the records provide, may find some different explanation more plausible.

3. *British Museum, Stowe MS. 366.*

This is a compilation of speeches and a narrative of proceedings in the House, consisting of 294 folio pages, $8\frac{1}{2} \times 13\frac{1}{2}$ in., covering the whole session (17 March–26 June). The manuscript is bound in brown museum binding. The title page reads: "Some notes taken in the cessions of parliament held at Westminster beginning the 17th of March 1627 and ending the 26 of June 1628". The name, "Sir William Borlase, Knight", that is written under the title may indicate ownership rather than authorship (see below). It bears no resemblance to the handwriting of the text, which is clearly the work of several different copyists. The hand, even the color of the ink, changes from day to day, sometimes in the middle of a day.

It is possible that this journal was intended for circulation, although there is no way of knowing what the circulation was.[119] The account of each day's business, starting always at the top of a new page, runs continuously to the end of the day, with no numbering of pages. At the end of each daily account its pages were folded in quarters, and the date was written at the top of one quarter (the verso); sometimes the packets so formed were creased slightly down the center. The packets were kept in chronological order. The folio numbers on the manuscript were added in pencil at a later time, perhaps when the daily accounts were unfolded and bound. Folio 289 seems to be the last that was folded; ff. 290–294 are in the same hand as the major portion of the narrative but appear to have been written separately, and were not folded. Mr. Hakewill's speech of 1 May on ff. 123–124v is unique; not included in the days' proceedings, it was evidently written separately, and then folded. On f. 292 at the end of the volume is "A Catalogue of the bills in the Commons House of Parliament this present session 1628", which indicates the number of times each bill was read and lists those that were voted down; the list is divided into two categories, public bills and private bills, and appears to be accurate and complete.[120] On f. 293 is a copy of "My L.D.'s [Lord Duke of Buckingham's] protestation against the mariners, 19 May 1628".

The only copy of Stowe MS. 366 known to be extant is in British Museum, Stowe MS. 367. Bound in brown leather with gold lettering, its binding reads: "Debates in the House of Commons 1618–1628, Brit. Mus., Stowe 367". The folios measure $7 \times 8\frac{3}{4}$ in., are written in one hand, and have not been folded. Folios 1–327 are the account of the 1628 proceedings, of which ff. 1–41 contain copies of some of the speeches at the conferences between the two Houses on 7 and 16 April. The final folios, ff. 329–344v, in a different hand, and on different paper, contain miscellaneous notes of speeches and public acts and declarations, some from the Civil War period, collected by a Mr. Morant.

---

pp. 58, 138, 191), but there is no evidence of his attending.

119. One copy, which is a later one, is Stowe MS. 367 (see below). Notestein stated (*Commons Debates for 1629*, p. xliii) that there was a third copy in the manu-

scripts of the Earl of Ashburnham. He did not realize that the Stowe manuscripts in the British Museum had come from the Ashburnham collection. See also pp. 11–12, above.

120. The list of bills will be printed in the Appendix.

The orderly arrangement of the account in Stowe MS. 367 indicates that it had not been put together from separate parts, but must have been copied after Stowe MS. 366 had been compiled. It contains occasional slight variations in wording.

The organization and nature of the record in Stowe MS. 366 indicate that it is based on the notes of one who was present as a member of parliament, but that it is not an actual diary. After reporting the King's speech on 17 March, for example, the writer added: "There is this left out, about the middle of the speech, which I did almost forget", and then he wrote down the omitted sentence.[121] There are also many marginal notes identifying persons mentioned in the debates, and numerous references to the time of day, or to "tomorrow"—all suggesting that the journal was written after a day's sitting, and was based on rough notes taken in the House or from memory. That it was actually rewritten is shown by its style, which is more finished than that of a true diary: there are no blanks, such as occur in each of the private diaries, indicating words not heard by the writer, and the writing flows smoothly, with syntactically complete sentences.[122] Furthermore, separates of speeches or messages were used at various times. The Hakewill speech mentioned above is one example. Another occurs on 2 May in relation to a message delivered from the King by Sir John Coke. First written was a summary of the message, but then it was crossed out, and a fuller version was given with a marginal note, "This is the true copy".[123] The note suggests that, while the writer was compiling his journal for the day, he received, perhaps from the Clerk's office, a "true copy" of the message, which he then substituted for the summary.

The reports of the debates in the Stowe MS. are more colorful and lively than the rather formal reporting which is provided in the Proceedings and Debates. The author had the knack, perhaps through the use of shorthand, of noting comments, almost asides, of various members. It was he who caught Sir John Eliot's pungent remark about Dr. Walter Balcanquhall, dean of Rochester, whose sermon for the fast was disliked, that he was "ill inhabited in his upper parts".[124] And he noted Sir Edward Coke's exclamation (26 May) that, "I am almost dead for joy", on learning of the Lords' consent to support the Petition of Right,[125] and, similarly, Coke's exultant, "I am half dead with joy", when, two weeks later, he heard that the King would accept the Petition.[126] He also included accounts of various humorous episodes that are not reported or are only briefly mentioned elsewhere. There was the time on 22 April, when he caught Coke's remarks about the shouts, "Commit it! Commit it!", after the puritanical Ignatius Jordan had spoken in favor of a bill "for the further punishment of adultery and fornication".[127] And there is the extended report he gives of the argument on 31 May between the Oxford and the Cambridge men over the precedency of their universities.[128] One can get the feeling, while reading the Stowe narrative, that he is actually present in the House, listening to the debates.

Furthermore, on several days, the Stowe MS. reports more speeches than do any of the other accounts. An example is the critical debate on supply that took place on 4 April in the committee of the whole House. For this debate the Stowe MS. lists 59 speakers; the Proceedings and Debates, 25; Newdegate, 45; Harleian MS. 2313, 27; and Nicholas, 32. At only one point in this debate did its author refer to a speaker as *Ignotus*. The fact that he

---

121. See Vol. II, p. 9 (17 March).

122. An example of this style is the report of a speech by Secretary Coke on 22 April (Vol. III, pp. 27–28). Since the Secretary had not prepared his remarks beforehand, copies of the speech would not have been available, as was sometimes the case.

123. See n. 51, 2 May.
124. Stowe MS. 366, f. 206.
125. Ibid., f. 192v.
126. Ibid., f. 225v.
127. Ibid., f. 97v.
128. Ibid., ff. 204v–207.

rarely left a speaker unidentified suggests either a familiarity with the membership or a special care to learn, possibly from someone sitting nearby, who was speaking. At times, perhaps as an aid to readers, he identified a member by his profession, e.g., "a lawyer".

The identity of the author of Stowe MS. 366 remains unknown. The name of Sir William Borlase on the title page is not conclusive, although the Borlase family of Buckinghamshire had frequently sent members to parliament. A comment on Aylesbury (20 March, Vol. II, p. 37) suggests that the diarist was familiar with political affairs in Buckinghamshire. Sir William Borlase, Senior, an M. P. in 1604 and 1614, was still living in 1628 and probably continued to be interested in news from parliament. His elder son Henry, M.P. in 1621 and 1624, died before 1628, and the second son and now heir, Sir William Borlase, Junior, sat in 1628. The latter had been educated by foreign travel rather than in the law, and had gained some reputation for his learning,[129] but his only parliamentary experience before 1628 had been in the brief session of 1614. His literary interests might give some basis for considering him as the author of Stowe MS. 366, with its evidence of wit and human interest, but whether one of limited parliamentary experience would have known so many of his fellow members may be open to question. The early speakers, of course, were mostly men of prominence. Borlase could have heard of them from other members of his family and from associates in London. By 4 April even a new member who attended regularly must have learned the names of many more.

There has been some speculation that the author was Sir Nathaniel Rich,[130] who kept diaries for the parliaments of 1621, 1624, and 1626, as well as some fragmentary notes for 1628 (21–22 May and 6–11 June).[131] Although there is some resemblance between the language of Stowe and the "conversational style" of Rich's diary of 1621, and although some usages with regard to dating are similar to those that appear in the Rich diaries of 1621 and 1626,[132] for several reasons Rich must be rejected as the author of Stowe MS. 366. In his own diaries Rich mentioned himself only occasionally, using the personal pronouns *I* or *myself*, and usually not reporting his own speeches; but in the 1628 Stowe manuscript Rich appears as one of the leading speakers in the Commons.[133] Furthermore, a close examination of the Rich notes for 1628, for example those of 22 May, shows that those notes cannot be considered as the base from which the fuller journal emerged: they differ greatly in listing the various speakers, and the longer journal includes material that is not in the briefer notes, but omits significant names that the notes record.

Nor can any other name be proposed,

---

129. *O.R.* The elder William had been named to the committee of privileges in 1614 (*C.J.*, I, 256), and was a friend of Ben Jonson. The younger William was a son-in-law of Sir Francis Popham. Personal details on William Borlase, father and son, are in George Lipscomb, *The History . . . of Buckingham* (4 vols., London, 1847), I, 310; and *Genealogist*, n. s., II, 229–235.

130. Notestein was once inclined toward this view, and identified Rich with the "Borlase" diary in a list drawn up in 1929. A copy of that list is in the files of the Yale Center for Parliamentary History.

131. Rich's diary for 1621 was published in Notestein, Relf, and Simpson, *Commons Debates 1621*; the unpublished diaries, photocopies of which are at the Yale Center for Parliamentary History, are mentioned in R. C. Johnson, "Parliamentary Diaries of the Early Stuart Period", *Bulletin of the Institute of Historical*

Research, XLIV (1971), 297–298. See also Section I,C, 6, of this Introduction.

132. Examples of the "conversational" tone in the Rich diary for 1621 are in *Commons Debates 1621*, I, 89–90. In Stowe MS. 366, as in the Rich diary for 1626 (photocopy, Yale Center for Parliamentary History), dates are regularly given by the day of the week as well as the day of the month. Similarities in spelling are inconclusive, since the Stowe MS. was done by copyists.

133. At one point in Stowe MS. 366 (f. 188v), on 23 May, the word *myself* appears in a speech by Sir Nathaniel Rich. It relates to the part in a conference with the Lords that was to be carried by "Sir Henry Marten, attended by Mr. Pym and myself". From its place in the speech, it is clear that *myself* refers to Rich as the reporter on plans for the conference. It was not the diarist's reference to himself. See Vol. III, p. 581.

since Stowe MS. 366 has come down to us only in the hands of several copyists and contains no identifying personal pronouns. All that can be concluded about its author, therefore, is that, while he did not know law well, he was a good observer, had learned to know his fellow members, and wished to tell a story well.

C. Diaries

Private diaries, either full or fragmentary, consist of or are based on notes kept by individual members of the Commons while they were actually sitting in the House. They differ from the compiled accounts in that they do not pretend to give an orderly report of each day's business, although in some of them there is evidence that the authors made corrections or additions at the close of a day or at some later date.[134] The notes are often hurried; blanks appear where parts of speeches were missed; errors occur because words were heard incorrectly; and there is little or no punctuation. In a few cases, shorthand notes are used. In many of the diaries the notes are incomplete because the diarist was absent or arrived late on a particular day. Often, however, the private diaries include speeches by less well-known members and, because of the writers' efforts to jot down exactly what was said, they tend to reveal much about the House of Commons and its members that is missing from the more formal accounts.

One parliamentary diary for 1628, that of Sir John Lowther, has been published previously (see below, Section I, C, 7). Professor Notestein, who searched widely for such records, secured photographic copies and initiated transcriptions of three diaries for 1628: Sir Richard Grosvenor's and the two

anonymous diaries contained in Harleian MSS. 2313 and 5324, and Harleian MS. 1601. For a fourth set of notes, those by Edward Nicholas, which are partly in shorthand and which had been used in a limited way by S. R. Gardiner,[135] Notestein and his students worked out an early transcription.[136] Rough transcripts of these diaries were made available by Notestein to a limited number of scholars. Brief excerpts from Grosvenor and Nicholas, relating to maritime and American matters, have been printed,[137] but none of the four diaries in the group mentioned above has until now been fully edited. Another diary, that of John Newdegate, was located by Notestein, but was not transcribed until the present edition was started.[138] Two other diaries for 1628 have been found since the establishment of the Yale Center for Parliamentary History, Henry Sherfield's and Sir Nathaniel Rich's. Of the three diaries in this latter group, with the possible exception of Rich's,[139] none has, to the Editors' knowledge, been used by students of the early Stuart period. The initial publication of these sets of notes taken by members, and the critical edition of Lowther's, should add considerably to the historian's knowledge of what occurred in the House of Commons in 1628.

Although the dates covered by the several diaries for 1628 differ (see Table of Manuscripts, below), they have been arranged in the text, and will be discussed in the following pages, in order of their fullness with respect to detail, beginning with that of Sir Richard Grosvenor.[140]

1. *Trinity MSS. E.5. 33–36, The diary of Sir Richard Grosvenor* [Trinity College Library, Dublin], is in four closely written small leatherbound books covering the period

---

134. Some examples of Sir Richard Grosvenor's insertion of fair copies of speeches are given in n. 144, below.

135. See below, n. 174.

136. See J. T. Gerould, ed., *Sources of English History of the Seventeenth Century . . . in the University of Minnesota Library* (Minneapolis, 1921), nos. 124–128, 132.

137. Leo F. Stock, ed., *Proceedings and Debates of the British Parliaments Respecting North America*, I, 79–95.

138. On Newdegate's diary, see below, Section I, C, 2.

139. See below, Section I, C, 6.

140. On the place of the Lowther diary in this order, see above, n. 2.

from 18 April 1628 through 21 June 1628. There were originally five books; the first of the surviving volumes is identified by the diarist as the "2nd book". The extant volumes constitute, for the days covered, the fullest private diary for the parliament. The first of the surviving volumes (E.5.33) has notes for the period from 18 April through 1 May and consists of 192 pages. There is no title page but there is at the start a brief table noting eight speeches and the dates on which they were delivered. The second (E.5.34) extends from 2 May through 17 May and numbers 189 pages; the third (E.5. 35), from 19 May through 3 June in 183 pages; and the fourth (E.5.36), from 4 June through 21 June in 189 pages.[141] The diary is all the more valuable in that its writer, unlike many of the other diarists, was remarkably faithful in his attendance at the meetings of the House, and was present regularly from 18 April through 21 June. The abrupt ending of the diary on the latter date was probably due to rumors that prorogation was imminent, and the writer, like many other members, may have started for his home. That the diary was Sir Richard Grosvenor's has been established by the hand, which is the same as that of the Grosvenor diary of 1626,[142] and also by the

notes on committees to which Grosvenor was named, and by the scratchy notes on his own speeches.[143]

Grosvenor's diary is written in a scrawling hand. The writer uses a system of abbreviations of his own devising. Some of the marginalia are difficult to read because of the present binding, which was added after the notes were written. At times Grosvenor inserted, in his own hand, fair copies of certain speeches.[144] Day by day, however, his own rougher notes give every indication that he was writing while he was in his seat at the House of Commons.

The diary indicates that Grosvenor attempted to get down in his notes as full an account of what was said and done while he was in the House as his writing speed allowed. In terms of the number of speeches reported, his notebooks are not equaled by any of the other diaries and accounts. Less well-known speakers are reported almost as often as the leaders of the House. Although no attempt has been made to count all recorded speeches, the following sampling, tabulated from the four major accounts (Proceedings and Debates, Stowe MS. 366, Grosvenor, and Newdegate), covering a period of five weeks, is revealing:

Comparison of the number of speeches recorded (21 April–24 May)

	P. & D.	Stowe	Grosvenor	Newdegate
21–26 April (6 days)	81	57	92	80
28 April–3 May (6 days)	85	98	133	68
5–10 May (6 days)	64	89	146	64
12–17 May (6 days)	90	65	142	62
19–24 May (6 days)	97	69	152	55
Totals	417	378	665	329

141. On the history of the Grosvenor diary of 1628, see Relf, *The Petition of Right*, p. 70n10. The missing first volume may not have covered all of the early weeks of the parliament. Grosvenor does not appear in other accounts as speaking until the subsidy debate of 4 April (Vol. II, p. 308), or as being named to a committee until after that date. The death of his third wife, Elizabeth, on 12 March 1628 may have delayed his start for Westminster. His notes for the 1629 session were used by Notestein and Relf for *Commons Debates for 1629*.

142. Trinity College Library, Dublin, MS. E.5. 17. A transcript of the 1626 diary is at the Yale Center for Parliamentary History.

143. See Relf's comments in *The Petition of Right*, p. 70n10.

144. Examples are a speech by the Archbishop of Canterbury at a conference on 25 April (MS. E.5. 33, p. 90); and the Lord Keeper's speech of 28 April (see n. 92, 28 April).

Thus the next most thorough account in the matter of entering speeches provides only five-eighths as many as Grosvenor does for the period of 21 April–24 May. Moreover, for no single week interval, with the exception of the first, does any other source give as many as three-fourths of the speaker entries that Grosvenor does. The Grosvenor diary includes notes on remarks by men whose presence there is not even noted in other accounts during the period tabulated above or earlier; for example, Thomas Godfrey, Richard Estcott, Sir Robert Crane, Sir Richard Molyneux, Sir William Spring, Sir William Pooley, and Sir William Twysden.

The Grosvenor diary has other merits. It is particularly good in reporting debates on legislation, even on minor bills, such as the private bills of this session. It is useful also for its record of debates in committees, especially that on religion. For example, Grosvenor reports in full the examination of Richard Burgess, vicar of Witney, on 5 May, while the Proceedings and Debates and Stowe give it scant mention, and the other diarists (Newdegate, Harleian MS. 5324, and Nicholas) omit it entirely. And Grosvenor was the only diarist to report the further proceedings of the committee of religion against Burgess on 26 May.[145]

Sir Richard Grosvenor had represented Chester in the parliament of 1621 and again in that of 1626. A member of an old and prominent Cheshire family, he was born at Eaton in January 1585, the son and heir of Richard Grosvenor and his wife, Christian, the daughter of Richard Brooke. He matriculated at Queen's College, Oxford, in 1599 and received his B.A. in 1602. He was knighted in 1612, and, upon his father's death in 1619,

inherited the family estates. Two years later he was made a baronet. Grosvenor played a prominent role in the affairs of his region, serving as sheriff of Cheshire in 1623–1624, and the next year as sheriff of Denbighshire.[146] In the parliament of 1621 he spoke at least nineteen times, on subjects that ranged from relief for the Palatinate, reforms in the law courts, and abuses by monopolists and by Trinity House, to the problems of Chester's trade; and he was named to an important subcommittee on the courts of justice.[147] As a speaker he was probably more earnest than polished. Edward Nicholas noted dryly in his diary on 27 November 1621, "Sir Richard Grosvenor here out of his papers read us a large lecture".[148] In the shorter parliament of 1626, according to his own diary, Grosvenor spoke but once, and was named to five committees.[149]

When he came to Westminster in 1628, Sir Richard was forty-three, and he may have arrived late.[150] This time he did not speak frequently, but he was fairly active in committee work, with appointments to fourteen committees. That he was interested in religious matters is indicated by the fact that his reporting of speeches on the subject is fuller than that of any of the other diarists.[151] In the second session of 1629 Grosvenor made a long report on "the proceedings of this House against Popery the last Session and what fruit hath been therein".[152]

But Grosvenor does not limit his interests to matters of religion, as the characteristics of his diary previously mentioned indicate. Because he reports what went on in the House more amply than any other diarist whose direct record of the proceedings survives, because he records the opinions of more members than

145. See 26 May, O.B.

146. An account of the Grosvenor family, and especially of Sir Richard Grosvenor, is in James Coston, *County Families of Lancashire and Cheshire* (London, 1887), pp. 297–340; see also *Alumni Oxonienses*.

147. *Commons Debates 1621*, III, 149, 185n11, 213, 268; VI, 262, 322, and Index.

148. *Proceedings and Debates in the House of Commons in 1620 and 1621* (Oxford, 1766), II, 219.

149. From the transcript of the 1626 diary mentioned in n. 142, above.

150. See above, n. 141.

151. Some idea of his sympathies may be drawn from his remark in 1621, during the discussion of Floyd's case, when he recommended that Floyd be punished by being sent to the Tower "with papers and his beads". *Commons Debates 1621*, III, 125.

152. *Commons Debates for 1629*, pp. 65–69.

does any other account, and because he gives notes on proceedings reported in no other source, Grosvenor provides us with a most valuable record of the debates in the Commons in 1628.

2. *CR 136/A.1, The diary of John Newdegate,* on loan from F. H. M. FitzRoy Newdegate, Warwick County Record Office [Shire Hall, Warwick]. The diary, consisting of three small notebooks (approximately $5\frac{3}{4} \times 3\frac{3}{4}$ in.) in the Newdegate Collection of family papers, has been in the local record office since 1950.[153] Although the parchment covers give no evidence of ownership, the diary has been identified as John Newdegate's because it has remained among the papers of the family and because John Newdegate was the only member of that family who sat in the parliament of 1628.[154] The notes cover the period from 21 March through 25 June, with Book I, 93 ff., containing the notes of 21 March through 11 April; Book II, 79 ff., those of 16 April through 4 June; and Book III, 58 ff., those of 5–25 June. In terms of the number of days covered, with only nine days of Commons business missing,[155] this is the most complete of all the known private diaries. The notes give every evidence of having been written while the author was sitting in the House; there are many abbreviations and interlineations, and many sentences are incomplete.

Although Newdegate was faithful in his attendance, his notes in the early days of the 1628 parliament indicate that he was unable to identify some of the speakers. Robert Goodwin, who spoke on 22 March, he identified as "a young gentleman". On 26 March he referred to Edward Kirton, one of the

thirty-odd most active members of the House, as "a gentleman above". Even Sir Nathaniel Rich appears in his notes at the committee of religion on 24 March as *Ignotus*.[156] By early April, however, he was much more sure about the identity of his fellow members. In the debate on the subsidy bill on 4 April, his identifications of forty-four of the members whose speeches he recorded check with those made by other reporters of the debate. In other respects, however, perhaps because he wrote in haste, or because he had difficulty in hearing, his notes are less reliable. He misquoted the Solicitor General on 25 March, for example, implying that he had been present at, instead of absent from, an argument in King's Bench. On the same date he misunderstood the name of the defendant in Coke's report on the case of John de Bildeston, a chaplain.[157] Later (22 May) in writing about a bill concerning abuses on the Lord's Day, he wrote "Lord Say[e]" instead of "Lord's Day".[158]

Newdegate usually reported speeches more briefly than the Proceedings and Debates, Stowe MS. 366, and the Grosvenor diary, but this does not diminish the importance of his record. During the first five weeks, Newdegate reported seventy-four speeches that are not included in the other accounts. On 1 April, in an important debate in the "grand committee for the liberty of the subject", when a petition was passed in opposition to arbitrary imprisonment, Newdegate reported thirty-four speakers, while Proceedings and Debates recorded only thirteen; Stowe MS. 366, only ten; and the other private diaries, no more than eight. Especially before the start of the surviving Grosvenor notes, the

---

153. The diary was found by Wallace Notestein in his searches of a generation ago, but it was not transcribed until a photocopy of the manuscript was rediscovered by R. C. Johnson in 1969 in the Sterling Memorial Library, Yale University.

154. The name is spelled "Nudigate" in *O.R.*, but the spelling customary for the family is Newdegate. The diarist's younger brother, Sir Richard Newdigate (1602–1678), a judge in the Cromwellian period (see *D.N.B.*), was the first to spell his name with an *i*. A

pedigree of the family and notes about its background are in *Gossip from a Muniment Room*, ed. by Lady Newdigate-Newdegate (London, 1897).

155. There are no notes for 17–20 March, 8 April, 12–15 April (the Easter season), 29–30 May, and 26 June.

156. See Vol. II, pp. 71, 133, 93.

157. See Vol. II, pp. 109, 110.

158. See Vol. III, p. 546.

Newdegate diary must be counted on for the less formal speeches and for the remarks of many of the less eminent members.

The diarist, John Newdegate, was a new-comer to parliament in 1628. Though elected by the borough of Liverpool, he came of a family once associated with Harefield, Middlesex, but seated since 1585 in Warwickshire. He was the son and heir of Sir John Newdegate of Arbury (d. 1610), and was born in 1600. Through his mother, Anne, eldest daughter of Sir Edward Fitton of Gawsworth, Cheshire, he was connected with families of prominence in the counties of Cheshire, Lancashire, and Shropshire, and with several persons at court.[159] Newdegate matriculated at Trinity College, Oxford, in November 1618. He took no degree, but was a student at Gray's Inn and the Inner Temple in 1620.[160] Unlike his younger brother Richard, however, he did not follow the law for a career. In 1621 he married Susanna, daughter of Arnold Luls, a Dutch merchant in London, and seems to have returned to Warwickshire before 1625, for he served in that year as sheriff of the county. It is impossible to say whether his election as M. P. for Liverpool, 3 March 1628, is to be traced to the influence of kinsmen on his mother's side in the Lancashire-Cheshire region, or to the influence of family friends at court.[161] Newdegate's fellow member for Liverpool, the courtier Henry Jermyn, almost certainly represented the patronage of the Duchy of Lancaster that was customary there.

John Newdegate died in 1642. Of his political or religious views his notes of 1628 reveal little. Whether he shared his brother's sympathies with parliament we do not know. There is no record that he ever spoke in the House, and he was appointed to only two committees. He seems to have been interested especially in keeping a record, either for his own personal satisfaction or for future reference, of what was being said and done in the House of Commons. That the importance of this parliament for his own time and the future did not escape him is shown by the way he caught, more than most of the other diarists, the emotional impact of Phelips's remarks on 30 April. After disclaiming any lack of confidence in the King, Phelips continued, according to Newdegate, "But our undertakings now are to bind future kings not to be able to hurt our posterity, and I hope that the child unborn will have cause to give thanks that he had a parent or friend in this parliament, and that our meeting now shall cause the safety of them in many subsequent ages. This I speak suddenly, and I pray pardon me".[162]

3. *Harleian MSS. 2313, 5324* [British Museum], an anonymous diary, consisting of two small tablets whose leaves measure $3\frac{1}{2} \times 6$ in., and covering the dates of 26 March 1628 through 24 May, with one entry for 4 June 1628. Originally in the form of tablets with pages fastened at the top, the manuscripts are now bound as notebooks, fastened on the side. The first volume, Harleian MS. 2313, 77 ff., has notes on the Commons debates from 26 March through 29 April, and also on the conference with the Lords of 16–17 April; the conference notes begin on the last folio and continue toward the middle of the volume, as the diarist reversed his tablet. The second volume, Harleian MS. 5324, 55 ff., covers 30 April to 24 May, and has a final entry for 4 June. The folios in the second volume have been numbered from the end, with f. 1v being 23 May

---

159. Biographical details are taken from *Alumni Oxonienses*; Burke's *Landed Gentry*, p. 923; and Lady Newdigate-Newdegate, *Gossip from a Muniment Room*. Among his mother's ancestors was the Elizabethan Lord President of Connaught, Sir Edward Fitton (see *D.N.B.*).

160. *Alumni Oxonienses*.

161. One family friend was William Knollys, Earl of Banbury. Philip Manwaring, who held various posts at court, had assisted Newdegate's mother with the problem of the wardship of her children in 1610. Lady Newdigate-Newdegate, *Gossip from a Muniment Room*, pp. 90–91, 139. On Manwaring, another 1628 M.P., see *D.N.B.*

162. See Vol. III, p. 179.

and f. 55v being 30 April; the diary is in correct sequence by date, but because the writer periodically turned his tablet around to begin a new set of notes, some of his accounts for a single day are all on verso sides, and some are all on recto. At times, also, he skipped folios. In editing these volumes, we have followed the diarist's correct order according to dates, and have indicated in the text, within square brackets, the folio numbers that are now on the manuscripts. Both volumes are bound in brown leather, with red leather on the spine, on which are marked the manuscript numbers and the fact that they contain notes of proceedings in the House of Commons.[163] At one time there were metal fasteners on the books, but these are no longer there.

Inside the cover of each notebook is a bookplate of "John Duke of Newcastle, Marquis and Earl of Clare, Baron Haughton[164] of Haughton, and Knight of the Most Noble Order of the Garter". The bookplate signifies that the volumes had been in the library of the only member of the Holles family to have the title of Duke of Newcastle (d. 1711), and that they were part of the Cavendish-Holles library at Welbeck Abbey in Nottinghamshire, which passed into the Harleian Collection in 1718.[165]

This 1628 diary, which is written in a hand that is usually clear and readable, has all the symptoms—abbreviations, deletions, interlineations, unfinished sentences, and almost complete lack of punctuation—of having been written while the Commons was in session. Although the identity of the author is unknown (see below), it seems probable that he was either a lawyer or one who had a keen interest in the law. Unlike Grosvenor or Newdegate, he did not try to record every

speech, but was more selective. If a speaker was less eminent than the great legalists of the House, or was not a lawyer, he tended to summarize the speech in a sentence or two, or else to omit any reference to it; but when such distinguished lawyers as Sir Edward Coke, John Selden, William Hakewill, or Edward Littleton presented their legal arguments, he took copious notes. Although his sentences frequently are unfinished, his initial citation of a legal precedent is usually accurate. Furthermore, this is the only diary that reports the complex legal arguments that occurred in the conferences with the Lords on 16 and 17 April and 23 May.

Harleian MSS. 2313 and 5324 report also the proceedings of committees meeting in the afternoon. For the meeting of the committee of privileges on 27 March, concerning the elections at Colchester and Lewes, only two accounts survive, Stowe MS. 366 and Harleian MS. 2313. The former sums up the proceedings in two sentences, while the Harleian MS. gives a full account. On other days, this diarist gives the best (and sometimes the only) firsthand account of the meetings of the committee of the whole House on grievances, notably on 26 and 28 March, 25 and 30 April, and 21 May.

There has been speculation concerning the authorship of Harleian MSS. 2313 and 5324, but nothing has been proved. Because of the bookplate (see above), Frances Helen Relf conjectured that the author might have been Denzil Holles.[166] The handwriting, however, does not resemble his. Mentioned also by Relf was another 1628 member, Henry Pelham, who was a lawyer, but this possibility seems more remote. Although the estates of John [Holles], Duke of Newcastle passed upon his

163. Harleian MS. 5324 is inaccurately described in the *Catalogue of the Harleian Manuscripts in the British Museum* as "Short Notes of what passed in the Commons, April and May, 1640, etc.".

164. The present spelling is Houghton.

165. The estates of Henry Cavendish, second Duke of Newcastle (d. 1691), passed, through a daughter, to her husband, the Earl of Clare, who was subsequently created Duke of Newcastle (see *D.N.B.*). On

the transfer of the Cavendish-Holles manuscripts into the Harleian collection, see Harl. MS. 4771, above, p. 7.

166. Relf, *The Petition of Right*, p. 71. John Holles, Marquis and fourth Earl of Clare and Duke of Newcastle (d. 1711), was a grandson of the second Earl of Clare, brother of Denzil Holles, and inherited in 1694 the estates of Denzil Holles (Baron Holles of Ifield). G.E.C., *Complete Peerage* (Gibbs ed.).

death to the family of Pelham (of Laughton, Sussex),[167] these diaries were among the Duke's manuscripts at Welbeck that were transferred to the Harleian library instead of being kept with other parts of the estates.[168] They can hardly be associated therefore with the Sussex Pelhams or with their kinsman, Henry Pelham of the 1628 parliament.[169]

The connection of the Harleian manuscripts with the Cavendish-Holles library at Welbeck suggests that one other 1628 member might be considered among the possible authors of the diary. This is Sir Charles Cavendish of Welbeck, M. P. in 1628 for Nottingham, the borough he had represented also in 1624. The younger brother of William, Earl, and later Duke, of Newcastle, the royalist commander of the Civil War period, Sir Charles was noted for his wide scholarly interests. Before his death in 1654, he had done some collecting of manuscripts and some writing of his own in the field of mathematics; but it is not known that he kept a parliamentary diary, nor is it known whether any of his papers survived at Welbeck as it went through the sequestration of the estates of royalists in the war years. John Aubrey records that a quantity of valuable manuscripts on mathematics that Sir Charles had collected abroad was destroyed through carelessness in the handling of his executor's affairs. Since he died unmarried, any papers he might have left at Welbeck passed, presumably, along with other Cavendish documents, to his brother and his heirs.[170]

As to internal evidence, the diarist referred to himself only once, when he noted briefly for 11 April: "Good Friday. I was absent. The subsidies agreed upon to be paid within the year".[171] The notes from the meeting of the committee of privileges give no clue as to authorship, since members of the House were free to attend those sessions even if they had not been named to serve on the committee (none of the three members mentioned above had been so named). The only noticeable peculiarity in his spelling or writing is that he wrote "by cause" instead of "because".

Whoever the diarist was, he attended faithfully during most of the session. Although his notes do not begin until 26 March, from that date until 24 May he was absent only twice—on Good Friday (11 April) and 21 April. There is no explanation as to why he kept no notes between 24 May and 4 June, if he was in attendance. Possibly his notes of 4 June can be explained by the fact that two days earlier the Commons had set that date for the House to be called, with the penalty of a fine of 20s. for anyone absent without leave.[172] If he had indeed been absent when the vote for a call was taken, his presence two days later suggests that he had been in London or its vicinity.

4. S.P. 16/97. The diary of Edward Nicholas [Public Record Office, London] is a small notebook of 92 folios, 4 × 11 in., covering the dates 21 March to 11 June 1628.[173] Originally the diary was written in five separate books that were tied together on the left side in two places with string, and were unnumbered. Book 1 (21 March–10 April), contains ff. 2–21v; Book 2 (11–28 April), ff.

---

167. Thomas Pelham, of Laughton, a nephew of John Holles, Duke of Newcastle, inherited the estates in 1711, changed his name to Pelham-Holles, and was in 1715 created Duke of Newcastle. G.E.C., *Complete Peerage*; and William Berry, *Pedigrees of the Families of the County of Sussex* (London, 1830), pp. 314–315.

168. See above, n. 165.

169. On the career of Henry Pelham, lawyer and parliamentarian, and his connections with the Sussex Pelhams, see Keeler, *L. P.*, and A. R. Maddison, *Lincolnshire Pedigrees* (Harleian Society, 1904), pp. 765–766.

170. For biographical details, see *D.N.B.* (Supplement); Arthur Collins, *Historical Collections of the Families of Cavendish, Holles* . . . (London, 1752), pp. 24–25; A. S. Turberville, *A History of Welbeck Abbey and its Owners* (2 vols., London [1938–1939]), I, 132; and John Aubrey, *Brief Lives*, ed. by Oliver Lawson Dick (Ann Arbor, 1957), p. 58. On the transfer of the Cavendish-Holles manuscripts from Welbeck, see above, n. 165.

171. See Vol. II, p. 422.

172. *C. J.*, I, 907.

173. A brief description of the diary, with attribution to Nicholas, is in *Cal. S.P. Dom., 1628–1629*, p. 31.

22–45; Book 3 (29 April–12 May), ff. 46–69; Book 4 (13 May–6 June), ff. 70–85; Book 5 (9–11 June), ff. 86–92. The books are now bound together as one, and on the outside binding is pasted a later key to the shorthand system Nicholas used in making his notes. It was never a part of the diary. There is no title page; the notes begin with the business of 21 March. The notebook is worn by time and the bottom sections of some pages are so spoiled by damp that they can no longer be read.

The Nicholas diary has numerous deletions and interlineations, and for most of the proceedings it provides a thin account, much less extensive than the notes taken by Nicholas of debates in 1621 and 1624.[174] The entries are usually brief. Most of the speeches reported here are to be found in much longer versions in the other diaries and accounts, although some of them are not to be found elsewhere—seven of them during the first five weeks of the session. Nicholas's attendance, as indicated by the number of entries in the diary, was irregular. He was absent on thirty of the eighty-seven days that parliament sat, and was usually late in arriving, having been detained, perhaps, by duties elsewhere. On days when the debate was very critical for the King's interests, however, Nicholas arrived early and left only when the debate was finished. Thus he was present for the entire debate on the subsidy bill on 4 April, and took notes on a total of thirty-two speeches, perhaps to report to his superiors the sentiments expressed by each of the speakers.

The career of Edward Nicholas is already well-known and need not be described here in detail.[175] He had sat for Winchelsea in the parliaments of 1621 and 1624; and in 1628, having failed first for election at Portsmouth, he secured a seat for Dover.[176] He was Clerk of the Council Extraordinary; and as an intimate of the Duke of Buckingham, he was much involved in the preparations for the expeditions to the Isle of Ré.

Although a member of the court group in parliament, Nicholas was not a useful spokesman for the crown. He appears to have spoken only once in the parliament of 1621, not at all in 1624, and but rarely in 1628.[177] In this parliament also he was named to no committees. His votes were probably on the side of the King, however, and his notes and unrecorded observations must have been useful to Buckingham. Occasionally a note, such as that regarding Sir James Bagg on 8 April,[178] suggests that he was jotting a reminder for himself more than recording action in the House. At times, also, perhaps when his attention wandered from the debate, he inserted casual notes on other subjects, such as a recipe for water to cleanse hawks.[179]

Although the Nicholas diary for 1628 is of less significance than his notes for 1621, he occasionally caught a flavor in a speech that other notetakers missed; for example, his note (31 March) that Phelips praised Sir Edward Coke as *monarcha juris*, who, though removed from the King's Bench on earth, might hope to have a place on King's Bench in heaven.[180]

174. The notes for 1621 were published in two volumes in 1766 under the title *Proceedings and Debates of the House of Commons in 1620 and 1621*, T. Tyrwhitt, ed.; and notes for 1624 are contained in P.R.O., S.P. 14/166. The diary for 1628 was transcribed and edited by Louise M. Sumner as a thesis (M.A.) at the University of Minnesota in 1913, but her transcript is filled with errors and has not been helpful to us. S. R. Gardiner made some use of the 1628 diary in his *History of England*, citing it a dozen times as "Nicholas's Notes". Probably because large parts are in shorthand, he appears not to have used all of the text as it is edited for *Commons Debates 1628*. Nicholas's notes for the 1629

session have been edited in Notestein and Relf, *Commons Debates for 1629*, pp. 107–172.

175. See Donald Nicholas, *Mr. Secretary Nicholas* (London, 1955).

176. *Cal. S. P. Dom., 1627–1628*, pp. 548, 584.

177. He spoke at least once on 5 June, and several times on 9 June, regarding naval matters.

178. Nicholas noted the mood of the House: "An inclination that Sir James Bagg shall be sent for". See Vol. II, p. 370.

179. 6 June, f. 85v.

180. See Vol. II, p. 224.

5. *Harleian MS. 1601* [British Museum], an anonymous diary, covering portions of three parliaments, 1626, 1628, and the Long Parliament. It is written on a tablet of fifty-six folios, measuring $4\frac{3}{4} \times 7\frac{1}{2}$ in., with the major part, ff. 4–41v, being a record of the proceedings of 17 March–8 May 1628.[181] On eighteen days within this time span there are no entries. The book is bound in maroon leather, with gold letters stamped on the binding that read: "House of Commons Diary, 1626–1641, British Museum, Harley MS. 1601". The handwriting is often difficult to read.

Of all of the personal accounts, this diary is the sketchiest. Its notes are brief, and it gives little information that cannot be found elsewhere. Fewer than ten speeches are reported that are not mentioned in other accounts.

It is not known which member of parliament kept this diary. The document contains no personal references, and the handwriting has not been identified. Even the fact that the diarist kept notes for three parliaments offers few clues. Of the nearly five hundred persons who were members in 1628, ninety-six sat also in both the parliament of 1626 and the Long Parliament.[182]

6. *Huntingdon and Peterborough County Council MS. D.D.M.58, Notes of Sir Nathaniel Rich* [Huntingdon Record Office]. This manuscript, from the papers of the Duke of Manchester, consists of two thin note pads. The first (seven folios) is labeled on the cover, "Concerning the additional clause and the bill of subscription", and contains notes for 21–22 May 1628; the second (five folios) has notes for 6–11 June.

The notes, which are hurriedly written and are difficult to read, have been identified as Sir Nathaniel Rich's through comparison with the handwriting and the shorthand style in other Rich documents, particularly his diaries for the parliaments of 1621 and 1626 and some of his private accounts.[183]

The career of Sir Nathaniel Rich, M.P. for Harwich, Essex, and a leader in this parliament, is well-known. His notes for 1628 relate to particular parts of the debates on the Petition of Right in May and to the Remonstrance to the King in June, but they add relatively little to the information provided by other accounts of this parliament.

7. *A Manuscript of the Earl of Lonsdale (unnumbered)*, the diary of Sir John Lowther [Cumberland and Westmorland Record Office], is a small quarto volume with notes for 4–26 June 1628, and also some notes for the 1629 session. A description of the document appears in the Historical Manuscripts Commission's *Thirteenth Report, Appendix*, Part VII, on the Manuscripts of the Earl of Lonsdale (pp. iii–iv). This is the only one of the diaries for 1628 that has been printed before.[184] Our decision to republish it is based on the following factors: (1) although the transcript made by J. J. Cartwright for the Historical Manuscripts Commission is generally good, certain portions of the diary are misdated; (2) Cartwright did not attempt a critical edition of the diary; and (3) few other private diaries cover the period from 4 June through 26 June, the span of the Lowther diary.

Why this account began so late in the session as 4 June is not known. Certainly its author, Sir John Lowther (see below), was present earlier, for he spoke on 4 and 9 April, and on 17 May his name was added to a committee list. Also, during the period of the diary—a total of twenty days—he was absent only four times. Perhaps there was an earlier notebook that is now lost. The diary kept by

---

181. For 1626, there are notes for 9–13 June (ff. 2–4); f. 42 is blank; and the last part of the volume (ff. 42v–56) covers 7 March–10 April 1641.

182. Information compiled from Keeler, *L. P.*

183. See above, n. 132. Mr. Christopher Thompson, who has used other Rich papers, concurs in this identification.

184. Historical Manuscripts Commission, *Thirteenth Report, Appendix*, Part VII, The Manuscripts of the Earl of Lonsdale (London, 1893), pp. 33–58. The Earls of Lonsdale were descendants of the seventeenth-century Lowther family.

the same author for 1626 also begins late, almost eleven weeks after the parliament opened.

Lowther took his notes carefully. He wrote in a relatively neat and legible hand, and his diary contains a minimum number of deletions, interlineations, and unfinished sentences. Usually each speech or item of business is set apart by a line drawn across the page. J. J. Cartwright's suggestion that the diary was reworked from rough notes or from memory seems unlikely. The order of the speakers is more accurate than would be possible for one relying on memory alone; and the number of blanks left with the names of speakers not filled in suggests that the diarist did not go over his notes again to insert the names.

Three members of the Lowther family sat in the parliament of 1628: Sir John Lowther of Lowther, John Lowther, Esq. (no doubt Sir John's son), both knights of the shire for Westmorland; and Richard Lowther, Gent., burgess for Appleby, Westmorland. The elder John, who was knighted on 6 June 1626, had sat in the parliaments of 1624 and 1626, and Richard had sat in the latter parliament also. The Lonsdale manuscripts include parliamentary diaries for 1624 and 1626, both written in the same hand as that for 1628. Since of the three 1628 members named Lowther only Sir John had sat in all three of these parliaments, it is clear that he must be the author of the 1628 diary as well as of the others. This identification was not established by Cartwright, since he was not aware of the 1624 diary.[185]

Sir John Lowther was a gentleman of prominence in northern England. His father, Sir Christopher, who was knighted in 1603 after having accompanied King James from the Scottish border to Newcastle, served on various commissions concerned with government in Cumberland and Westmorland. Following Sir Christopher's death in 1617, his son John continued in the same tradition. In 1624 he was elected to parliament for Westmorland, and he was returned likewise for the first two parliaments of Charles I. On 26 June 1626, shortly before the dissolution of that year's parliament, he was knighted. In 1627 Sir John was appointed to the King's Council in the Northern Parts. He served in that year also as one of the commissioners for the forced loan, and paid his own contribution.[186] Reelected for his county in 1628, Sir John was among those members who approved the grant of five subsidies for the King.

Lowther's diary adds much to our knowledge of the proceedings in the Commons during the last three weeks that parliament sat. By the time his diary began, the House was "growing thin", and a number of the other diarists had departed or were about to leave. In his concluding sentence on 26 June, he well summed up the feelings of many in the House toward the King's action: "And this was the end of this session, with no great content, for they desired an adjournment or recess".[187]

8. *Manuscript on deposit of J. L. Jervoise (xxiii7)*, the diary of Henry Sherfield [Hampshire Record Office], is an account extending from 8 April through 23 May 1628. Parts of the diary that were written in pencil are so faded that they can be read now only under ultraviolet light; and other parts are almost unreadable because of being spoiled by damp. The diary was written in a combination of English and Law French, interspersed with

185. Cartwright, who examined the 1626 and 1628 diaries, but not that of 1624, established by internal evidence that the 1626 notes were taken by either Sir John or Richard Lowther. For information on the 1624 diary, which has only recently been found, we are indebted to Robert E. Ruigh.

186. See Joseph Nicholson and Richard Burn, *The History and Antiquities of the Counties of Westmorland and*

Cumberland (2 vols., London, 1777), I, 431–432.

187. Lowther was not wholly in sympathy with his fellow members. The use of the word *they* instead of *we*, the personal pronoun by which other diarists usually referred to the House of Commons, suggests that this diarist may not have been in full agreement with all that had been done. His comments regarding the debate on the remonstrance (11 June) also suggest this.

many Latin words and phrases. Because the condition of the manuscript has prevented us from transcribing it according to the principles followed for the other diaries, we have decided not to include it with the other texts, but to print as much of it as can be transcribed in the Appendix volume.

The diarist, Henry Sherfield, M.P. for Salisbury, Wiltshire, was a well-known Puritan lawyer who had sat in three previous parliaments (1614, 1621, and 1624). See *D.N.B.*

D. Collections of Speeches of the Parliament of 1628

There are numerous collections of separates; that is, single speeches or other items, or groups of them. Such collections are often found among family papers. One from the Alford family has been mentioned previously (Harleian MSS. 6799 and 6800).[188] The separates among the Alford manuscripts contain no new speeches; but there are some copies of petitions in Harleian MS. 6800, and occasionally some meaningful variants of passages of speeches or versions of the proceedings. Excerpts from this collection have been used in footnotes and, in a few instances, have been included with the supplementary materials at the end of the proceedings for a day.[189] References to different separates, some of which were printed in Rushworth or used by Cobbett, have been made at times in footnotes.

One large collection, Braye MSS. 89 in the House of Lords Record Office, differs from many others in that its arrangement is not chronological but topical, with special emphasis on the Petition of Right. Once in the possession of John Browne, Clerk of the Parliaments, 1638–1649, it bears the long title: "A Journal Book containing True Relations of the most important and weighty affairs done and handled in the Commons House of Parliament holden at Westminster in the third and fourth years of the reign of King Charles: Together with the true copies of all the arguments made concerning the Petition of Right, all which arguments as well as the Petition itself and the King's full answer thereunto are upon record in the House of Commons". In spite of its title, it gives no account of the proceedings such as is found in Proceedings and Debates. Because most of the materials it contains can be found in other collections or accounts, usually although not always verbatim, we have not published the Braye MSS. 89 in full. As in the case of Harleian MS. 6800, however, we have used excerpts from the Braye MSS. when they provide a meaningful variant or some special insight. An example is the comment on Sir John Eliot's speech of 22 March, "He did passionately and rhetorically set forth our late grievances . . . ".[190]

E. Contemporary Correspondence

A final source of information about the parliament of 1628 consists of letters written by members of parliament or persons knowledgeable about parliamentary affairs. One member, Sir Francis Nethersole, a prolific letter writer, corresponded regularly during the course of the parliament with Elizabeth, Queen of Bohemia; and another, Christopher Lewkenor, wrote about parliamentary matters to the Earl of Northumberland.[191] A third, Thomas Alured, wrote to Sir John Coke after the latter had left London for Portsmouth in May.[192] Another letter from Alured to "old Mr. Chamberlain of the Court of Wards", published by Rushworth in his *Historical Collections* (I, 609–610), vividly described the agitation in the Commons in early June when many members feared the imminent dissolution of parliament.

188. See above, Section I, B, 1.

189. E.g., Warner's petition on 25 March; and reports on the Selden/Suffolk business, 14–17 April. See the O.B. for each date.

190. See n. 15, 22 March.

191. See above, pp. 11–12 and n. 69.

192. Coke had left London for Portsmouth on 19 May. Alured wrote to him there on 21 June. H.M.C., *Twelfth Report, Appendix*, Part I, MSS. of the Earl Cowper, pp. 343, 350.

Although usually such letters merely summarize the proceedings and debates in the House, they sometimes contain information or opinions not found elsewhere. We learn from a Nethersole letter, for example, his view that at least until 14 April "Sir Thomas Wentworth . . . hath the greatest sway in this parliament".[193] On 5 June, the Commons received a message from the King that in view of his intention to prorogue the parliament the House should not proceed with the Remonstrance. Two days after this incident, Nethersole wrote to Elizabeth of Bohemia, "Sir Robert Phelips could not speak for weeping; others blamed those that wept; and one said though they wept yet they had hearts and hands and swords to cut the throats of the enemies of the King and kingdom".[194] Thomas Alured described the same scene and, after remarking that "yesterday was a day of desolation amongst us . . .", he added, "Sir Robert Phelips spake, and mingled his words with weeping".[195] Another member whose published correspondence has been of use was Sir Thomas Wentworth.[196]

In editing the debates, if a passage from a member's correspondence serves to clarify a point of procedure or gives some insight into the debate of a particular day or adds material not found elsewhere, we have included the appropriate excerpt in a footnote. The texts of letters of members so used, if not elsewhere in print, will be found in the Appendix volume.

Besides letters by members of the Commons, other correspondence has occasionally been used. We have not searched all records of this kind, which for this period exist in such abundance, but have utilized several well-

known types of correspondence. One such is the anonymous newsletter. A major series of such letters, bearing the caption "Letter from London", was sent to Joseph Mead of Cambridge (Harleian MSS. 389–390). Some, but not all, of these were transcribed by Thomas Birch for his *Court and Times of Charles I.* Although their author is not known,[197] he was obviously someone in London who was sending to a group of subscribers in the country his reports on what was occurring in the city. His comments on proceedings at Westminster are brief, but he often included bits of information that do not appear elsewhere. His letter of 21 March, for example, mentioned that a peer was heard to say when parliament opened, that the members of the Commons "were able to buy the Upper House (his Majesty excepted), thrice over".[198] From letters in this series, and others in the Harleian MSS. 389–390, such as those written by Mead himself, we have drawn an occasional footnote (e. g., n. 51, 24 March). Texts of such letters, if previously unprinted, and a number that relate to elections, will be found in the Appendix volume.

Among the State Papers, besides the Nethersole letters mentioned above, is the Conway correspondence, from which several excerpts have been taken. As for the dispatches of foreign ambassadors, always interested observers of English affairs, relatively little valuable comment on proceedings in the parliament has been found. Neither the French nor the Spanish court had a representative in London in 1628. The chief proceedings of the parliament were routinely reported by Alvise Contarini to the Doge and Senate of Venice, but he noted little that cannot be obtained from other sources. We have in-

---

193. Nethersole to Elizabeth, Queen of Bohemia, 14 April 1628. S.P. 16/101:4.

194. Letter of 7 June 1628. S.P. 16/106:55.

195. Rushworth, *Historical Collections*, I, 609.

196. In addition to W. Knowler's edition of *The Earl of Strafford's Letters and Despatches* (London, 1739), we have used J. P. Cooper's edition of *Wentworth Papers,*

1597–1628 (London, 1973).

197. An additional correspondent, whose letters Mead mentioned at times, was John Pory. On Pory's career and on his activities as a correspondent after 1624, see *D.N.B.*

198. Newsletter from London, 21 March 1628. Harleian MS. 390, f. 365.

cluded in footnotes, however, a few of his remarks. The same may be said regarding the dispatches of Amerigo Salvetti, ambassador from the Grand Duke of Tuscany, although Salvetti appears to have had somewhat better information about parliamentary affairs than did his Venetian counterpart. Some of his observations have been useful.[199]

II. EDITING COMMONS DEBATES 1628

In preparing *Commons Debates 1628* for publication, the Executive Editor, with the advice and counsel of the Editorial Board and the Advisory Board of the Yale Center for Parliamentary History, has made a number of decisions with respect to editorial procedure, aids for the use of scholars, and editorial conventions. Where there were several alternative solutions to a particular editorial problem, we made our choices on the grounds of convenience to the users of the work, of a reasonable economy with respect to editorial and publishing costs, and of maximizing the speed with which usable portions of the proceedings in the House of Commons in 1628 could be put in the hands of scholars. Needless to say the foregoing considerations were not always perfectly compatible with each other. And of course they have given way to the overriding object of the editorial project: to make available to scholars an accurately edited version of what went on in the House of Commons between 17 March 1628, when the members of parliament first assembled, and 26 June 1628, when the King prorogued the first session of the parliament of 1628–1629.

What immediately follows is an explanation of the four major editorial decisions that have determined the form in which *Commons Debates 1628* appears.

A. Completeness of Reproduction of the Surviving Manuscripts

Since all accounts and diaries of the proceedings of the House of Commons in 1628 are accounts of the *same* proceedings, they inevitably in some measure duplicate each other. Indeed it would be surprising and disconcerting if they did not. This duplication, however, raises for the editors the question of how completely the manuscript sources should be reproduced in the printed version of *Commons Debates 1628*. The theoretical alternatives range from complete reproduction of all surviving manuscripts to full reproduction of only one of them, the most copious and complete. In the latter case, proceedings not "covered" in the most complete account, but "covered" in some other account, could be inserted in footnotes or in segments of text subordinated to the main account. The late Wallace Notestein, who first attempted the systematic editing of all surviving manuscript accounts of individual parliaments, followed such a procedure in editing the accounts of the early months of the Long Parliament.[200] In that case, one account, the parliamentary diary of Sir Simonds D'Ewes, was so much more copious and complete than any other, that Notestein published it alone in full and used the other surviving accounts to fill out the places where D'Ewes happened to be thin.

No one systematically editing the accounts of a single parliament or a single session of a parliament has ever published *all* the surviving manuscripts of such accounts. The reason for this is that for each of the parliaments or sessions (1610, 1621, 1629) so edited duplicate or multiple copies of one account or another have survived. There can be no good reason for publishing in full two accounts of proceedings in the House of Commons that differ one from the other only as the consequence of the errors of a copyist.

This stricture applies with even greater force to the parliament of 1628–1629 as a consequence of the existence of the narrative that we have called Proceedings and Debates for the session of 1628, and of the one that

199. The Salvetti Correspondence in H. M. C., *Eleventh Report, Appendix*, Part I.

200. *The Journal of Sir Simonds D'Ewes*, ed. by Wallace Notestein (New Haven, 1923).

Notestein and Relf called the True Relation for the session of 1629. We had found thirteen versions[201] of this account when we stopped searching on the grounds that, as far as increasing our information was concerned, we had reached the point not only of diminishing but of negligible returns. We were confirmed in our view of the futility of a more zealous search by the experience of Notestein and Relf. In a marvelous feat of manuscript-hunting they had dug up forty-eight versions of the True Relation and collated thirty-four of them.[202] The yield in additional insight and information of this effort fell sadly short of the energy that was invested in it. Among the forty-eight manuscripts, the editors were unable to identify an *Ur*-version, much less to identify the initial compiler of the narrative; nor were they able to offer an entirely convincing hypothesis to explain how the narrative was actually gathered and put together.[203] Moreover, well before they had got past the collation of a dozen manuscripts of the True Relation, the collating process had ceased yielding anything much but variants of copyist errors. Finally, if the hypothesis about the origins of Proceedings and Debates offered above (Section I, B) is correct, variants in Proceedings and Debates are even less significant than in the True Relation.

It is evident then that our editorial practice in dealing with the thirteen versions of Proceedings and Debates had to be different from our practice in dealing with the two versions of the Stowe MSS. (Stowe MSS. 366 and 367), the second of which was clearly a later copy of the first. In effect we produced from the collation of thirteen manuscripts a synthetic version of Proceedings and Debates, on

principles described below in Section II, B, Texts and Annotations.

As to the remaining accounts, we will publish in full the manuscript journal of the House of Commons, the narratives in Harleian MS. 6799 and the original copy of the account in Stowe MS. 366, and seven diaries by men in parliament dealing with what went on in the House of Commons in 1628. That is, we are publishing *in full* all known *independent* accounts of the proceedings of the House of Commons in 1628.[204] The grounds for publishing in full sources that frequently overlap each other in substance have been succinctly stated by Professor Geoffrey Elton of Cambridge University in what we like to think of as Elton's First Law. Our aim has been one that he proposed, "to make all recourse to the originals superfluous".[205]

The reasoning behind Elton's Law is clear enough. The systematic publication of all known manuscript records of proceedings in a particular session of a pre-Hansard House of Commons is not a once-in-a-lifetime, or a once-in-a-century, but a once-ever thing. The primary justification for so ambitious an enterprise is that it will provide scholars forever with a convenient printed version of related records that are now in manuscripts widely scattered and often difficult to decipher. Under such circumstances, for an editor to provide scholars with only so much of a particular account of the proceedings in the House of Commons as in his great wisdom he deemed important would verge on the pride that goes before the fall. In 1975 we do not know and have no way of knowing what scholars (if there are any) in the year 2100 will think important, any more than scholars

---

201. Several imperfect copies in addition to the thirteen that have been collated for our text were found also. See above, Section I, B, 2.

202. *Commons Debates for 1629*, p. 276.

203. The sections (ibid., pp. xv–xli) that Notestein and Relf devoted to the discussion of the True Relation in its many versions and to the related "separates" (see above, Section I, B, 2) are models of historical erudition, but with respect to the problems mentioned

above they do not answer all the questions.

204. We hope that our search has uncovered all surviving accounts of proceedings in parliament in 1628. If any other account comes to light after the publication of the first volumes of *Commons Debates 1628* and before the last volume goes to press, we shall incorporate it into the last volume.

205. G. R. Elton, "Studying the History of Parliament", *British Studies Monitor*, II (1971), 7.

in 1850 knew what historians in 1975 would think important.[206] Therefore we have not tried to guess what in the records of proceedings of the House of Commons in 1628 will interest scholars during the next 125 years. We have rather published in full all known independent accounts of what went on in the House in 1628, and left it to other scholars now and hereafter to decide what in those accounts interests them.

B. Texts and Annotations

The range of editorial effort that could be invested in publishing the texts of and annotations to the independent accounts of the proceedings in the House of Commons in 1628 is broad. Leaving aside for a moment the problematic, multiple-version Proceedings and Debates, minimal editing of all other accounts of the proceedings would be attainable by publishing photocopies of those accounts with no annotation at all. On the other end of the spectrum, besides "modernizing" the texts, an editor could provide in the footnotes a running commentary on and explication of the proceedings of the House with full treatment of their antecedents and consequences. He could thus produce a text that ran as a thin trickle between Alpine massifs of footnotes.

The second alternative did not seem desirable. It appeared to us that the function of the editors of *Commons Debates 1628* was to prepare not a definitive *treatise on*, but a convenient *edition of* the records of proceedings in Commons in 1628 for the use of other scholars. Sensibly the Research Division of the National Endowment for the Humanities, which generously and patiently supported the project so conceived, would, we believe, have rejected the more ambitious enterprise with its larger requirement of time and money.

On the other hand, the minimal program seemed equally unwise. What men said and did in the parliament of 1628 should be of interest and therefore accessible not only to historians of early Stuart parliaments, but to scholars interested in the general history of England; in the constitutional history and law of England, the United States, and the states of the British Commonwealth; in the history of liberty, of political ideas, of representative institutions, and of elites; and finally in matters whose relation to the parliament of 1628 we can not even conceive of. Assuming a potential cluster of users so extensive and so amorphous, we have prepared a "modernized" text and provided annotations and other editorial aids and devices that, given a reasonable expenditure of effort, will enable reasonably assiduous researchers to figure out what, insofar as it was recorded, was going on in the House of Commons from 17 March to 26 June 1628. In Section II, E, below, readers will find a description of the editorial aids provided in *Commons Debates 1628*, and in Section II, F they will find a description of the canons of modernization adhered to and of the specific editorial conventions used in these volumes. Through those aids and conventions we hope to comply with Elton's Second Law on the editing of sources, "to make historical evidence not only accessible but also manageable and comprehensible".[207]

Some peculiarities of the manuscript texts could not be dealt with through any simple procedural rules. One such involved the personal names of some of the members who took part in debate or served on committees, but who in some accounts were not identified by personal name. Such was the case with several members holding office under the crown. In the manuscript accounts they

---

206. Most of us have perhaps encountered even in respectable collections of source materials of 125 years ago the sort of bracketed statement of which the following is a characteristic though fictitious example: "[The next 50 folios indicate the itemized monthly expenditures of this humble family of six between

March 1672 and January 1675. We have omitted this material as being of insufficient general interest to our readers]".

207. G. R. Elton, "Studying the History of Parliament", *British Studies Monitor*, II (1971), 7.

appear as, for example, Mr. Secretary, Mr. Solicitor, Mr. Treasurer. In the text we have reproduced the titles as they occur in the manuscripts. However, in the Order of Business (see below, pp. 44–46) we have listed all officials by their personal names. A more acute difficulty arises with members who had surnames identical with or similar to that of other members: the Alfords, the Goodwins, the Joneses, and so on. Fortunately, a good many of the "doubled" members had titles of honor. The custom was that the given name (or at least initial) of a knight or baronet was set down along with his title and surname. This takes care of the three Howards who were knights and the two-dozen-odd other titled commoners who shared a surname with another member. It does not take care of Sir Robert and Sir Rowland Cotton, much less of Sir Thomas Fanshawe (M.P., Hertford) and Sir Thomas Fanshawe (M.P., Lancaster). Often when a Cotton speaks he is designated as "Sir Robert", but we cannot be sure which Cotton the "Sir Ro." appointed to the committee on the estates of William Morgan was.[208] There is no way to tell which Sir Thomas Fanshawe is speaking in the House or serving on a committee. Identity of surname creates greater perplexity among untitled commoners. Often neither the Commons Journal, nor the compilers of the narratives, nor the diarists set down the given names of such commoners.

This awkward situation makes it hard to know which of three Welsh Mr. Joneses is which, and whether the "Mr. Browne, a lawyer", who made an important speech on 28 March, was George or John, since both had had a legal education. Worse, it makes it not quite certain who three of the apparently most active members of the House actually were. Was "Mr. Alford" Edward or John, "Mr. Rolle" John or Henry? And "Mr. Littleton", was he Edward or Thomas?

Judged by the extent of their participation in debate and service on committee, Alford and Rolle were important members, if they were each one man. And "Mr. Littleton", Edward or Thomas or both, was so busy—chairman of the committee of the whole House for most of the proceedings that eventuated in the Petition of Right, and active in many other ways besides—that he *might* have been *two* leading members of the House.

Nor does the trouble end with identical surnames. There is, for instance, Mr. Pim or Pym or Pimme. He is John Pym, who a dozen years later was to be the most effective member of either House in the Long Parliament. Or is he? If he is Mr. Pimme, probably. But if he is Mr. Pim or Pym, he might be John or Hugh Pyne. Seventeenth-century spelling and writing are erratic enough to embrace this possibility. Nor was there always a perfect consensus among our keepers of accounts whether a certain speaker was Mr. Sherfield [Henry], Mr. Sherland [Christopher], or Mr. Sherwill [Thomas].[209]

Yet, if one will grant one probability and make an inference from one certainty, something can be done to diminish some of the uncertainties in identifying members. The probability is that lawyers were more likely than laymen to address themselves to legal issues and serve on committees that dealt with matters of law. The certainty is that freshman members were a very quiet lot. The most garrulous of the freshman members of 1628 whose identity is clear spoke eight times; most new members spoke not at all.[210] The inference is that freshman M.P.'s who were untitled and who bore the same name as another member behaved the way most other freshmen did: either they did not speak at all, or the diarists made no note when they did.

Application of the two tests regarding training as lawyers and previous experience in

208. 15 April.

209. Disagreements among the manuscripts regarding these names appear on 21 and 24 March.

210. Of 135 members of the 1628 House about

whose names there is no ambiguity, and who had not sat within the past decade, 106 are not recorded as speaking at all from 17 March to 27 May 1628.

parliament, which have just been described, makes it fairly safe to infer that the Alford and the Littleton who show up in the records of proceedings in 1628 are almost always the Edwards,[211] the Rolle is usually Henry,[212] and that the Mr. Pym, Pim, Pine, or Pyne, is more often John Pym than Hugh Pyne or John Pyne.[213] We can be reasonably confident also that it was one of the lawyers, Christopher Sherland or Henry Sherfield, who made several speeches concerned with the law, and not Thomas Sherwill, the merchant.[214]

In all cases we have left the name in the text as it occurred in the manuscript. When the evidence seemed to warrant, we have supplied what appeared to us the correct name in the Order of Business (see below, pp. 44–46). In the committee lists, on the basis of our knowledge of the particular interests and experience of some of the members, we have occasionally inserted in the text in brackets an identifying first name for a member listed. Both in the Order of Business and in committee lists we have always inserted first names when there is no doubt about the identification. When a diarist wrote down the name of a speaker but made no record of the speech that followed, we have printed the name as it occurs in the manuscript.

Although some of the texts of the manuscript accounts posed frequent and considerable paleographic difficulties, happily they did not present the editors with very many insoluble problems of meaning. On occasion, however, diarists did set down notes in a confused or careless way that left the meaning of a passage unintelligible. In such instances, via footnotes, we have referred readers to accounts more cogently setting forth the speech or the proceedings in question. Occasionally, too, a diarist (usually Newdegate)[215] put in his notes a patently absurd statement. In such cases we have inserted "[sic]" at the end of the statement or after an incongruous word. Once in a while entirely intelligible accounts of the same speech or action will disagree as to what was actually said or done. We call attention to such disagreements by means of footnotes.

Sometimes in the press of notetaking a diarist failed to finish writing a sentence. Where this happened we have inserted a virgule [/] in the text. Less frequently a writer left space in an account, apparently with the intention of later inserting a word or phrase. In such cases we have inserted "[blank]".

The thirteen copies of Proceedings and Debates confront an editor with a problem different in dimensions and kind from that of the single-copy diaries and from that of Stowe MSS. 366 and 367. Although it has been possible to divide the thirteen manuscripts of Proceedings and Debates into two groups and even to offer a tenuous hypothesis as to how that account was first put together,[216] we have not been able to work out a plausible genealogy of the manuscripts nor,

---

211. John Alford had never before sat in the House. Edward Alford, his father, had been a member at least five times before, beginning in 1604, and in the 1620s had sat in all the parliaments save that of 1626, from which Charles I barred him by pricking him sheriff. Thomas Littleton, not a lawyer, had not sat before 1628. Edward Littleton, already a distinguished lawyer and a future Chief Justice of Common Pleas, had served as M.P. at least three times previously. The latter was more probably the Mr. Littleton who spoke often on legal issues. From other sources, we know that he often chaired the committees of the whole House.

212. John Rolle, merchant, had been a member once before. His brother Henry, a future Chief Justice of King's Bench, had served four times, and was more probably the Mr. Rolle whose speeches and com-

mittee appointments were often concerned with the law.

213. John Pym had sat four times before in the 1620s; John Pyne had served twice before. Hugh Pyne, though a new M.P., was known as an outspoken critic of royal policies. Birch, *Court and Times of Chas. I*, I, 292, 295; Keeler, *L.P.*, p. 319.

214. Sherland had been a member three times before in the 1620s, and Sherfield, four times before. The problem of identity arises only when accounts disagree; often the two lawyers are clearly identified.

215. E.g., the Solicitor's speech on 25 March (Vol. II, p. 109): "Because his health did hinder him from being absent . . .".

216. A description of the manuscripts collated for this edition, with the numbers by which they are re-

except where there were manifest copyist errors, to argue that the version of a passage in one manuscript was closer to the original than the version in any other manuscript. The laborious and time-consuming effort of collating the thirteen manuscripts yielded little insight into their lines of descent and only an occasional variant that was not the consequence of an omission or a copyist's error. What collation did yield was a few commonsense rules for editing Proceedings and Debates under the constraints that our uncertainties about the manuscripts imposed on us.

Under the circumstances it made sense first to begin construction of the version of Proceedings and Debates to be published on the foundation of one of the most complete manuscripts and one that presented a minimum of paleographic obscurities. Trumbull Add. MS. 50 met these requirements.

Second, it made no sense to footnote words or phrases from the other Proceedings and Debates manuscripts that varied from the Trumbull MS. but had no effect on the meaning of a passage. Therefore, we have footnoted only in places where variations altered the sense of a passage.

Third, when the text of more than one-half of the other manuscripts (i.e., seven of them) made sense of a passage and/or enlarged it by the use of an additional word or phrase, and the Trumbull MS. did not make sense or gave a briefer account, we substituted the reading of the fullest and most intelligible text. The substituted passages are not indicated by footnotes but are simply incorporated into the Trumbull account, making a composite text. In a few instances less than half of the manuscripts had a variant word that agreed with the diaries and the Stowe MS. 366 account. Believing the diarists to reflect more accurately what was actually said, because they wrote in the House at the time the speeches were being made, the editors have inserted such "correct" variants

from the other accounts into the published Proceedings and Debates text.

Finally, when any manuscripts had alternate readings significantly different from the Trumbull MS. we inserted footnotes to give the variant readings and the numbers of the manuscripts in which these readings occur.

In this Section II, B of the Introduction we have described several situations in which, in order to provide a text making maximum sense, we have had recourse to annotation in footnotes. All further annotation has been undertaken to give necessary editorial assistance to the users of *Commons Debates 1628*. The general rules and bounds followed in providing this assistance will be described in Section II, E, below.

C. Arrangement of the Edited Texts

The editors recognized three alternatives—one ideal, two practical—for arranging the edited manuscripts of *Commons Debates 1628*.

Ideally it was possible to arrange the manuscripts in parallel columns with all accounts of a speech or action coordinated horizontally, as Matthew, Mark, and Luke are arranged in synoptic versions of the first three Gospels. However convenient such an arrangement might be, and it would indeed be most convenient, the potential publishing costs were astronomical.

More practical was the possibility of using the individual account as the unit of editing, thus publishing *Commons Debates 1628* diary-by-diary. In one sense, this is the natural way to arrange the narratives since it is in effect the way they were written, one-by-one. Moreover, it is the arrangement adopted by Professor Notestein for publishing the massive *Commons Debates 1621*, and more recently by Elizabeth Read Foster for *Proceedings in Parliament 1610*. Of the five volumes of text in *Commons Debates 1621* the last two contain twelve different accounts of proceedings in the House. Scholars who have worked with the

---

ferred to in footnotes, is in Section I, B, 2 of this Intro-   duction.

sources thus disposed have found the arrangement somewhat cumbersome.

Although the accounts of a parliament were set down one-by-one, that is not the way the parliament itself actually happened. It happened day-by-day.[217] The day is a second practical unit for arranging the accounts of what went on in the House; and it is the one we have adopted for *Commons Debates 1628*. This arrangement will enable scholars to find all accounts of the proceedings in Commons for a single day together, arranged in a standard sequence: first the Journal of the House of Commons, then the narratives, then the diaries, followed, on a few days, by separates that include some summaries of debates.[218] The place in the sequence either of a narrative or of a diary, with the exception of Lowther's,[219] depends on the fullness and detail it offers over all.

The order of the narratives and diaries in the text is as follows: Harleian MS. 6799, Proceedings and Debates, Stowe MS. 366, Grosvenor, Newdegate, Harleian MSS. 2313 and 5324, Nicholas, Harleian MS. 1601, Rich, Lowther. The dates covered by each account are shown in the Table of Manuscripts,[220] and the order of the several accounts on any day is shown at the start of the section for that day in a table of page references.

After the last of the diary entries for a day we have placed in the text supplementary materials—texts of petitions, texts of special messages from the King, and so on—which serve to make some of the proceedings for the day more intelligible.

Besides the daily sessions of the House, the Commons had three special conferences with the Lords on 7 April, 16 April, and 17 April that all members were free to attend. These conferences were lengthy and of great importance in the history of the parliament of 1628 and of the Petition of Right. We have given each of these conferences a section separate from the regular proceedings on the day on which it took place. The sources used for the conference texts, which include a printed pamphlet (1642) with which the Proceedings and Debates manuscripts have been collated, are described in n. 22, 7 April, Volume II.

D. Publication

We estimated that *Commons Debates 1628* could be issued in three volumes for text, a volume for Introduction and Reference Materials, and a final volume for appendixes and general index. It would have been theoretically possible to issue all of the volumes of *Commons Debates 1628*, as *Commons Debates 1621* was issued, at the same time. Reasonable considerations of economy in use of staff time barred such a publication schedule.

The other obvious alternative, that of issuing the work volume-by-volume was barred by the peculiar historical contours of the parliament of 1628. The first sensible breakpoint in proceedings comes on 27 May. On that day the Lords finally approved the Petition of Right as the Commons had sent it up to them almost three weeks earlier. Moreover if the first published parts of *Commons Debates 1628* were to be immediately useful for scholars, they would need to include at least the remarkable discussions in consequence of which the House of Commons rejected, first, the Lords' proposed alterations in the Petition and, second, the "saving clause" for the King's prerogative, which the Lords wished to add to the Petition. For these reasons it seemed to us that the best procedure was to publish first the proceedings of Commons through 27 May, when the House of Lords agreed to the Petition of Right verbatim as the Commons had sent it to them on

---

217. And of course hour-by-hour and minute-by-minute. But the accounts themselves all note the passage of days, while none of them marks the passage of minutes or hours.

218. The collection of speeches in Harl. MS. 6800 has been used for this purpose on 2, 14, and 15 April.

219. See above, Section I, C.

220. See below, Section II, E.

8 May.[221] These ten weeks of debates are far too massive to put in one volume. They require at least two. Although publishing with 27 May as the final date for the second of these volumes of text leaves for the final volume the crisis that developed over the form of the King's consent to the Petition, it nevertheless permits the inclusion of all the theoretical and legal arguments in connection with the Petition, in which the members of the House justified the constraints they were imposing on the freedom of action of the King.

So the first two volumes of the debates (Volumes II and III) extending from 17 March through 27 May now appear together. With them, bound separately for convenience in use, are the Introduction and Reference Materials (Volume I). The final volume of debates (Volume IV), carrying the proceedings of the House to the prorogation on 26 June, will appear separately, as will the volume containing the appendixes and the General Index (Volume V).

E. Editorial Aids for Scholars Using *Commons Debates 1628*

Editors need to work out ways to help scholars who may use the sources they are editing. There were particular circumstances that demanded special care on the part of the editors of *Commons Debates 1628*. First, because the initial volumes will appear well in advance of the General Index, some provisional devices had to be deployed to render these volumes usable by scholars despite the temporary lack of a General Index. Second, early on the House of Commons got into a discussion of legal issues from which grew a thicket of citations to statutes, *Year Books*, reports, and treatises, so dense that all the scholars in the world, except a dozen highly specialized students of legal history, would get lost in it without a trace. We have tried

to work out some ways to help scholars who are not among the dozen.

Beyond these particular problems we have had three other concerns in providing editorial help. First, as we mentioned before, we wanted to make these volumes useful to a reasonably broad spectrum of scholars and researchers, not just, so to speak, to a narrow ultraviolet band. Second, we wanted to make them useful to scholars who do not have regular access to a great library. Finally, we wanted to produce an edition of *Commons Debates 1628* that by provision of adequate editorial aids brought the gratuitous nuisance of using the volumes down to an irreducible minimum. In this section of the Introduction we will try to offer a description of the scholarly aids included in this edition, which is accurate and precise enough to enable scholars to use them efficiently. *We strongly recommend that researchers planning to use Commons Debates 1628 read this section carefully before proceeding with their work.*

Tabs. Given the day-by-day arrangement of *Commons Debates 1628*, it is essential that researchers be able to turn easily to the proceedings for a given day. To make this possible we have included date tabs to show the sequence of days of the session. In the introductory volume we have also tabbed separately several editorial aids: Table of Manuscripts; Lists; Abbreviations and Short Titles; Glossary of Foreign Words and Phrases; and Legal Citations (see below under these headings).

Table of Manuscripts. One disadvantage of the day-to-day arrangement of *Commons Debates 1628* is that it breaks the continuity of each account once, so to speak, every twenty-four hours. This regular interruption makes it more difficult than an account-by-account arrangement would for the reader to get an impression of the peculiar charac-

---

221. More precisely, on 19 and 20 May the Commons accepted insignificant changes in wording that the Lords had asked them to consider. Of the changes proposed by the Lords these were the only ones they accepted.

teristics of any particular narrative or diary. To make it easier for a reader to follow a single account as far as he wishes, we have included a Table of Manuscripts in which he will be able to find the dates on which a given account appears, as well as the manuscript pages (folios) of the account which cover each day. The pages of the text that are covered by each account are listed at the top of the Order of Business for each day.[222]

Lists. There are three kinds of information likely to be useful to scholars working with *Commons Debates 1628*, that can most conveniently be provided by lists:

Members of the House of Commons. The *Official Returns*[223] lists the members of the House in 1628. Its arrangement is complex. It lists English counties alphabetically, then Welsh counties alphabetically. Under each county it lists first the knights of the shire. Then follow the parliamentary boroughs of the county alphabetically ordered, with the members for each. In a list so arranged it is difficult to find which constituency a given M. P. sat for, or which M. P. sat for a given constituency. We have provided two lists of the members for 1628, the first arranged alphabetically by family names of the members, the second alphabetically by the names of the constituencies. In the first list we have referred to various standard works that contain biographical information about many of the members.[224] For the rules followed with respect to the spelling of the names of members and of constituencies, see section on *Spelling* in Section II, F, below.

Officials mentioned in Commons Debates 1628. To help readers identify men who are referred to in the accounts of proceedings by a a title of office, we have compiled two lists

of officers, one arranged alphabetically by the titles of the offices held, the second alphabetically by surnames of the officers. The lists include persons mentioned in debate as officers of parliament, the central administration, the judiciary, the church, and the city of London.

Abbreviations and Short Titles. Abbreviations used in *Commons Debates 1628* are listed alphabetically on pp. 81–87. This section includes abbreviated titles of works frequently cited in footnotes.

Glossary of Foreign Words and Phrases. Frequently speakers in the House in 1628 interspersed their English discourse with Latin, dropping phrases, sayings, adages, and maxims, sometimes from classical authors, sometimes from the Bible, sometimes from the statute books or other legal sources. We have arranged these Latin tags (and a very few in French) alphabetically in a glossary and provided translations for them.[225] An explanation of the arrangement of the information provided by the glossary will be found in the introduction to that section.

In most cases, to find the translation, the reader can refer directly from the quotation to the glossary. If a different version of the same quotation appears in another account or in a later speech, a footnote at that point will direct the reader to the appropriate entry in the glossary. If a Latin passage is long (several phrases or clauses) the translation and the source are given in a footnote to the first occurrence of the passage. When the passage recurs in subsequent accounts, the reader will be referred by a footnote to the initial translation. If the text itself provides a Latin citation with a correct translation, there will be no entry in the glossary and no footnote.

---

222. See below, p. 45.

223. *Return of the Name of Every Member of the Lower House of Parliament . . . 1213 to 1874*, (2 vols., London, 1878).

224. For more detailed information about the lists of M.P.s, see the introduction to them, p. 52.

225. It seems to us unrealistic snobbery to pretend that every scholar who might wish to use *Commons Debates 1628* will be able to read Latin. Professor Coburn V. Graves of Kent State University did much of the work on the Latin phrases, identifying the sources from which they came and suggesting translations.

For any foreign words and phrases occurring in the final volume of the debates (Volume IV), which have not been included in the original glossary, a supplement to the glossary will be provided in that volume.

Legal Citations. For an editor of parliamentary proceedings, the accounts of the debates in the House of Commons in 1628 present a problem, if not unique, surely uniquely acute. What creates the problem is the density of legal citations in the debates.

During the latter half of November, 1627, four months before parliament opened, five gentlemen imprisoned for refusing to pay the forced loan levied by the King's government had sought to be freed. Writs of *habeas corpus* issued to their jailers, their counsel claimed in King's Bench, had been returned without showing lawful cause for their detention. This suit, the so-called Five Knights' or Darnel case, had elicited a major deployment of legal learning by the lawyers for each side, and the Justices of King's Bench. The gentlemen were not released but returned to custody. In late January, for lack of funds, Charles I had to reconcile himself to summoning a parliament. Everywhere it was evident that the preeminent grievances to be considered would be the imprisonment of those who had resisted the illegal loan, and the refusal of the crown to show legal cause for holding them, and of the judges to release them. Early in the session, the lawyers made it clear to all that at the root of the country's grievances were violations of the law of the land by the King's officials. That being so, it was essential to show how the law had been violated, and therefore to show what the law was. The distinguished lawyers in the House then began to fill the air with legal citations drawn from all the recognized sources of the Common Law:[226] reports, *Year Books*, court rolls, statutes, treatises. Debate was at times immersed in precedents.

When the recorded speeches of some members get close to being strings of legal citations casually linked by scraps of prose, it is difficult to make out what such members are talking about unless one has a notion of what legal sources they are citing and what the sources say. How to provide that notion in the most convenient way (or in fact at all) confronted the editors of *Commons Debates 1628* with their most perplexing editorial problem. If the reader finds the solution finally adopted a bit awkward, we ask him both to contrive an alternative solution and to think through all the editorial consequences of it.

The foundation for our dealing with the law-boundedness of much of the debate in the House in 1628 is a collection we have called "Legal Citations", which is placed in this introductory volume. It includes the citation for each of the legal authorities that occurs in the debates from 17 March through 27 May and for those treatises most frequently cited; a supplementary list will be provided at the end of the final volume of the debates (Volume IV). In this collection the reader will find listed *in correct form* the legal precedents cited in the text. He will find there also an introduction explaining the nature of the sources, and the arrangement of the precedents. For the convenience of the reader to whom the sources may not be readily available, and to enable all readers to discover quickly the substance of a major case or statute referred to, we have included additional material in the form of either a quotation or a brief summary to provide that information. This procedure has been followed for each of the cases and statutes that, because they have been referred to repeatedly in the debates, can be recognized as being central to the argument. In organizing these materials, the editors have been much beholden to the expert and generously given advice of Dr. Charles M. Gray.

The Order of Business. When a reader uses a tab to turn to the record of the proceeding in

---

226. And a few unrecognized ones. Sir Edward Coke cited Paul's claim to the protection of Roman law

from Acts 25:27. See Vol. II, p. 102

the House on a particular date, he will not immediately be confronted by the Commons Journal, always the first account of the proceedings for that day. The first thing he will see will be the Order of Business.[227] At the top of the first page of each day's Order of Business the reader will find a page index to the transcribed manuscripts—the accounts and supplementary material—of the day's proceedings, arranged in the sequence in which the accounts appear in the text.

Then follows the Order of Business proper. It is essentially a chronological page-index to those events that took place in the House, in committees, or in conferences, which left a mark on the surviving record. This of course includes speeches, which sometimes are major events in a deliberative body.

The following matters are noted in the Order of Business: (1) the readings, commitments, engrossments, and other actions of the House upon bills and petitions; (2) the orders and decisions of the House and committees of the House; (3) the creation and meetings of committees; (4) the speakers.

Once a subject is introduced into the Order of Business, the speakers listed may be presumed to be speaking to that matter until another subject is noted in the Order. If a speech itself alters the subject or direction of debate, as for example when a speech turns debate from consideration of granting a subsidy to consideration of the amount to be granted, the new subject is listed after the speaker's name.

The Order of Business was produced by comparing all the accounts of proceedings in the House to determine as far as possible exactly what happened and the precise sequence of happenings. By this process we have usually been able to locate a probable place for every event mentioned in every account of the day's business. On a few occa-

sions this has not been possible. These occur in three different sets of circumstances. (1) At times it is not possible to make even an informed guess as to the *sequence* of speakers. When we have been unable to determine the order of speakers, we have italicized the *names* in the Order of Business. (2) Sometimes the author of a particular account is so imprecise or so diverges from other accounts as to cause *confusion* or to suggest that he is in *error*. In that case we have italicized in the Order of Business the *page number* of the account where the perplexity occurs. (3) Finally, there is sometimes a reasonable *uncertainty* about whether an event mentioned in an account actually happened in the way in which it is recorded. In this situation the entire entry in the Order of Business is in italics.

The page-index to each event listed in the Order of Business directs the reader to every description of that event in the accounts for the day, and makes it easy for readers to find in the accounts every version of each speech and action.

As a further aid for the reader, certain key words in the Order of Business have been put in boldface type so that the subjects of bills, proceedings, orders, and debates can be picked out at a glance.

Where the manuscript (and therefore the text) identifies a member only by last name (Mr. Selden), the Order of Business lists him by his full name (John Selden). When a speech or action is ascribed to different members in different accounts we have retained in the printed text the manuscript identification but have indicated in the Order of Business all the alternative identifications. Where an account records what was going on in the House in regular session, we print in capitals the names of the members mentioned as speaking in the proceed-

---

227. The daily Orders of Business are unique to *Commons Debates 1628*. They are rendered possible by the fact that the accounts are arranged day-by-day. As Associate Editor, Mrs. Maija Cole began to sketch out orders of business for her own convenience in per-

forming her editorial tasks. It soon became evident that what was convenient for her would be even more helpful to scholars using *Commons Debates 1628* for research. The Orders of Business as they appear here are refinements of those that Mrs. Cole first worked out.

ings. In all other instances, including the actions and speeches of members in the committee of the whole House or in select committees and conferences, the names of the members are printed in the usual way. The names of members that appear in the Order of Business are always given in full there: title of honor, if any, given name, surname. Officers of the crown and the Speaker appear not by title of office as in the text (e.g., Treasurer of the Household) but by name (Sir Thomas Edmondes). When a member reports from a committee, presents a petition, or brings a message, in the Order of Business his name follows in parentheses the listing of the activity.

When a petition, message, etc., noted in the Order of Business as being read in the House is printed in full somewhere within the text of *Commons Debates 1628*, a bracketed entry refers the reader to the page where the document is printed. Entries in the Order of Business are bracketed also when they refer to editorial insertions into the text, such as those that show separation between a morning and an afternoon session or between sittings of the House and meetings of the committee of the whole House. Election cases are referred to in Order of Business entries by constituency; but on the *first* (and only the first) entry about such a case the names of the contesting parties are given in brackets.

A system of cross-referencing in the Order of Business will enable the reader to follow specific topics through *Commons Debates 1628*. If such a topic came up more than once in the course of a *single day's debate*, to mark the fact we have used "[*see above*]" and "[*see below*]" following the appropriate entries in the day's Order of Business. Cross-references to Orders of Business for other days are by *date* (8/4 for 8 April). They *follow* the page references for the entry. There will sometimes appear a single date, sometimes several dates. A *single* date refers the reader to the *principal entry* for the particular piece of business under consideration, usually the date at which it was introduced into the House.

At the principal entry the reader will find cross-references indicating *every date* included in the volume *on which that particular piece of business was discussed*. If on the day to which there is a cross-reference the matter referred to came up more than once, the number of references to it on that day is indicated in parentheses after the date. At the principal entry in the first volume of the debates (Volume II), the reader will also find references to the *first date* on which that business was taken up in the next volume (Volume III). At the first entry in the second volume of debates where a piece of old business is taken up, the reader will find a back-reference to the main entry in the preceding volume and if necessary a forward-reference to the third volume of debates (Volume IV). All volumes are similarly cross-referenced.

The Provisional Index. The Order of Business for each day makes it feasible to compile a provisional index to each volume of the texts of *Commons Debates 1628*. The provisional index will enable scholars to make reasonably effective use of the volumes as they are published, before the large general index appears in Volume V. Moreover, despite its limitation, the provisional index may be a more convenient means than the general index for pursuing certain topics through *Commons Debates 1628*. Essentially the provisional index combines with the daily Orders of Business to create a two-step page-index to the accounts of proceedings in the House. The number-references in the provisional index are *to dates, not to pages*. They refer the reader to the Order of Business for a given date. There he can find page-directions to the particular item he seeks. The provisional index is thus really an index to the Orders of Business.

The user of the provisional indexes is asked to remember that they are *provisional*. They do not and are not intended to replicate for each volume what will appear in the General Index at the end of the final volume.

The General Index. The cumulative Index at

the end of Volume V will be modeled on the superb Index to Notestein, Relf, and Simpson's *Commons Debates 1621*; that is to say, it will be a highly detailed and subdivided alphabetical index to dates and pages.

Footnotes. We have already indicated above, in Section II, B, certain recurring circumstances in which we use footnotes as a matter of editorial convenience. We have also laid down a general editorial rule restrictive of footnotes: *Commons Debates 1628* is to be an edition of accounts of proceedings in parliament in 1628, not a commentary at large on those proceedings.

There remain nonetheless some residual matters concerning which we have exercised editorial discretion in the matter of footnoting. Primarily we have used footnotes to correct or clarify matters in the text. We have used them to identify, when we were able, persons and events named but not identified in the text. We have put in footnote references to, and sometimes explanations from, modern historical works that provide information about matters adverted to in the accounts but inadequately described by them. Sometimes it is hard to make out from the accounts what course the Commons are entering on and why. To guide the reader we have introduced in the footnotes, when it seemed necessary or useful, information on the rules and customs of parliamentary procedure. Footnotes related to legal material are described in the section on Legal Citations. Occasionally we have included contemporary comment (i.e., from Birch, *Court and Times*) which has seemed to throw light on a particular debate. Biblical allusions have been identified when we could detect them.

F. Editorial Conventions

Once we decided to "modernize" the text, certain residual *arbitrary* decisions on rules about spelling, punctuation, and capitalization became necessary. On a certain number of other matters convenience suggested the adoption of consistent conventions in the printed text.

Spelling. In modernizing the spelling in the text of *Commons Debates 1628*, where possible we have followed American usage as established in Webster's *New International Dictionary*. When a word is without contemporary American equivalent, we have adopted the spelling in the *Oxford English Dictionary*. For place names we have used as a guide the *Oxford Dictionary of English Place Names*. For names of persons holographs for all members have not been available; nor could we rely wholly on one compiled source for a standard of orthography, since not all such names appear in any one modern publication. We have, therefore, established a source preference list as a guide. This list in order of decreasing preference follows: *D.N.B., O.R., Cal. S.P. Dom.,* and *A.P.C.*

Capitalization. Seventeenth-century capitalization being even more unruly than seventeenth-century spelling, we have modernized it. That is, we have followed the recent practice of capitalizing sparsely rather than abundantly, so that few but the most proper nouns are awarded capitals. Following the convention established by Notestein, we have set names of members in capitals when they spoke in the House in regular session. In all the other circumstances in which members' names appear in the text, we have printed them in the ordinary way. The same procedures have been followed in the daily Order of Business.

Punctuation. We have also modernized punctuation since the idiosyncratic seventeenth-century punctuation of the manuscript sources is as likely to obscure the meaning of the text as to clarify it. We have supplied such modern punctuation as in our judgment helped make the best possible sense of the text, on the grounds that making sense was part of the original intention of the authors of the diaries and of the compilers of the narratives. Frequently, comparisons of the several accounts have guided us in our choice of one way of punctuating over another. It must be emphasized, however, that our procedure with respect to punctuation lacks the neutrality of our modernization of spelling and capitalization. In the latter cases we have not blotted out alternative possible meanings of the words modernized, since there are, in fact, no alternative meanings to blot out. Often this is not true in the case of punctuation. At times punctuating the identical series of words in a different way will give it a different and equally intelligible meaning. In a sense the punctuation we have imposed on a word series has the effect of a particular *gestalt*, overlaying and obscuring alternative meanings that the series might have. Readers should feel free to try their hand at revising the punctuation in any part of the text that in their view makes unsatisfactory sense as it stands, or might make different but equal sense if punctuated in a different way.

Abbreviations. Abbreviations of the names of monarchs in citations of regnal years (4 *H. VI, 2 Jac.* 1) have been standardized. Single-letter abbreviations of men's first names (Sir D. Digges) in an account, and references to law books customarily abridged in print *(Liv. Ass.)* have not been altered in the printed text. We have extended all other abbreviations and contractions (e.g., *gentleman* for *gent.*, *parliament* for *parlt.*, *Edward* for *Ed.*). Where we made such an extension as the result of reasonable inference rather than practical certainty we have enclosed it in square brackets.

Numbers in Text. With a few exceptions, numbers are given in the printed text in the form in which they appear in the manuscript accounts. When Proceedings and Debates, however, spells out the regnal year, we substitute the arabic numeral, for example, "24 *Eliz.*" for "twenty-four *Eliz.*". In headings and footnotes we have followed modern calendar custom and used 1 January rather than 25 March as the date for the change to a new year. Thus, for example, the first of January after 31 December 1623 is 1 January 1624, not 1 January 1623.

Italics, Quotation Marks, and Brackets. We have italicized all foreign language statements in the text including abbreviations for books with non-English titles (e.g., *Rot. Parl.* for *Rotuli Parliamentorum*) and abbreviations of Latinized names of rulers (e.g., *Jac.* for *Jacobus*, that is, James). Quotation marks are used in the text only when the speaker is quoting verbatim from a source. Brackets have been used only where letters or words have been inserted in the text by the editors for purposes of correction or clarification.

Folio and Page Numbers. We have inserted in the printed text, within brackets, the numbers of the folios or pages of each account as they occur in the manuscripts.[228] This will make it easier for scholars who wish to attack illegibilities that defeated us or to check our transcriptions against the manuscripts.

---

228. Most of the accounts have page or folio numbers but, in the case of the third volume of the Newdegate diary and all of Lowther's, numbers are lacking.

REFERENCE MATERIALS

TABLE OF MANUSCRIPTS

The following table lists the daily sequence of pages/folios for each manuscript used in the text.

	Journal of the House of Commons (pp.)	Proceedings and Debates (Trumbull Add. MS. 50) (ff.)	Stowe MS. 366 (ff.)	Grosvenor (pp.)	Newdegate (pp. & ff.)*	Harleian MSS. 2313 and 5324 (ff.)	Nicholas (ff.)	Harleian MS. 1601 (ff.)	Lowther (ff.)	Other MSS. (ff.)
				MS.E. 5.33	v.I	MS. 2313				Harleian MS.6799
17 March	1	1–3v	2–3v							
19 March	2	3v–7v	4–4v							
20 March	3–8	8–9	5–6v					4v		
21 March	9–11	9–9v	7–8		* 1–5		2	4v–5		288–289
22 March	11	9v–15v	9–12v		5–23			5–5v		289v–292 335–336
24 March	12–14	15v–19	13–14v		23–39		2v			
25 March	14	19v–23	15–17v		39–53			7–8v		
26 March	14–16	23–27	19–22		53–67	1v–5v	3–4v	8v–10		
27 March	16–17	27–31v	23–25		*35–41v	5v–9		10–11		
28 March	17–20	31v–33v	27–28v		41v–49v	9–12v		11–11v		
29 March	20–21	33v–36	29–32v		50–55	13–18v	4v–6	11v–12v		
31 March	21–22	36–38v	33–34v		55–59v	19–21	6			
1 April	22–23	39–40v	35–36v		59v–64v	21v–23	6v–7	13–14v		
2 April	23–24	40v–46	37–40v		65–71	23v–27v	7v–9v	14v–16		
3 April	25–29	46–48	41–42		71–78v	28–31	10	16–18		
4 April	30–31	48–51	43–50		78v–83	31–34v	10v–14v			
5–6 April (The fast)			(50v)							
7 April (Conference)	32–34	51v–53v (223–228)	53–54v		83–84	34v–35v	15		19v	
8 April	34–35	53v–55v	55–59v			36v–37v	15–17			
9 April	35–38	55v–59	61–64v		84–88	38–39	17v–19v		20v	
10 April	38–40	59v–60v	65–67v		88–89	39v–40	20–20v		21v–22	
11 April	40–41	60v–62v	69–72		89–93	40	22			
12 April	41–43	63–65v	73–76			40v–41	22v–23v		23v–24	
14 April	43–46	65v–70	77–79			42–42v	23–24v			
15 April	46–47	70–74	81–83		v.II 2–4	43–47	24v–27v		25v–26v	
16 April (Conference)	47–49	74–75v	85–86v		(77v–72v)	48–49v	27–29			

	Journal of the House of Commons (pp.)	Proceedings and Debates (Trumbull Add. MS. 50) (ff.)	Stowe MS. 366 (ff.)	Grosvenor (pp.)	New-degate (pp. & ff.)*	Harleian MSS. 2313 and 5324 (ff.)	Nicholas (ff.)	Harleian MS. 1601 (ff.)	Low-ther	Other MSS. (ff.)
17 April (Conference)	49–56	76–77	87–88	MS.E.5.33	4–7v	50–52	29–31v	27v–28		
		(77–78)				(72v–68v)				
		(228v–230v)								
18 April	56	78–81v	89–92v	3–27	7v–10v	52–53v	31v–33v			
19 April	57–58	81v–82v	93–94v	27–40	10v–13	54–54v	33v–34v			
21 April	58–60	82v–84	95–96v	41–52	13–17		34v–36			
22 April	60–61	84–85v	97–100	53–66	17–20	55–56v	36–37v	29v–30		
23 April	62–65	86–87	101–102	67–75	20–22v	56v–57	37v–38v			
24 April	65–68	87–88	103–104	76–80	22v–23	57–58	38v–39	31v		
25 April	68–70	88–92	105–107v	80–94	23–24v	58v–61v	39–40			
26 April	70–71	92–95	109–111v	101–123	25–30v	61v–64	40–43v			
28 April	71–74	95–99	113–115v	124–144	30v–32v	64–65	43v–44v			
29 April	74–75	99–101v	117–118v	148–165	32v–36	66–67v	46–49	32v–33		
						†MS. 5324				
30 April	76–77	101v–102v	119–120v	166–170	36–37v	55v–52v	49–51			
1 May	77–78	103–105	121–122v	171–187	38–40	51v–44v	51–54	34v–35		
				MS.E.5.34						
2 May	79–80	105–107v	125–128v	5–26	40v–42	44v–41v	54–57	35v–36		
3 May	81	107v–109	131–134	26–39	42–43	40v–37v	57–58v	36v–37		
5 May	82–83	109–110v	135–137v	40–55	43v–44	37v–35v	59–60v			
6 May	84	111–113v	139–144v	56–78	44–47	35v–27v	60v–64	38v–40		
7 May	84–87	114–115v	145–146v	78–101	47–48	27v	64v–65	40v		
8 May	87–89	116–116v	147–148v	102–106	48–48v	26v–24v	65–65v	41v		
9 May	89–91	116v–120	155–156	107–114	48v–49v	24v–22v	65v–66v			
10 May	91–95	120–120v	157–158v	114–125	49v–50v	21v–20v				
12 May	96–100	120v–123	159–160v	126–145	50v–51v	20v	66v–68			
13 May	100–102	123–124	163–164v	146–165	51v–54	19v–17v	70v			
14 May	103–104	124v–125v	165–167v	166–171	54–55v	17v–15v	70–71			
15 May	105–106	125v–126	169–169v	172–178	55v–56	14v–13v	71			
16 May	106–108	126–128v	171–172v	178–185	56–58	13v	71v–73			
17 May	108–111	128v–130	173–174v	186–189	58–59	13v–12v	73–74v			
				MS.E.5.35						
19 May	112–115	130–131v	175–177	3–27	59–61v	12v–11v	74v			Rich
20 May	116–118	131v–133	178–180v	28–49	61v–64v	10v–8v	74v–75v			Notes
21 May	118–121	133–133v	182–183	50–57	64v–66	7v–6v	75v–76v			1–2v
22 May	121–122	134–139	184–187	58–76	66–68v	5v–4v	77–78v			2v–7v
23 May	122–124	139–149	188–189v	77–91	68v–70	3v–4	78v–79			
24 May	125–127	149–151v	190–191v	92–100	70v–72	4–7	79–79v			
26 May	127–129	151v–152v	192–193v	101–108	72–73		79v–81			
27 May	130–132	152v–155	194–195	109–116	73–74v					
28 May	132–134	155–157	196–196v	117–126	74v					
29 May	134–135	157–157v	198–200v	127–132						
30 May	135–136	158–160	202–203	133–148						

	Journal of the House of Commons (pp.)	Proceedings and Debates (Trumbull Add. MS. 50) (ff.)	Stowe MS. 366 (ff.)	Grosvenor (pp.)	Newdegate (pp. & ff.*)	Harleian MSS. 2313 and 5324 (ff.)	Nicholas (ff.)	Harleian MS. 1601 (ff.)	Lowther	Other MSS. (ff.)
31 May	137–138	160–160v	204–207v	148–159	74v–75					
2 June	138	160v–161v	210–211v	159–161	75–75v		81			
3 June	139–140	161v–166v	212–214v	161–183	75v–77		81–81v			
				MS.E.5.36						
4 June	140–143	166v–168v	216–217v	9–16	77v–79	11–13			*X	
					v.III					Rich Notes
5 June	143	168v–171	218–220v	17–42	*X				X	
6 June	144	171–176	222–223v	43–77	X		81v–85v		X	1–3v
7 June	144–146	176–177v	224–226	78–98	X			84v	X	3v,5v
9 June	146–147	177v–180v	230–231v	98–116	X		86–86v			3v–4v
10 June	147–148	181–181v	232–233v	116–130	X				X	
11 June	149–150	181v–188	234–241	131–143	X		87–91v		X	4v–5
12 June	151	188	242–242v	144–147	X					
13 June	152–155	188–190	244–247v	148–156	X					
14 June	156–157	190–204	248–250	156–163	X				X	
16 June	157–159	204v–206	251–253v	163–167	X				X	
17 June	159–160	206–207v	255–269	167–172	X				X	
18 June	161–162	207v–209	270–271	173–176	X					
19 June	162–163	209–210	272–273v	177–180	X				X	
20 June	163–166	210–211v	274–275v	180–183	X				X	
21 June	166–169	211v–214	276–278	183–189	X				X	
23 June	169–173	214–216v	280–281v		X				X	
24 June	173–174	216v–218v	282–284v		X				X	
25 June	175–176	219–221v	286–287v		X				X	
26 June	176–177	221v–222	288–289		X				X	

*The Newdegate diary MS. has been paginated through 26 March, and thereafter in volume I as well as throughout volume II, is numbered only by folios. Volume III of the Newdegate diary and the entire MS. of the Lowther diary have no page or folio numbers. We have used Xs in this table to indicate days for which entries occur in these diaries.

†The folios of Harleian MS. 5324 are numbered from the end of the notebook.

MEMBERS RETURNED TO THE HOUSE OF
COMMONS IN 1628

The following list contains the names of 507 men returned to the House in 1628. Resolutions involving disputed elections resulted in the returns of seventeen persons being voided during the course of the session. However, in some cases these decisions were not reached until after the person had been sitting in the House for some time. The return for Sir Thomas Savile was not voided until 23 April, while the election of Robert Greville and Francis Lucy was not invalidated until 31 May. Two other members, Edward Alford, Sr., and Sir William Killigrew, had been doubly returned and so retained a seat in the House even after one of their returns had been declared void. Another member, Sir Edmund Sawyer, was expelled from the House on 21 June; and three more (Sir George Goring, Sir Baptist Hicks, and Sir Edward Howard) were elevated to the peerage. Thus, at the end of the session, total membership stood at 488, with several places still to be filled by by-elections.

All of the above actions, with relevant dates, are noted in the following list. The list further indicates, with italics, the preferred constituencies of the eleven M.P.s who were "doubly returned". Asterisks (*) are used to denote the twenty-three members who had been confined for refusing to subscribe to the forced loan, and notes on these confinements are appended to the list. The three members who were privy councillors are marked with daggers (†). The seven members of this House who later signed the death warrant of Charles I are noted by double daggers (‡).

The list of members was compiled from the O.R., the Crown Office List, and information provided by the text of the 1628 debates. For the convenience of the reader who wishes to learn additional details of the lives of many of the M.P.s, references are given to the following biographical works: D.N.B. (Dictionary of National Biography); L.P. (Mary Frear Keeler, The Long Parliament, 1640–1641); A.C. (John Venn and J. A. Venn, eds., Alumni Cantabrigienses); and A.O. (Joseph Foster, ed., Alumni Oxonienses). Also useful in this regard is G. E. C[okayne]'s Complete Baronetage.

Alford, Edward, Sr., Esq.
    Steyning, Sussex; Colchester, Essex (Colchester return voided 28 March)
Alford, John, Gent., of Offington, Sussex (L.P.; A.O.)
    Arundel, Sussex
Alford, Sir William, Kt.
    Beverley, Yorkshire
Alured, Thomas, Gent. (A.C.)
    Hedon-in-Holderness, Yorkshire
Annesley, Sir Francis, Kt. and Bart. (D.N.B.)
    Newton, Lancashire
*Armine, Sir William, Bart. (D.N.B.; L.P.; A.C.)
    Lincolnshire
Arnold, Nicholas, Esq., of Lantony, Monmouthshire (A.O.)
    Monmouthshire
Arundel, John, Esq., of Trerice (D.N.B.)
    Tregony, Cornwall
Ashburnham, John, Esq. (D.N.B.; L.P.; A.C.)
    Hastings, Cinque Port
Ashton, William, Esq.
    Appleby, Westmorland
*Ayscough, Sir Edward, Kt. (L.P.; A.C.)
    Lincoln, Lincolnshire

Baber, John, Esq., Recorder of Wells (A.O.)
    Wells, Somerset
Backhouse (Bakehouse), Sir John, K.B.
    Marlow, Buckinghamshire
Badger, Sir Thomas, Kt.
    Lostwithiel, Cornwall (vice Sir Robert Carr)
Bagg, Sir James, Kt.
    Plympton, Devonshire
Bagot, Sir Harvey, Bart. (L.P.; A.O.)
    Staffordshire
Ball, Peter, Esq. (A.O.)
    Tiverton, Devonshire
Bampfield, John, Esq. (A.O.)
    Devonshire
Bancroft, Thomas, Esq.
    Castle Rising, Norfolk
Bankes, John, Esq. (D.N.B.; A.O.; A.C.)
    Morpeth, Northumberland

Barker, John, Merchant
  Bristol, Gloucestershire
*Barnardiston, Sir Nathaniel, Kt. (*D.N.B.*; *L.P.*)
  Suffolk
Barnham, Sir Francis, Kt. (*D.N.B.*; *L.P.*; *A.C.*)
  Maidstone, Kent
*Barrington, Sir Francis, Kt. and Bart. (*A.C.*)
  Essex
Barrington, Robert, Esq.
  Newtown (Isle of Wight), Hampshire
Barrington, Sir Thomas, Kt. (*L.P.*)
  Newtown (Isle of Wight), Hampshire
Barwis, Richard, Esq. (*L.P.*)
  Carlisle, Cumberland
Bashe, Sir Edward, Kt. (*A.C.*)
  Stamford, Lincolnshire
Bedell (Beadle), Sir Capel, Bart. (*A.C.*)
  Huntingdonshire
Beecher, Sir William, Kt. (*A.C.*)
  New Windsor, Berkshire
Belasyse, Henry, Esq. (*L.P.*; *A.C.*)
  Yorkshire
Bellingham, Henry, Esq. (*A.C.*; *A.O.*)
  Chichester, Sussex
Bellingham, Richard, Esq. (*D.N.B.*; *A.O.*)
  Boston, Lincolnshire
Benson, Henry, Esq., of Knaresborough (*L.P.*)
  Knaresborough, Yorkshire
Berkeley, Sir Charles, Kt. (*A.O.*)
  Heytesbury, Wiltshire
Berkeley, Sir Henry, Kt. (*L.P.*; *A.O.*)
  Ilchester, Somerset
Bindlose (Bindlosse), Sir Francis, Kt. (*A.C.*)
  Lancaster, Lancashire
Bludder, Sir Thomas, Kt. (*L.P.*; *A.C.*)
  Reigate, Surrey
Bluett, John Esq. (*A.O.*)
  Tiverton, Devonshire
Borlase, Sir William, Jr., Kt. (*A.O.*)
  Chipping Wycombe, Buckinghamshire
Bowes, Sir Talbot, Kt., of Streatlam, Durham
  Richmond, Yorkshire
Bowyer, Sir Thomas, Bart. (*L.P.*)
  Bramber, Sussex
Bradshaw, Joseph, Esq.
  Westminster, Middlesex
Brereton, Sir William, Bart. (*D.N.B.*; *L.P.*; *A.O.*)
  Cheshire
Brett, Thomas, Esq.
  New Romney, Cinque Port
Bridgeman, Edward, Esq.
  Wigan, Lancashire

Bridgeman, George, Esq.
  Much Wenlock, Shropshire
Bridges, Sir Giles, Bart.
  Herefordshire
Bromley, Sir Thomas, Kt. (*A.O.*)
  Worcestershire
Brooke, Sir Robert, Kt. (*A.C.*)
  Dunwich, Suffolk
Brooke, Sir William, K.B. (*A.C.*)
  Rochester, Kent
Browne, Sir Ambrose, Bart. (*L.P.*; *A.C.*)
  Surrey
Browne, George, Esq., of Taunton
  Taunton, Somerset
Browne, John, Esq.
  Gloucester, Gloucestershire
Browne, John, Esq., of Frampton, Dorset (*L.P.*; *A.O.*)
  Bridport, Dorset (return voided 12 April)
Bulkeley, Richard, Esq.
  Anglesey, Wales
Buller, Francis, Esq. (*L.P.*; *A.C.*)
  Mitchell (Michael), Cornwall (return voided 21 May)
Buller, Sir Richard, Kt. (*L.P.*)
  Saltash, Cornwall
Bulstrode, Sir William, Kt.
  Rutland
*Bunce, James, Leatherseller
  London, Middlesex
Button, Sir William, Kt. and Bart. (*D.N.B.*; *A.O.*)
  Wiltshire
Byron, Sir John, K.B. (*D.N.B.*; *A.C.*)
  Nottinghamshire
Bysshe, Edward, Esq.
  Blechingley, Surrey

Cage, William, Esq. (*L.P.*)
  Ipswich, Suffolk
Canon (Cannon), Sir Thomas, Kt. (*A.O.*)
  Haslemere, Surrey
Carleton, Sir John, Bart. (*A.O.*)
  Cambridgeshire
Carnaby, Sir William, Kt. (*L.P.*)
  Northumberland
Carr, Sir Robert, Kt.
  Preston, Lancashire; Lostwithiel, Cornwall
Cary, Henry Lord (*A.O.*)
  Grampound, Cornwall
Cary, Thomas, Esq.
  St. Mawes, Cornwall
Cavendish, Sir Charles, Kt. (*D.N.B.*; *A.O.*)

Nottingham, Nottinghamshire
‡Cawley, William, Esq. (*D.N.B.*; *L.P.*; *A.O.*)
  Chichester, Sussex
Chaffin (Chafin), Bampfield, Esq., of Folke, Dorset
  Bridport, Dorset (vice John Browne)
Cheeke, Sir Thomas, Kt. (*L.P.*; *A.C.*)
  Colchester, Essex
Chudleigh, Sir John, Kt. (*A.C.*)
  Lostwithiel, Cornwall
Clare, Sir Ralph, K.B. (*D.N.B*; *A.O.*)
  Bewdley, Worcestershire
Clifton, Sir Gervase, K.B. and Bart. (*L.P.*; *A.C.*)
  Nottinghamshire
Clitherow, Christopher, Alderman (*D.N.B*; *A.O.*)
  London, Middlesex
Cokayne, Charles, Esq.
  Reigate, Surrey
Coke, Clement, Esq. (*A.C.*)
  Aylesbury, Buckinghamshire
Coke, Sir Edward, Kt. (*D.N.B.*; *A.C.*)
  Buckinghamshire; Suffolk
†Coke, Sir John, Kt., Principal Secretary of State (*D.N.B.*; *A.C.*)
  Cambridge University
Compton, Sir Henry, K.B. (*A.O.*)
  East Grinstead, Sussex
‡*Constable, Sir William, Kt. and Bart. (*D.N.B.*)
  Scarborough, Yorkshire; Callington, Cornwall
Conway, Ralph, Esq. (*A.O.*)
  Andover, Hampshire
Corbet (Corbett), Sir Andrew, Kt. (*A.O.*)
  Shropshire
‡Corbet, Miles, Esq., Recorder of Great Yarmouth (*D.N.B.*; *L.P.*; *A.C.*)
  Great Yarmouth, Norfolk
*Coryton, William, Esq. (*D.N.B.*; *L.P.*)
  Cornwall
Cosewarth (Cosworth), John, Esq.
  Mitchell (Michael), Cornwall (vice Francis Buller)
Cottington, Sir Francis, Kt. and Bart. (*D.N.B.*)
  Saltash, Cornwall
Cotton, Sir Robert, Kt. and Bart. (*D.N.B.*; *A.C.*)
  Castle Rising, Norfolk
Cotton, Sir Roland, Kt. (*A.C.*)
  Newcastle-under-Lyme, Staffordshire
Cotton, Thomas, Esq. (*D.N.B.*; *A.C.*)
  St. Germans, Cornwall
Coventry, Thomas, Esq.
  Worcestershire
Cowcher (Coucher), John, Esq. (*L.P.*)
  Worcester, Worcestershire

Cowper (Cooper), Sir John, Kt. and Bart.
  Poole, Dorset
Coxe, William, Esq., of Southwark
  Southwark, Surrey
Cradock, Matthew, Esq.
  Stafford, Staffordshire
Crane, Sir Robert, Kt. and Bart. (*L.P.*)
  Sudbury, Suffolk
Cresheld (Creswell), Richard, Esq. (*L.P.*)
  Evesham, Worcestershire
Crew, John, Esq., of Steane, Northamptonshire (*D.N.B.*; *L.P.*; *A.O.*)
  Banbury, Oxfordshire
Crofts, Sir William, Kt.
  Malmesbury, Wiltshire
Croke, Sir Henry, Kt. (*A.O.*)
  Christchurch, Hampshire
Croke, Sir John, Kt. (*A.O.*)
  Shaftesbury, Dorset
Crompton, Thomas, Esq.
  Staffordshire
‡Cromwell, Oliver, Esq. (*D.N.B.*; *L.P.*; *A.C.*; *A.O.*)
  Huntingdon, Huntingdonshire
Crossing, Francis, Esq. (*A.O.*)
  Camelford, Cornwall
Crow, Sir Sackville, Kt. and Bart.
  Bramber, Sussex
Culpeper (Colepeper), Sir Thomas, Kt. (*D.N.B.*; *A.O.*; *A.C.*)
  Tewkesbury, Gloucestershire
Curwen, Sir Patrick, Bart. (*L.P.*; *A.C.*)
  Cumberland
Curzon (Curson), John, Esq. (*L.P.*; *A.O.*)
  Brackley, Northamptonshire

Dacres, Sir Thomas, Kt. (*L.P.*; *A.C.*)
  Hertfordshire
Dalston, Sir George, Kt. (*L.P.*; *A.C.*)
  Cumberland
Daniel, Richard, Gent.
  Truro, Cornwall
‡Danvers, Sir John, Kt. (*D.N.B.*; *A.O.*)
  Oxford University
Darcy, Sir Francis, Kt. (*A.O.*)
  Middlesex
Darley, Henry, Esq. (*L.P.*; *A.C.*)
  Aldborough, Yorkshire
Day, Edmund, Gent.
  Ipswich, Suffolk
Debney, Robert, Esq.
  Norwich, Norfolk

Delbridge, John, Merchant (*A.C.*)
    Barnstaple, Devonshire
Denton, Sir Thomas, Kt. (*A.O.*)
    Buckingham, Buckinghamshire
Denys (Dennys), Sir Edward, Kt.
    Yarmouth (Isle of Wight), Hampshire
Devereux, Sir Walter, Kt. (*L.P.*; *A.O.*)
    Tamworth, Staffordshire
Digby, Philip, Esq., of London
    Milborne Port, Somerset
Digges, Sir Dudley, Kt. (*D.N.B.*; *A.O.*)
    Kent
Digges, Richard, Serjeant at Law (*A.O.*)
    Marlborough, Wiltshire
Dodington, Herbert, Esq. (*A.O.*)
    Lymington, Hampshire
Doughty, John, Alderman
    Bristol, Gloucestershire
Doughty, William, Gent., Alderman of King's Lynn (*A.C.*)
    King's Lynn, Norfolk
Drake, Sir Francis, Bart. (*A.O.*)
    Devonshire
Drake, Francis, Esq., of Ashurst, Surrey
    Bridport, Dorset (return voided 12 April)
Dunch, Edmund, Esq. (*L.P.*)
    Wallingford, Berkshire
Dyott, Richard, Esq. (*A.O.*)
    Lichfield, Staffordshire
Dyve, Sir Lewis, Kt. (*D.N.B.*; *A.O.*)
    Weymouth and Melcombe Regis, Dorset

Eden, Thomas, LL.D., a Master in Chancery (*D.N.B.*; *L.P.*; *A.C.*)
    Cambridge University
Edgcombe, Piers, Esq. (*A.O.*; *A.C.*)
    Newport, Cornwall
Edgcombe, Sir Richard, Kt.
    Bossiney, Cornwall
†Edmondes, Sir Thomas, Kt., Treasurer of the Household (*D.N.B.*)
    Penryn, Cornwall
Edwards, Evan, Esq.
    Camelford, Cornwall
*Eliot, Sir John, Kt. (*D.N.B.*; *A.O.*)
    Cornwall
Erle (Earle), Christopher, Esq. (*A.O.*)
    Lyme Regis, Dorset
*Erle (Earle), Sir Walter, Kt. (*L.P.*; *A.O.*)
    Dorset
Escott, Richard, Esq., of Lincoln's Inn (*A.O.*)
    Launceston (Dunheved), Cornwall

Estcourt, Sir Giles, Kt. and Bart. (*A.O.*)
    Cirencester, Gloucestershire
Evelyn, John, Esq. (*L.P.*; *A.C.*)
    Blechingley, Surrey
Eversfield, Nicholas, Esq. (*A.C.*)
    Hastings, Cinque Port
Eyre, Sir John, Kt.
    Chippenham, Wiltshire

Fairfax, Sir Ferdinando, Kt., of Denton (*D.N.B.*; *L.P.*)
    Boroughbridge, Yorkshire
Fane, Sir George, Kt. (*A.C.*)
    Maidstone, Kent
Fane, Mildmay, Lord Le Despenser (*D.N.B.*; *A.C.*)
    Peterborough, Northamptonshire
Fanshawe, Sir Thomas, K.B. (*D.N.B.*; *L.P.*)
    Hertford, Hertfordshire
Fanshawe, Sir Thomas, Kt. (*A.C.*)
    Lancaster, Lancashire
Farnefold, Sir Thomas, Kt. (*L.P.*)
    Steyning, Sussex
Fenwick, Sir John, Kt. (*D.N.B.*; *L.P.*)
    Northumberland
Fettiplace, John, Esq. (*L.P.*)
    Berkshire
Fiennes, James, Esq. (*L.P.*; *A.C.*)
    Oxfordshire
Finch, Francis, Esq. (*A.O.*; *A.C.*)
    Eye, Suffolk
Finch, Sir John, Kt. (*D.N.B.*; *A.C.*)
    Canterbury, Kent
Finch, Sir Thomas, Kt. and Bart. (*A.C.*)
    Kent
Fleetwood, Sir Miles, Kt. (*L.P.*)
    Woodstock, Oxfordshire
Fleetwood, Sir William, Kt. (*A.O.*)
    Buckinghamshire
Fleming, Philip, Esq. (*A.O.*)
    Newport (Isle of Wight), Hampshire
Fotherley (Fotherby), Thomas, Esq.
    Rye, Cinque Port
Foxe, Sir Edward, Kt.
    Bishops Castle, Shropshire
Frankland, William, Esq.
    Thirsk, Yorkshire
Franklin (Franklyn), Sir John, Kt., of Wilsdon, Middlesex (*L.P.*; *A.C.*)
    Wootton Bassett, Wiltshire
Freeman, Sir Ralph, Kt. (*D.N.B.*)
    Winchelsea, Cinque Port

Fretchvile (Frechville), John, Esq.
    Derbyshire

George, John, Esq. (*L.P.*; *A.O.*)
    Cirencester, Gloucestershire
Gerard (Garrard), George, Esq.
    Preston, Lancashire
Gifford, Sir Richard, Kt.
    Stockbridge, Hampshire
Giles, Sir Edward, Kt. (*A.O.*)
    Totnes, Devonshire
Glanville, Sir Francis, Kt.
    Tavistock, Devonshire
Glanville, John, Esq. (*D.N.B.*; *A.O.*)
    Plymouth, Devonshire
Gleane, Sir Peter, Kt. (*A.C.*)
    Norwich, Norfolk
*Godfrey, Thomas, Esq.
    New Romney, Cinque Port
Godolphin, Francis, Esq., of Godolphin, Cornwall
    (*L.P.*; *A.O.*)
    St. Ives, Cornwall
Godolphin, Sidney, Esq. (*D.N.B.*; *L.P.*; *A.O.*)
    Helston, Cornwall
Gollop, George, Alderman (*L.P.*)
    Southampton, Hampshire
Goodwin, Ralph, Esq., of Ludlow Castle, Shrop-
    shire (*L.P.*; *A.O.*)
    Ludlow, Shropshire
Goodwin, Robert, Esq. (*L.P.*)
    East Grinstead, Sussex
Gorge (Gorges), Sir Robert, Kt. (*A.O.*)
    Ilchester, Somerset
Goring, Sir George, Kt. (*D.N.B.*; *A.C.*; *A.O.*)
    Lewes, Sussex (created Baron Goring of
    Hurstpierpoint 14 April 1628)
Goring, Sir William, Bart.
    Sussex
Graham (Grayme), Richard, Esq.
    Carlisle, Cumberland
*Grantham, Sir Thomas, Kt. (*A.O.*)
    Lincoln, Lincolnshire
Greene, Giles, Gent. (*L.P.*)
    Corfe Castle, Dorset
Greene, Richard, Esq.
    Coventry, Warwickshire
Grenville, Bevil, Esq. (*D.N.B.*; *L.P.*; *A.O.*)
    Launceston (Dunheved), Cornwall
Grenville, Sir Richard, Kt. (*D.N.B.*)
    Fowey, Cornwall

Gresley, Sir George, Bart. (*A.O.*)
    Newcastle-under-Lyme, Staffordshire
Greville, Robert, Esq. (*D.N.B.*; *A.C.*)
    Warwick, Warwickshire (return voided 31
    May)
Griffith, John, Esq. (*L.P.*; *A.O.*)
    Caernarvonshire, Wales
*Grimston, Sir Harbottle, Kt. and Bart. (*L.P.*)
    Essex
Grosvenor, Sir Richard, Kt. and Bart. (*A.O.*)
    Cheshire
Grymes, George, Esq.
    Haslemere, Surrey

Hakewill, William, Esq. (*D.N.B*; *A.O.*)
    Amersham, Buckinghamshire
Hales, Sir John, Kt. (*A.O.*)
    Queenborough, Kent
*Hampden, John, Esq. (*D.N.B.*; *L.P.*; *A.O.*)
    Wendover, Buckinghamshire
Hanbury, John, Esq.
    Gloucester, Gloucestershire
Hare, Sir John, Kt.
    King's Lynn, Norfolk
Harley, Sir Robert, K.B. (*D.N.B.*; *L.P.*; *A.O.*)
    Evesham, Worcestershire
Harris, John, Esq. (*L.P.*)
    Liskeard, Cornwall
Harrison, John,[1] Esq. (*L.P.*)
    Scarborough, Yorkshire
Harrison, Sir Richard, Kt. (*A.O.*)
    Berkshire
Hartopp, Sir Edward, Bart.
    Leicestershire
Harvey, Sir William, Kt.
    Bury St. Edmunds, Suffolk
Haselocke, John, Esq.
    Worcester, Worcestershire
Hastings, Ferdinand Lord (*A.C.*)
    Leicestershire
Hatcher, Thomas, Esq. (*D.N.B.*; *L.P.*; *A.C.*)
    Grantham, Lincolnshire
Hatton, Sir Thomas, Kt.
    Stamford, Lincolnshire
Hawtrey, Ralph, Esq.
    Wendover, Buckinghamshire
Hele (Heale), Sir Thomas, Bart. (*L.P.*; *A.O.*)
    Plympton, Devonshire
Herbert, Edward, Esq. (*D.N.B.*; *L.P.*; *A.O.*;
    A.C.)

---

[1]"John Herris" in Crown Office List.

Downton, Wiltshire

Herbert, Sir William, Kt.
Montgomeryshire, Wales; Wilton, Wiltshire

Herne (Heron), John, Esq., of Lincoln's Inn (*D.N.B.*; *A.C.*)
Newport, Cornwall (return voided 14 April)

Herris, Sir Arthur, Kt. (*A.C.*)
Maldon, Essex

Herris, Christopher, Esq. (*A.C.*)
Harwich, Essex

*Heveningham, Sir John, Kt. (*A.C.*)
Norfolk

Hewett, Thomas, Esq. (*A.C.*)
New Windsor, Berkshire

Heyman, Sir Peter, Kt. (*D.N.B.*; *L.P.*; *A.C.*)
Hythe, Cinque Port

Hicks, Sir Baptist, Kt. and Bart. (*D.N.B.*; *A.C.*)
Tewkesbury, Gloucestershire (created Baron Hicks of Ilmington and Viscount Campden 5 May 1628)

Hicks, Sir William, Kt. and Bart. (*A.C.*)
Tewkesbury, Gloucestershire (vice Sir Baptist Hicks)

Hildyard (Hilliard), Sir Christopher, Kt. (*A.C.*)
Hedon-in-Holderness, Yorkshire

Hill, John, Merchant
Dorchester, Dorset

Hippisley, Sir John, Kt., Lieutenant of Dover Castle (*L.P.*)
Dover, Cinque Port

Hobart, Sir Miles, Kt. (*D.N.B.*; *A.O.*)
Marlow, Buckinghamshire

Hoby, Sir Thomas Posthumus, Kt. (*A.O.*)
Ripon, Yorkshire

Holcroft, Sir Henry, Kt.
Newton, Lancashire

Holles, Denzil, Esq. (*D.N.B.*; *L.P.*; *A.C.*)
Dorchester, Dorset

Hopton, Sir Ralph, K.B. (*D.N.B.*; *L.P.*)
Wells, Somerset

Horner, Thomas, Gent. (*A.C.*)
Minehead, Somerset

Hoskins, John, Esq., Serjeant at Law (*D.N.B.*; *A.O.*)
Hereford, Herefordshire

*Hotham, Sir John, Kt. and Bart. (*D.N.B.*; *L.P.*)
Beverley, Yorkshire

Howard, Sir Charles, Kt., of Newlodge, Berkshire
Gatton, Surrey

Howard, Sir Edward, K.B. (*D.N.B.*)
Hertford, Hertfordshire (created Baron Howard of Escrick 12 April 1628)

Howard, Sir Robert, K.B. (*D.N.B.*; *L.P.*)
Bishops Castle, Shropshire

Howell, James, Esq. (*D.N.B.*; *A.O.*)
Richmond, Yorkshire

Hoyle, Thomas, Alderman of York City (*L.P.*)
York, Yorkshire (vice Sir Thomas Savile)

Hungerford, Sir Edward, K.B. (*D.N.B.*; *L.P.*; *A.O.*)
Cricklade, Wiltshire

Hutton, Sir Richard, Kt. (*A.C.*)
Knaresborough, Yorkshire

Hyde, Lawrence, Esq., of Heale, Wiltshire (*A.O.*)
Hindon, Wiltshire

Ingram, Sir Arthur, Sr., Kt., of York City (*D.N.B.*; *L.P.*)
York, Yorkshire

Irby, Sir Anthony, Kt. (*L.P.*; *A.C.*)
Boston, Lincolnshire (vice Richard Okely)

Jackson, Sir John, Kt. (*A.O.*)
Pontefract, Yorkshire

Jay, Sir Thomas, Kt.
Ludgershall, Wiltshire

Jenens, Owen, Gent.
Portsmouth, Hampshire

Jenner, Robert, Gent. (*L.P.*)
Cricklade, Wiltshire

Jennings, Sir John, K.B. (*L.P.*)
St. Albans, Hertfordshire

Jephson, Sir John, Kt.
Whitchurch, Hampshire

Jermyn, Henry, Esq. (*D.N.B.*)
Liverpool, Lancashire

Jermyn, Sir Thomas, Kt. (*L.P.*; *A.C.*)
Bury St. Edmunds, Suffolk

Jermyn, Thomas, Esq. (*L.P.*; *A.C.*)
Clitheroe, Lancashire

Jervoise, Sir Thomas, Kt. (*L.P.*)
Whitchurch, Hampshire

Jones, Charles, Esq.
Beaumaris, Anglesey, Wales

Jones, Richard, Esq., of Trewerne, Radnorshire
Radnorshire, Wales

Jones, Robert, Esq.
Flintshire, Wales

Jordan, Ignatius, Esq.
Exeter, Devonshire

Keightley, Christopher, Esq.
Old Sarum, Wiltshire

Kemeys (Kemys), Nicholas, Esq., of Lanvayre,

Monmouthshire
  Monmouthshire
Kent, Thomas, Gent.
  Devizes, Wiltshire
Killigrew, Sir Robert, Kt., of Cornwall (*D.N.B.*; *A.O.*)
  Bodmin, Cornwall
Killigrew, Sir William, Kt. (*D.N.B.*; *A.O.*)
  Penryn, Cornwall; Newport, Cornwall (Newport return voided 14 April)
Kirkham, Robert, Esq. (*A.O.*)
  St. Albans, Hertfordshire
Kirton, Edward, Esq. (*L.P.*; *A.O.*)
  Great Bedwyn, Wiltshire
*Knightley, Richard, Esq. (*D.N.B.*)
  Northamptonshire
Knollys, Sir Francis, Jr., Kt. (*L.P.*; *A.O.*)
  Reading, Berkshire
Knollys, Sir Robert, Kt. (*A.O.*)
  Wallingford, Berkshire

Lake, Sir Thomas, Kt. (*A.O.*)
  Gatton, Surrey (return voided 26 March)
Lambert (Lambart), Charles Lord (*D.N.B.*; *A.C.*)
  Bossiney, Cornwall
Lane, Thomas, Esq. (*L.P.*)
  Chipping Wycombe, Buckinghamshire
Lawley, Thomas, Esq.
  Much Wenlock, Shropshire
Leech, Sir Edward, Kt.
  Derbyshire
Le Groos (Le Grosse), Sir Charles, Kt. (*L.P.*; *A.C.*)
  Orford, Suffolk
Leigh, Sir Thomas, Kt. and Bart. (*A.O.*)
  Warwickshire
Leving, Timothy, Esq. (*A.O.*)
  Derby, Derbyshire
Lewis, James, Esq., of Abertnantbychan (*A.O.*)
  Cardiganshire, Wales
Lewkenor, Christopher, Esq. (*L.P.*; *A.O.*)
  Midhurst, Sussex
Lewkenor, Richard, Esq. (*A.O.*)
  Sussex
Lister, John, Esq.[2] (*L.P.*; *A.O.*)
  Kingston-on-Hull, Yorkshire
Littleton, Edward, Esq. (*D.N.B.*; *A.O.*)
  Caernarvon, Caernarvonshire, Wales; Leominster, Herefordshire
Littleton, Thomas, Esq., of Henley, Shropshire
  Leominster, Herefordshire (vice Edward

Littleton, Esq.)
Lloyd, Richard, Gent.
  Montgomery, Montgomeryshire, Wales
Long, Robert, Esq. (*D.N.B.*; *A.O.*)
  Devizes, Wiltshire
Long, Walter, Esq. (*L.P.*)
  Bath, Somerset
Lowe, George, Sr., Esq. (*L.P.*)
  Calne, Wiltshire
Lowther, Sir John, Kt., of Lowther
  Westmorland
Lowther, John, Esq., of Lowther
  Westmorland
Lowther, Richard, Gent.
  Appleby, Westmorland
Lucy, Francis, Esq. (*A.O.*)
  Warwick, Warwickshire (vice Sir Thomas Puckering; return voided 31 May)
Lucy, Sir Thomas, Kt. (*D.N.B.*; *L.P.*; *A.O.*)
  Warwickshire
*Luke, Sir Oliver, Kt. (*L.P.*; *A.C.*)
  Bedfordshire
Lynne, John, Gent.
  Exeter, Devonshire
Lytton, Sir William, Kt. (*L.P.*; *A.C.*)
  Hertfordshire
Lyveley, Edward, Esq.
  Berwick-on-Tweed, Northumberland

Mallory, William, Sr., Esq. (*L.P.*; *A.C.*)
  Ripon, Yorkshire
Maltravers, Henry Lord
  Arundel, Sussex
Mansell, Sir Robert, Kt., Vice Admiral for the county of Glamorgan, Wales (*D.N.B.*; *A.O.*)
  Glamorganshire, Wales
Manwaring (Mainwaring), Philip, Esq. (*D.N.B.*; *A.C.*)
  Derby, Derbyshire
Marlott, William, Gent. (*L.P.*)
  Shoreham, Sussex
Marten, Sir Henry, Kt., LL.D. (*D.N.B.*; *A.O.*)
  Oxford University
Martyn, Nicholas,[3] Gent.
  Exeter, Devonshire (return voided 26 March)
*Masham, Sir William, Bart. (*L.P.*; *A.O.*)
  Colchester, Essex (vice Edward Alford, Sr.)
Mason, Rober , Esq. (*D.N.B.*)
  Winchester, Hampshire
Matthew, Roger, Merchant (*L.P.*)

---

[2]Lister was knighted 23 May 1628.

[3]"Michael Martyn" in *O.R.*; see Appendix: Elections.

Dartmouth, Devonshire

†May, Sir Humphrey, Kt., Chancellor of Duchy
of Lancaster (*D.N.B.*; *A.O.*)
    Leicester, Leicestershire

Maynard, Sir John, K.B. (*D.N.B.*; *A.C.*)
    Calne, Wiltshire

Mayor, John, Alderman
    Southampton, Hampshire

Meautys, Thomas, Esq.
    Cambridge, Cambridgeshire

Middleton (Myddelton), Sir Hugh, Bart. (*D.N.B.*)
    Denbigh, Denbighshire, Wales

Middleton, John, Esq.
    Horsham, Sussex

Mildmay, Sir Henry, Kt., Master of the Jewel
House (*D.N.B.*; *L.P.*; *A.C.*)
    Maldon, Essex

Miller (Meller), Sir John, Kt., of Little Breddy,
Dorset
    Wareham, Dorset

Molyneux, Sir Richard, Kt. and Bart. (*D.N.B.*;
A.O.)
    Lancashire

Montagu, James, Esq. (*A.C.*)
    Huntingdon, Huntingdonshire

Moody, Sir Henry, Kt. and Bart.
    Malmesbury, Wiltshire

Moore (More), Poynings, Esq., of Loseley (*L.P.*)
    Guildford, Surrey

More, Alexander, Jr., Esq. (*A.C.*)
    Grantham, Lincolnshire

Morgan, Lewis, Esq. (*A.O.*)
    Cardiff, Glamorganshire, Wales

Morgan, Sir Thomas, Kt.
    Wilton, Wiltshire

Morgan, William, Esq., of the Middle Temple,
London (*L.P.*)
    Monmouth, Monmouthshire

Morley, Robert, Esq.
    Shoreham, Sussex

Morris, Thomas, Esq.
    Westminster, Middlesex

Morrison, Sir Charles, K.B. and Bart.
    Hertford, Hertfordshire (vice Sir Edward
    Howard)

Moulson, Thomas, Alderman
    London, Middlesex

Moundeford, Edmund, Esq., of Feltwell, Norfolk
(*L.P.*; *A.C.*)
    Thetford, Norfolk

Murray, William, Esq. (*D.N.B.*)
    East Looe, Cornwall

Napier, Gerard, Esq., of More Crichel, Dorset
(*D.N.B.*; *L.P.*)
    Wareham, Dorset

Napier, Sir Nathaniel, Kt., of More Crichel,
Dorset (*A.O.*)
    Milborne Port, Somerset

Napier, Sir Robert, Jr., Kt. (*L.P.*; *A.O.*)
    Weymouth and Melcombe Regis, Dorset

Nethersole, Sir Francis, Kt. (*D.N.B.*; *A.C.*)
    Corfe Castle, Dorset

Nevill, Francis, Esq., of Reate
    Boroughbridge, Yorkshire

Newdegate, John, Esq. (*A.O.*)
    Liverpool, Lancashire

Newport, Sir Richard, Kt. (*D.N.B.*; *A.O.*)
    Shropshire

Nicholas, Edward, Esq. (*D.N.B.*; *A.O.*)
    Dover, Cinque Port

Nichols (Nicolls), Francis, Esq. (*D.N.B.*; *A.O.*)
    Northamptonshire

Nichols, Humphrey, Esq., of Cornwall
    Bodmin, Cornwall

North, Sir Dudley, K.B. (*D.N.B.*; *L.P.*; *A.C.*)
    Horsham, Sussex

North, Sir Roger, Kt. (*L.P.*)
    Eye, Suffolk

Norton, Sir Daniel, Kt.
    Hampshire

Nowell, William, Gent.
    Clitheroe, Lancashire

Noy, William, Esq. (*D.N.B.*; *A.C.*; *A.O.*)
    Helston, Cornwall

Oglander, Sir John, Kt. (*D.N.B.*; *A.O.*)
    Yarmouth (Isle of Wight), Hampshire

Okely, Richard, Esq.
    Boston, Lincolnshire (return voided 8 May)

Oldisworth, Michael, Esq. (*D.N.B.*; *L.P.*; *A.O.*)
    Old Sarum, Wiltshire

Oliver, Richard, Esq.
    Buckingham, Buckinghamshire

Onslow, Sir Richard, Kt. (*D.N.B.*; *L.P.*; *A.C.*)
    Surrey

Osborne, Sir Edward, Bart. (*A.C.*)
    East Retford, Nottinghamshire

Owen, Hugh, Esq. (*L.P.*)
    Pembroke, Pembrokeshire, Wales

Owen, Thomas, Esq.
    Shrewsbury, Shropshire

Owen, Sir William, Kt.
    Shrewsbury, Shropshire

Owfield (Oldfield), Samuel, Esq., of Gatton

(*L.P.*; *A.C.*)
    Gatton, Surrey

Packer, John, Esq. (*D.N.B.*; *A.C.*)
    West Looe, Cornwall
Palmer, Sir Roger, K.B. (*L.P.*)
    Queenborough, Kent
Palmes, Sir Guy, Kt. (*L.P.*)
    Rutland
Paramore, Thomas, Esq.
    Lyme Regis, Dorset
Parkhurst, Robert, Jr., Gent. (*L.P.*; *A.O.*)
    Guildford, Surrey
Paule, Sir George, Kt. (*D.N.B.*)
    Bridgnorth, Shropshire
Payne, John, Esq., of Pallenswicke, Middlesex
    St. Ives, Cornwall
Payne, Sir Robert, Kt.
    Huntingdonshire
Peke (Peake), Peter, Esq.
    Sandwich, Cinque Port
Pelham, Henry, Esq. (*L.P.*; *A.C.*)
    Great Grimsby, Lincolnshire
Percy, Henry, Esq. (*D.N.B.*; *L.P.*; *A.O.*)
    Marlborough, Wiltshire (vice Sir Francis Seymour)
Perrott, Sir James, Kt. (*D.N.B.*; *A.O.*)
    Haverfordwest, Pembrokeshire, Wales
Petty, Maximilian, Esq. (*A.O.*)
    Westbury, Wiltshire
Phelips, Sir Robert, Kt. (*D.N.B.*)
    Somerset
Philipot, John, Esq., Somerset [Herald] (*D.N.B.*; *A.O.*)
    Sandwich, Cinque Port
Pierrepont, Henry, Esq. (*D.N.B.*; *A.C.*; *A.O.*)
    Nottingham, Nottinghamshire
Pooley (Poley), John, Esq.
    Wilton, Wiltshire (vice Sir William Herbert)
Pooley (Poley), Sir William, Kt. (*A.C.*)
    Sudbury, Suffolk
Popham, Sir Francis, Kt. (*D.N.B.*; *L.P.*; *A.O.*)
    Chippenham, Wiltshire
Popham, John, Esq.
    Bath, Somerset
Portman, Sir Hugh, Bart., of Orchard, Somerset (*A.O.*)
    Taunton, Somerset
Potter, Thomas
    Coventry, Warwickshire (return voided 9 April)
Poulett (Powlett, Paulet), Thomas, Esq., of Burton,

Dorset (*A.O.*)
    Bridport, Dorset (vice Francis Drake)
*Poyntz, Sir Robert, K.B. (*D.N.B.*; *A.O.*)
    Gloucestershire
Prestwood, Thomas, Gent. (*A.O.*)
    Totnes, Devonshire
Price, Charles, Esq. (*L.P.*)
    Radnor, Radnorshire, Wales
Puckering, Sir Thomas, Kt. and Bart. (*D.N.B.*)
    Tamworth, Staffordshire; Warwick, Warwickshire
Purchas, Thomas, Alderman
    Cambridge, Cambridgeshire
‡Purefoy, William, Esq. (*D.N.B.*; *L.P.*; *A.C.*)
    Coventry, Warwickshire
Pye, Sir Robert, Kt. (*L.P.*)
    Grampound, Cornwall
Pye, Sir Walter, Kt., Attorney of the Court of Wards (*D.N.B.*)
    Herefordshire; Brecon, Breconshire, Wales
Pye, Walter, Esq.
    Brecon, Breconshire, Wales (vice Sir Walter Pye)
Pym, John, Esq. (*D.N.B.*; *L.P.*; *A.O.*)
    Tavistock, Devonshire
Pyne, Hugh, Esq.
    Weymouth and Melcombe Regis, Dorset
Pyne, John, Esq. (*L.P.*)
    Poole, Dorset

Radcliffe, Sir Alexander, K.B.
    Lancashire
Ramsden, Sir John, Kt.
    Pontefract, Yorkshire
Rashleigh, Robert, Esq.
    Fowey, Cornwall
Ratcliffe, John, Alderman
    Chester, Cheshire
Ravenscroft, William, Esq. (*A.O.*)
    Flint, Flintshire, Wales
Reynell (Raynall), Sir Thomas, Kt. (*A.O.*)
    Morpeth, Northumberland
Rich, Sir Nathaniel, Kt. (*D.N.B.*; *A.C.*)
    Harwich, Essex
Riddell, Sir Peter, Kt.
    Newcastle-on-Tyne, Northumberland
Riddell, Sir Thomas, Kt. (*D.N.B.*; *A.C.*)
    Newcastle-on-Tyne, Northumberland
Rivers, Sir George, Kt.
    Lewes, Sussex (return voided 3 April)
Rodney, Sir Edward, Kt. (*L.P.*)
    Somerset

Rolfe, William, Esq.
  Heytesbury, Wiltshire
Rolle, Henry, Esq. (*D.N.B.*; *A.O.*)
  Truro, Cornwall
Rolle, John, Merchant (*D.N.B.*; *L.P.*)
  Callington, Cornwall
Rous (Rowse), Anthony, Esq., of Fatcham, Surrey
  Wootton Bassett, Wiltshire
Rous, Francis, Esq. (*D.N.B.*; *L.P.*; *A.O.*)
  Tregony, Cornwall
Roydon, Marmaduke, Esq., [Captain] (*D.N.B.*)
  Aldeburgh, Suffolk
Rudyard, Sir Benjamin, Kt. (*D.N.B.*; *L.P.*; *A.C.*; *A.O.*)
  Downton, Wiltshire

St. John, Sir Alexander, Kt. (*A.C.*)
  Barnstaple, Devonshire
St. John, Sir Anthony, Kt. (*A.C.*)
  Wigan, Lancashire
*St. John, Sir Beauchamp, Kt. (*L.P.*; *A.C.*)
  Bedford, Bedfordshire
St. John, Oliver, Lord of Bletsoe (*D.N.B.*; *A.C.*)
  Bedfordshire
Sandys, Sir George, K.B.
  Higham Ferrers, Northamptonshire
Sandys, Sir Miles, Kt. and Bart. (*A.C.*)
  Cambridgeshire
Saunders, John, Esq. (*A.O.*)
  Reading, Berkshire
Savage, Edward, Esq.
  Midhurst, Sussex
Savile, Sir Thomas, Kt. (*D.N.B.*; *A.C.*)
  York, Yorkshire (return voided 23 April)
Sawyer, Sir Edmund, Kt.
  Berwick-on-Tweed, Northumberland (expelled from the House 21 June)
Scott, Sir Edward, K.B. (*A.O.*)
  Hythe, Cinque Port
Scott, Thomas, Esq.
  Canterbury, Kent
Scudamore, Sir John, Kt. and Bart. (*D.N.B.*; *A.O.*)
  Hereford, Herefordshire
Selden, John, Esq. (*D.N.B.*; *L.P.*; *A.O.*)
  Ludgershall, Wiltshire
Seymour, Sir Francis, Kt. (*D.N.B.*; *L.P.*)
  Wiltshire; Marlborough, Wiltshire
Shelton (Sheldon, Shilton), Sir Richard, Kt., Solicitor General (*D.N.B.*; *A.C.*)
  Bridgnorth, Shropshire
Sherfield, Henry, Esq., Recorder of Salisbury (*D.N.B.*)

Salisbury, Wiltshire
Sherland, Christopher, Esq., Recorder of Northampton
  Northampton, Northamptonshire
Sherwill, Thomas, Merchant
  Plymouth, Devonshire
Smythe (Smith), Thomas, Esq. (*L.P.*; *A.O.*)
  Bridgwater, Somerset
Sparke, John, Esq. (*A.O.*)
  Mitchell (Michael), Cornwall
Speccott, Paul, Esq. (*A.O.*)
  East Looe, Cornwall
Spencer, Richard, Esq. (*A.O.*)
  Northampton, Northamptonshire
Spiller, Sir Henry, Kt.
  Middlesex; Thetford, Norfolk
Spring, Sir William, Kt. (*A.C.*)
  Suffolk (vice Sir Edward Coke)
Stanhope, Sir Henry, K.B. (*A.O.*)
  East Retford, Nottinghamshire
Stanhope, Sir John, Kt., of Elvaston, Derbyshire
  Leicester, Leicestershire
Stapleton, Robert, Esq.
  Aldborough, Yorkshire
‡Stapley, Anthony, Esq. (*D.N.B.*; *L.P.*; *A.C.*)
  Lewes, Sussex
Stephens, Nathaniel, Esq. (*L.P.*)
  Gloucestershire
Steward, Sir Simeon, Kt. (*D.N.B.*; *A.C.*)
  Aldeburgh, Suffolk
Stonehouse, John, Esq. (*A.O.*)
  Abingdon, Berkshire
*Strangways, Sir John, Kt. (*L.P.*; *A.O.*)
  Dorset
Strode, William, Gent. (*D.N.B.*; *L.P.*; *A.O.*)
  Bere Alston, Devonshire
Stuart, Sir Francis, K.B. (*A.O.*)
  Liskeard, Cornwall

Talmache (Tollemache), Sir Lionel, Kt. and Bart.
  Orford, Suffolk
Taverner, Edmund, Esq. (*A.O.*)
  Woodstock, Oxfordshire
Taylor, Richard, Esq.
  Bedford, Bedfordshire
Thelwall, Sir Eubule, Kt. (*D.N.B.*; *A.C.*; *A.O.*)
  Denbighshire, Wales
Thomas, Edward, Esq. (*L.P.*)
  West Looe, Cornwall
Thoroughgood, John, Esq.
  Shaftesbury, Dorset
Thynne, Charles, Esq. (*A.O.*)

Westbury, Wiltshire

Thynne, Sir Thomas, Kt., of Longleat, Wiltshire (*A.O.*)
  Hindon, Wiltshire

Tichborne, Benjamin, Esq.
  Petersfield, Hampshire

Tichborne, Sir Richard, Kt.
  Winchester, Hampshire

Tomkins, James, Esq. (*A.O.*)
  Leominster, Herefordshire

Tomkins, Nathaniel, Esq.
  Christchurch, Hampshire

Tomkins, William, Esq. (*L.P.*)
  Weobley, Herefordshire

Tomlins (Tomlyns), Richard, Esq., of Westminster (*A.O.*)
  Ludlow, Shropshire

Tookie, Bartholomew, Alderman
  Salisbury, Wiltshire

Towerson, William, Gent. (*A.O.*)
  Portsmouth, Hampshire

Townshend, Sir Roger, Bart.
  Norfolk

Trefusis, Nicholas, Esq.
  Newport, Cornwall

Trevor, Sir John, Jr., Kt. (*D.N.B.*; *L.P.*; *A.C.*)
  Great Bedwyn, Wiltshire

Tufton, Richard, Esq. (*A.O.*)
  Rye, Cinque Port

Twysden, Sir William, Kt. and Bart. (*A.C.*)
  Winchelsea, Cinque Port

Upton, John, Esq. (*L.P.*; *A.O.*)
  Dartmouth, Devonshire

Uvedale, Sir William, Kt. (*L.P.*; *A.O.*)
  Petersfield, Hampshire

Valentine, Benjamin, Esq. (*D.N.B.*; *L.P.*)
  St. Germans, Cornwall

Vane, Sir Henry, Kt. (*D.N.B.*; *L.P.*; *A.O.*)
  Thetford, Norfolk (vice Sir Henry Spiller)

Vaughan, Henry, Esq. (*D.N.B.*; *L.P.*)
  Carmarthen, Carmarthenshire, Wales

Vaughan, John,[4] Esq., of Trawscoed, Cardiganshire (*D.N.B.*; *L.P.*; *A.O.*)
  Cardigan, Cardiganshire, Wales

Vaughan, Richard, Esq.
  Merionethshire, Wales

Vaughan, Sir Richard, K.B. (*D.N.B.*)
  Carmarthenshire, Wales

Verney, Sir Edmund, Kt. (*D.N.B.*; *L.P.*; *A.O.*)
  Aylesbury, Buckinghamshire

Vivian (Vyvian), Hannibal, Esq., of Lostwithiel (*A.O.*)
  St. Mawes, Cornwall

Walden, Isaac, Esq.
  Coventry, Warwickshire (return voided 9 April)

Waller, Edmund, Esq. (*D.N.B.*; *L.P.*; *A.C.*)
  Amersham, Buckinghamshire

Waller, Henry, Clothworker
  London, Middlesex

Wallop, Sir Henry, Kt. (*L.P.*; *A.O.*)
  Hampshire

Wallop, Robert, Esq. (*D.N.B.*; *L.P.*; *A.O.*)
  Andover, Hampshire

Walsingham, Sir Thomas, Jr., Kt. (*L.P.*; *A.C.*)
  Rochester, Kent

Walter, Sir William, Kt.
  Lichfield, Staffordshire

Walter, William, Esq.
  Weobley, Herefordshire

Waltham, Henry, Alderman
  Weymouth and Melcombe Regis, Dorset

Wandesford, Christopher, Esq. (*D.N.B.*; *A.C.*)
  Thirsk, Yorkshire

Watkinson, James, Esq.
  Kingston-on-Hull, Yorkshire

Wenman, Sir Francis, Kt.
  Oxfordshire

Wenman, Sir Thomas, Kt. (*D.N.B.*; *L.P.*; *A.O.*)
  Brackley, Northamptonshire

Wentworth, Sir John, Kt.
  Great Yarmouth, Norfolk

*Wentworth, Sir Thomas, Kt. and Bart. (*D.N.B.*; *A.C.*)
  Yorkshire

Wentworth, Thomas, Esq.
  Oxford, Oxfordshire

Weston, Jerome, Esq. (*D.N.B.*; *A.C.*)
  Gatton, Surrey (return voided 26 March)

Whistler, John, Esq. (*L.P.*; *A.O.*)
  Oxford, Oxfordshire

Whitaker, Lawrence, Esq. (*L.P.*; *A.C.*; *A.O.*)
  Peterborough, Northamptonshire

Whitby, Edward, Esq., Recorder (*A.O.*)
  Chester, Cheshire

Whitehead, Sir Henry, Kt. (*A.O.*)
  Stockbridge, Hampshire

4"James Vaughan" in the Crown Office List.

Whitehead, Richard, Esq. (*L.P.*; *A.O.*)
Lymington, Hampshire
Wilde, George, Esq. (*A.O.*)
Droitwich, Worcestershire
Wilde, John, Esq. (*D.N.B.*; *L.P.*; *A.O.*; *A.C.*)
Droitwich, Worcestershire
Williams, Henry, Esq.
Breconshire, Wales
Windham (Wyndham), Edmund, Gent., of Lincoln's Inn (*L.P.*; *A.O.*)
Minehead, Somerset
Wingfield, William, Esq.
Stafford, Staffordshire
Winterton, Francis, Gent.
Dunwich, Suffolk
Wise (Wyse), Thomas, Esq. (*L.P.*; *A.C.*)
Bere Alston, Devonshire
Wogan, John, Esq. (*L.P.*; *A.O.*)
Pembrokeshire, Wales
Wolstenholme, Sir John, Kt. (*D.N.B.*)
Newport, Cornwall (return voided 14 April)
Wray, Sir Christopher, Kt. (*D.N.B.*; *L.P.*)
Great Grimsby, Lincolnshire
*Wray, Sir John, Kt. and Bart. (*D.N.B.*; *L.P.*; *A.C.*)
Lincolnshire
Wrothe, Sir Thomas, Kt. (*D.N.B.*; *A.O.*)
Bridgwater, Somerset

Yarwood, Richard, Esq., of Southwark
Southwark, Surrey
Yelverton, Sir Christopher, Jr., Kt. (*L.P.*)
Newport (Isle of Wight), Hampshire

NOTES ON THOSE M.P.S WHO WERE COMMITTED OR CONFINED FOR REFUSING THE FORCED LOAN.[5]

Sir William Armine: 24 April 1627, appearance before the Privy Council (*A.P.C., 1627*, p. 240); 29 April, committed to the Fleet (ibid., p. 252); 30 June, committed to the custody of the sheriff of Oxfordshire (ibid., pp. 395, 430); 30 September, to be interrogated by the Attorney General (*A.P.C., 1627–1628*, p. 58); 2 January 1628, released from custody (ibid., p. 217).

Sir Edward Ayscough: 29 April 1627, committed to the Gatehouse (*A.P.C., 1627*, p. 253); 30 June, committed to the custody of the sheriff of Surrey (ibid., p. 396); another order to the same effect (ibid., p. 430); 6 August, committed to the custody of the sheriff of Suffolk (ibid., p. 475); 2 January 1628, released from custody (*A.P.C., 1627–1628*, p. 217).

Sir Nathaniel Barnardiston: 30 June 1627, committed to the custody of the sheriff of Sussex (*A.P.C., 1627*, p. 396); 20 July, committed to the custody of the sheriff of Lincolnshire (ibid., p. 430); 2 January 1628, released from custody (*A.P.C., 1627–1628*, p. 217).

Sir Francis Barrington: no date of commitment; 14 June 1627, suit in his behalf for release as a prisoner in the Marshalsea; order by the Privy Council to deliver him to the custody of the sheriff of Surrey (*A.P.C., 1627*, pp. 346–347); 2 January 1628, released from custody (*A.P.C., 1627–1628*, p. 217).

James Bunce: 15 June 1627, committed to the Gatehouse (as "James Dunce") (*A.P.C., 1627*, p. 351); 20 July, committed to the custody of the mayor of Halifax, Yorkshire (ibid., p. 429); 5 September, order to appear before the Privy Council (*A.P.C., 1627–1628*, p. 7); 30 September, to be interrogated by the Attorney General (ibid., p. 58); 2 January 1628, released from custody (ibid., p. 218).

Sir William Constable: 29 June 1627, order to appear before the Privy Council (*A.P.C., 1627*, p. 382); 17 July, appearance before the Privy Council; order "to attend the Board until further order from their Lordships" (ibid., p. 418); 9 September, another order to appear before the Privy Council (*A.P.C., 1627–1628*, p. 17); 6 October, appearance before the Privy Council; order to remain in the custody of the messenger until he was discharged (ibid., p. 75);

---

[5]At least three other M.P.s (Thomas Alured, Sir Anthony Irby, and William Purefoy) were called before the Council for their opposition to the loan but do not appear to have been confined. See *A.P.C., 1627*, pp. 52, 85, 142; S.P. 16/50: 54; 56: 39, 70.

2 January 1628, released from custody (ibid., p. 217).

William Coryton: 27 April 1627, order to appear, with Sir John Eliot, before the Privy Council (*A.P.C., 1627*, p. 248); 28 May, appearance before the Privy Council; order by the Privy Council "to give their attendance until they shall be dismissed by their Lordships" (ibid., p. 298); 30 June, order by the Privy Council to deliver Coryton into the custody of the sheriff of Sussex (ibid., p. 396); 27 July, order by the Privy Council "to the warden of the Fleet to receive [Coryton] from the keeper of the Marshalsea . . ." (ibid., p. 447); 7 September, apparently again put in the custody of the sheriff of Sussex (*A.P.C., 1627–1628*, p. 10); 30 September, order to the Attorney General to interrogate Coryton and others (ibid., p. 58); 2 November, order of the Privy Council to "fetch [Coryton] out of the county of Devon" (ibid., p. 126); 2 January 1628, released from the Gatehouse (ibid., p. 218).

Sir John Eliot: 27 April 1627, order to appear, with William Coryton, before the Privy Council (*A.P.C., 1627*, p. 248); 28 May, appearance before the Privy Council; order by the Privy Council "to give their attendance until they shall be dismissed by their Lordships" (ibid., p. 298); 30 June, order by the Privy Council to deliver him into the custody of the sheriff of Sussex (ibid., p. 396); 30 September, order to interrogate Eliot and others (*A.P.C., 1627–1628*, p. 58); 2 January 1628, released from the Gatehouse (ibid., p. 218).

Sir Walter Erle: 22 January 1627, appearance of Erle before the Privy Council (*A.P.C., 1627*, p. 30); 29 January, warrant to be imprisoned in the Fleet (ibid., p. 40); 15 August, warrant to commit Erle "close prisoner to the Fleet, and not to have any suffered to come unto him, saving only one servant" (ibid., p. 490); 30 September, order to the Attorney General to interrogate Erle and others (*A.P.C., 1627–1628*, p. 58); 7 Novem-

ber, warrants for detaining in prison Erle and four other persons "in the several prisons to which they were committed" (ibid., p. 131); 2 January 1628, released from the Fleet (ibid., p. 218).

Thomas Godfrey: 24 April 1627, appearance before the Privy Council (*A.P.C., 1627*, p. 241); 29 April, warrant to commit him and others "safe prisoners" to the Gatehouse (ibid., p. 253); 30 June, committed to the custody of the sheriff of Somerset (ibid., p. 395); 20 July, another order to the same effect (ibid., p. 430); 30 September, order to the Attorney General to interrogate Godfrey and others (*A.P.C., 1627–1628*, p. 58); 2 January 1628, released from custody (ibid., p. 217).

Sir Thomas Grantham: 24 April 1627, appearance before the Privy Council (*A.P.C., 1627*, p. 241); 29 April, warrant to commit Grantham and others "safe prisoners" to the Gatehouse (ibid., p. 253); 30 June, committed to the custody of the sheriff of Dorset (ibid., p. 395); 20 July, committed to the custody of the sheriff of Kent (ibid., p. 430); 2 January 1628, released from custody (*A.P.C., 1627–1628*, p. 217).

Sir Harbottle Grimston: 4 May 1627, warrant to the warden of the Fleet to receive Grimston into his custody (*A.P.C., 1627*, p. 262); 27 July, order to the sheriff of Northamptonshire to receive Grimston in his custody (ibid., p. 449); 2 January 1628, released from the Fleet (*A.P.C., 1627–1628*, p. 218).

John Hampden: 29 January 1627, appearance before the Privy Council (*A.P.C., 1627*, p. 39); 31 January, warrant to the keeper of the Gatehouse to receive Hampden into custody (ibid., p. 46); 27 July, committed to the custody of the sheriff of Hampshire (ibid., p. 449); 2 January 1628, released from custody (*A.P.C., 1627–1628*, p. 217).

Sir John Heveningham: 21 January 1627, appearance before the Privy Council (*A.P.C., 1627*, p. 28); 29 January, warrant to the keeper of the Marshalsea to receive Heven-ingham into his custody (ibid., p. 40); 27 June, order for his temporary release (ibid., p. 370); 30 June, committed to the custody of the sheriff of Salop (ibid., p. 395); 30 September, to be interrogated by the At-torney General (*A.P.C., 1627–1628*, p. 58); 7 November, warrant to detain him in prison (ibid., p. 131); 2 January 1628, released from the Marshalsea (ibid., p. 218).

Sir John Hotham: 29 June 1627, order to appear before the Privy Council (*A.P.C., 1627*, p. 382); 17 July, appearance before the Privy Council; order "to attend the Board until further order from their Lord-ships" (ibid., p. 418); 9 September, another order to appear before the Privy Council (*A.P.C., 1627–1628*, p. 17); 6 October, ap-pearance before the Privy Council; order to remain in the custody of the messenger until he was discharged (ibid., p. 75); 2 January 1628, released from custody (ibid., p. 217).

Richard Knightley: 19 January 1627, ap-pearance before the Privy Council (*A.P.C., 1627*, p. 25); 30 June, committed to the cus-tody of the sheriff of Southampton (ibid., p. 395); 20 July, again committed to the sheriff of Southampton (ibid., p. 430); 2 January 1628, released from custody (*A.P.C., 1627–1628*, p. 217).

Sir Oliver Luke: 4 July 1627, warrant to commit Luke "safe prisoner" to the Gate-house (*A.P.C., 1627*, p. 403); 21 November, temporarily released from custody to go to London and Westminster "in regard of many suits and other urgent occasions which he hath concerning himself and divers of his friends, which do necessarily require his personal attendance this term" (*A.P.C., 1627–1628*, p. 147); 2 January 1628, released from custody (ibid., p. 217).

Sir William Masham: 30 June 1627, committed to the custody of the sheriff of Somerset (*A.P.C., 1627*, p. 395); 2 January 1628, released from confinement (*A.P.C., 1627–1628*, p. 217).

Sir Robert Poyntz: 9 March 1627, order to appear before the Privy Council (*A.P.C., 1627*, p. 125); 24 March, appearance before the Privy Council (ibid., p. 157); 27 June, warrant to the warden of the Fleet to receive Poyntz into his custody (ibid., p. 374); 27 July, committed to the custody of the sheriff of Northamptonshire (ibid., p. 449); 2 January 1628, released from confinement (*A.P.C., 1627–1628*, p. 217).

Sir Beauchamp St. John: 21 February 1627, order to appear before the Privy Coun-cil (*A.P.C., 1627*, p. 74); 26 February, ap-pearance before the Privy Council (ibid., p. 86); 6 July, again ordered to appear before the Privy Council (ibid., p. 404); 23 July, warrant to commit him "safe prisoner" to the Gatehouse (ibid., 439); 2 January 1628, released from custody (*A.P.C., 1627–1628*, p. 217).

Sir John Strangways: 29 January 1627, appearance before the Privy Council (*A.P.C., 1627*, p. 38); 29 January, warrant to the warden of the Fleet to receive Strangways into custody (ibid., p. 40); 5 June, warrant to the warden of the Fleet for the temporary release of Strangways, in response to Strang-ways's suit to the King "to grant him such liberty, whereby he may apply himself to the cure of an infirmity that he is subject unto, for which he is advised by the physician to go unto the Bath" (ibid., pp. 318–319); 30 June, committed to the custody of the sheriff of Bedfordshire (ibid., p. 395); 17 July, an-other temporary release for Strangways (ibid., p. 424); 29 September, again put into the custody of the sheriff of Bedfordshire (*A.P.C., 1627–1628*, p. 57); 2 January 1628, released from confinement (ibid., p. 217).

Sir Thomas Wentworth: 15 June 1627, appearance before the Privy Council (*A.P.C., 1627*, p. 352); 4 July, warrant to commit Wentworth "safe prisoner" to the Marshalsea (ibid., p. 402); released into the custody of the sheriff of Kent (ibid., p. 449); 4 Novem-ber, temporary release of Wentworth, after

LIST OF MEMBERS BY CONSTITUENCY

Names in brackets represent those whose
returns were voided and those who, having
been doubly returned, chose another seat.

Abingdon, Berkshire
  John Stonehouse
Aldborough, Yorkshire
  Henry Darley
  Robert Stapleton
Aldeburgh, Suffolk
  Sir Simeon Steward
  Marmaduke Roydon
Amersham, Buckinghamshire
  William Hakewill
  Edmund Waller
Andover, Hampshire
  Robert Wallop
  Ralph Conway
ANGLESEY, WALES
  Richard Bulkeley
Appleby, Westmorland
  Richard Lowther
  William Ashton
Arundel, Sussex
  Henry Lord Maltravers
  John Alford
Aylesbury, Buckinghamshire
  Sir Edmund Verney
  Clement Coke
Banbury, Oxfordshire
  John Crew
Barnstaple, Devonshire
  Sir Alexander St. John
  John Delbridge
Bath, Somerset
  John Popham
  Walter Long
Beaumaris, Anglesey, Wales
  Charles Jones
Bedford, Bedfordshire
  Sir Beauchamp St. John
  Richard Taylor
BEDFORDSHIRE
  Oliver Lord St. John of Bletsoe
  Sir Oliver Luke
Bere Alston, Devonshire
  William Strode
  Thomas Wise
BERKSHIRE
  Sir Richard Harrison

John Fettiplace
Berwick-on-Tweed, Northumberland
  Sir Edmund Sawyer
  Edward Lyveley
Beverley, Yorkshire
  Sir John Hotham
  Sir William Alford
Bewdley, Worcestershire
  Sir Ralph Clare
Bishops Castle, Shropshire
  Sir Robert Howard
  Sir Edward Foxe
Blechingley, Surrey
  Edward Bysshe
  John Evelyn
Bodmin, Cornwall
  Humphrey Nichols
  Sir Robert Killigrew
Boroughbridge, Yorkshire
  Sir Ferdinando Fairfax
  Francis Nevill
Bossiney, Cornwall
  Sir Richard Edgcombe
  Charles Lord Lambert
Boston, Lincolnshire
  Richard Bellingham
  Sir Anthony Irby
  [Richard Okely]
Brackley, Northamptonshire
  Sir Thomas Wenman
  John Curzon
Bramber, Sussex
  Sir Thomas Bowyer
  Sir Sackville Crow
Brecon, Breconshire, Wales
  Walter Pye
  [Sir Walter Pye]
BRECONSHIRE, WALES
  Henry Williams
Bridgnorth, Shropshire
  Sir Richard Shelton
  Sir George Paule
Bridgwater, Somerset
  Sir Thomas Wrothe
  Thomas Smythe
Bridport, Dorset
  Thomas Poulett
  Bampfield Chaffin
  [Francis Drake]
  [John Browne]
Bristol, Gloucestershire
  John Doughty

John Barker
Buckingham, Buckinghamshire
 Sir Thomas Denton
 Richard Oliver
BUCKINGHAMSHIRE
 Sir Edward Coke
 Sir William Fleetwood
Bury St. Edmunds, Suffolk
 Sir Thomas Jermyn
 Sir William Harvey
Caernarvon, Caernarvonshire, Wales
 Edward Littleton
CAERNARVONSHIRE, WALES
 John Griffith
Callington, Cornwall
 John Rolle
 [Sir William Constable]
Calne, Wiltshire
 Sir John Maynard
 George Lowe
Cambridge, Cambridgeshire
 Thomas Meautys
 Thomas Purchas
Cambridge University
 Sir John Coke
 Thomas Eden
CAMBRIDGESHIRE
 Sir Miles Sandys
 Sir John Carleton
Camelford, Cornwall
 Evan Edwards
 Francis Crossing
Canterbury, Kent
 Sir John Finch
 Thomas Scott
Cardiff, Glamorganshire, Wales
 Lewis Morgan
Cardigan, Cardiganshire, Wales
 John Vaughan
CARDIGANSHIRE, WALES
 James Lewis
Carlisle, Cumberland
 Richard Barwis
 Richard Graham
Carmarthen, Carmarthenshire, Wales
 Henry Vaughan
CARMARTHENSHIRE, WALES
 Sir Richard Vaughan
Castle Rising, Norfolk
 Sir Robert Cotton
 Thomas Bancroft
CHESHIRE

 Sir Richard Grosvenor
 Sir William Brereton
Chester, Cheshire
 Edward Whitby
 John Ratcliffe
Chichester, Sussex
 William Cawley
 Henry Bellingham
Chippenham, Wiltshire
 Sir Francis Popham
 Sir John Eyre
Chipping Wycombe, Buckinghamshire
 Sir William Borlase
 Thomas Lane
Christchurch, Hampshire
 Nathaniel Tomkins
 Sir Henry Croke
Cirencester, Gloucestershire
 Sir Giles Estcourt
 John George
Clitheroe, Lancashire
 Thomas Jermyn
 William Nowell
Colchester, Essex
 Sir Thomas Cheeke
 Sir William Masham
 [Edward Alford, Sr.]
Corfe Castle, Dorset
 Sir Francis Nethersole
 Giles Greene
CORNWALL
 Sir John Eliot
 William Coryton
Coventry, Warwickshire
 William Purefoy
 Richard Greene
 [Thomas Potter]
 [Isaac Walden]
Cricklade, Wiltshire
 Sir Edward Hungerford
 Robert Jenner
CUMBERLAND
 Sir George Dalston
 Sir Patrick Curwen
Dartmouth, Devonshire
 John Upton
 Roger Matthew
Denbigh, Denbighshire, Wales
 Sir Hugh Middleton
DENBIGHSHIRE, WALES
 Sir Eubule Thelwall
Derby, Derbyshire

Philip Manwaring
Timonthy Leving

DERBYSHIRE
Sir Edward Leech
John Fretchvile

Devizes, Wiltshire
Robert Long
Thomas Kent

DEVONSHIRE
John Bampfield
Sir Francis Drake

Dorchester, Dorset
Denzil Holles
John Hill

DORSET
Sir John Strangways
Sir Walter Erle

Dover, Cinque Port
Sir John Hippisley
Edward Nicholas

Downton, Wiltshire
Sir Benjamin Rudyard
Edward Herbert

Droitwich, Worcestershire
John Wilde
George Wilde

Dunwich, Suffolk
Sir Robert Brooke
Francis Winterton

East Grinstead, Sussex
Sir Henry Compton
Robert Goodwin

East Looe, Cornwall
William Murray
Paul Speccott

East Retford, Nottinghamshire
Sir Henry Stanhope
Sir Edward Osborne

ESSEX
Sir Francis Barrington
Sir Harbottle Grimston

Evesham, Worcestershire
Sir Robert Harley
Richard Cresheld

Exeter, Devonshire
Ignatius Jordan
John Lynne
[Nicholas Martyn]

Eye, Suffolk
Sir Roger North

Francis Finch

Flint, Flintshire, Wales
William Ravenscroft

FLINTSHIRE, WALES
Robert Jones

Fowey, Cornwall
Sir Richard Grenville
Robert Rashleigh

Gatton, Surrey
Samuel Owfield
Sir Charles Howard
[Sir Thomas Lake]
[Jerome Weston]

GLAMORGANSHIRE, WALES
Sir Robert Mansell

Gloucester, Gloucestershire
John Browne
John Hanbury

GLOUCESTERSHIRE
Sir Robert Poyntz
Nathaniel Stephens

Grampound, Cornwall
Henry Lord Cary
Sir Robert Pye

Grantham, Lincolnshire
Thomas Hatcher
Alexander More, Jr.

Great Bedwyn, Wiltshire
Edward Kirton
Sir John Trevor, Jr.

Great Grimsby, Lincolnshire
Sir Christopher Wray
Henry Pelham

Great Yarmouth, Norfolk
Sir John Wentworth
Miles Corbet

Guildford, Surrey[1]
Poynings Moore
Robert Parkhurst, Jr.

HAMPSHIRE
Sir Henry Wallop
Sir Daniel Norton

Harwich, Essex
Sir Nathaniel Rich
Christopher Herris

Haslemere, Surrey
George Grymes
Sir Thomas Canon

Hastings, Cinque Port
John Ashburnham,

[1]O.R. indicates that another indenture naming Sir   Francis Carew was returned.

Nicholas Eversfield
Haverfordwest, Pembrokeshire, Wales
    Sir James Perrott
Hedon-in-Holderness, Yorkshire
    Sir Christopher Hildyard
    Thomas Alured
Helston, Cornwall
    William Noy
    Sidney Godolphin
Hereford, Herefordshire
    Sir John Scudamore
    John Hoskins
HEREFORDSHIRE
    Sir Walter Pye
    Sir Giles Bridges
Hertford, Hertfordshire
    Sir Thomas Fanshawe
    Sir Charles Morrison; vice
    Sir Edward Howard
HERTFORDSHIRE
    Sir William Lytton
    Sir Thomas Dacres
Heytesbury, Wiltshire
    Sir Charles Berkeley
    William Rolfe
Higham Ferrers, Northamptonshire
    Sir George Sandys
Hindon, Wiltshire
    Sir Thomas Thynne
    Lawrence Hyde
Horsham, Sussex
    Sir Dudley North
    John Middleton
Huntingdon, Huntingdonshire
    James Montagu
    Oliver Cromwell
HUNTINGDONSHIRE
    Sir Capel Bedell
    Sir Robert Payne
Hythe, Cinque Port
    Sir Peter Heyman
    Sir Edward Scott
Ilchester, Somerset
    Sir Henry Berkeley
    Sir Robert Gorge
Ipswich, Suffolk
    William Cage
    Edmund Day
KENT
    Sir Thomas Finch
    Sir Dudley Digges
King's Lynn, Norfolk

Sir John Hare
    William Doughty
Kingston-on-Hull, Yorkshire
    John Lister
    James Watkinson
Knaresborough, Yorkshire
    Sir Richard Hutton
    Henry Benson
LANCASHIRE
    Sir Richard Molyneux
    Sir Alexander Radcliffe
Lancaster, Lancashire
    Sir Francis Bindlose
    Sir Thomas Fanshawe
Launceston (Dunheved), Cornwall
    Bevil Grenville
    Richard Escott
Leicester, Leicestershire
    Sir Humphrey May
    Sir John Stanhope
LEICESTERSHIRE
    Ferdinand Lord Hastings
    Sir Edward Hartopp
Leominster, Herefordshire
    James Tomkins
    Thomas Littleton
    [Edward Littleton]
Lewes, Sussex
    Sir George Goring
    Anthony Stapley
    [Sir George Rivers]
Lichfield, Staffordshire
    Sir William Walter
    Richard Dyott
Lincoln, Lincolnshire
    Sir Thomas Grantham
    Sir Edward Ayscough
LINCOLNSHIRE
    Sir John Wray
    Sir William Armine
Liskeard, Cornwall
    Sir Francis Stuart
    John Harris
Liverpool, Lancashire
    Henry Jermyn
    John Newdegate
London, Middlesex
    Thomas Moulson
    Christopher Clitherow
    Henry Waller
    James Bunce
Lostwithiel, Cornwall

Sir John Chudleigh
Sir Thomas Badger
[Sir Robert Carr]
Ludgershall, Wiltshire
John Selden
Sir Thomas Jay
Ludlow, Shropshire
Richard Tomlins
Ralph Goodwin
Lyme Regis, Dorset
Christopher Erle
Thomas Paramore
Lymington, Hampshire
Herbert Dodington
Richard Whitehead
Maidstone, Kent
Sir George Fane
Sir Francis Barnham
Maldon, Essex
Sir Henry Mildmay
Sir Arthur Herris
Malmesbury, Wiltshire
Sir William Crofts
Sir Henry Moody
Marlborough, Wiltshire
Richard Digges
Henry Percy
[Sir Francis Seymour]
Marlow, Buckinghamshire
Sir John Backhouse
Sir Miles Hobart
MERIONETHSHIRE, WALES
Richard Vaughan
MIDDLESEX
Sir Henry Spiller
Sir Francis Darcy
Midhurst, Sussex
Christopher Lewkenor
Edward Savage
Milborne Port, Somerset
Philip Digby
Sir Nathaniel Napier
Minehead, Somerset
Thomas Horner
Edmund Windham
Mitchell, Cornwall
John Sparke
John Cosewarth
[Francis Buller]
Monmouth, Monmouthshire
William Morgan
MONMOUTHSHIRE

Nicholas Kemeys
Nicholas Arnold
Montgomery, Montgomeryshire, Wales
Richard Lloyd
MONTGOMERYSHIRE, WALES
Sir William Herbert
Morpeth, Northumberland
Sir Thomas Reynell
John Bankes
Much Wenlock, Shropshire
Thomas Lawley
George Bridgeman
New Romney, Cinque Port
Thomas Godfrey
Thomas Brett
New Windsor, Berkshire
Sir William Beecher
Thomas Hewett
Newcastle-on-Tyne, Northumberland
Sir Thomas Riddell
Sir Peter Riddell
Newcastle-under-Lyme, Staffordshire
Sir George Gresley
Sir Roland Cotton
Newport, Cornwall
Nicholas Trefusis
Piers Edgcombe
[Sir William Killigrew]
[John Herne]
[Sir John Wolstenholme]
Newport (Isle of Wight), Hampshire
Sir Christopher Yelverton
Philip Fleming
Newton, Lancashire
Sir Henry Holcroft
Sir Francis Annesley
Newtown (Isle of Wight), Hampshire
Sir Thomas Barrington
Robert Barrington
NORFOLK
Sir Roger Townshend
Sir John Heveningham
Northampton, Northamptonshire
Christopher Sherland
Richard Spencer
NORTHAMPTONSHIRE
Richard Knightley
Francis Nichols
NORTHUMBERLAND
Sir John Fenwick
Sir William Carnaby
Norwich, Norfolk

Sir Peter Gleane
Robert Debney
Nottingham, Nottinghamshire
    Sir Charles Cavendish
    Henry Pierrepont
NOTTINGHAMSHIRE
    Sir Gervase Clifton
    Sir John Byron
Old Sarum, Wiltshire
    Michael Oldisworth
    Christopher Keightley
Orford, Suffolk
    Sir Charles Le Groos
    Sir Lionel Talmache
Oxford, Oxfordshire
    John Whistler
    Thomas Wentworth
Oxford University
    Sir Henry Marten
    Sir John Danvers
OXFORDSHIRE
    James Fiennes
    Sir Francis Wenman
Pembroke, Pembrokeshire, Wales
    Hugh Owen
PEMBROKESHIRE, WALES
    John Wogan
Penryn, Cornwall
    Sir William Killigrew
    Sir Thomas Edmondes
Peterborough, Northamptonshire
    Mildmay Fane, Lord Le Despenser
    Lawrence Whitaker
Petersfield, Hampshire
    Sir William Uvedale
    Benjamin Tichborne
Plymouth, Devonshire
    John Glanville
    Thomas Sherwill
Plympton, Devonshire
    Sir Thomas Hele
    Sir James Bagg
Pontefract, Yorkshire
    Sir John Jackson
    Sir John Ramsden
Poole, Dorset
    Sir John Cowper
    John Pyne
Portsmouth, Hampshire
    Owen Jenens
    William Towerson
Preston, Lancashire

Sir Robert Carr
George Gerard
Queenborough, Kent
    Sir Roger Palmer
    Sir John Hales
Radnor, Radnorshire, Wales
    Charles Price
RADNORSHIRE, WALES
    Richard Jones
Reading, Berkshire
    Sir Francis Knollys, Jr.
    John Saunders
Reigate, Surrey
    Sir Thomas Bludder
    Charles Cokayne
Richmond, Yorkshire
    Sir Talbot Bowes
    James Howell
Ripon, Yorkshire
    Sir Thomas Posthumus Hoby
    William Mallory, Sr.
Rochester, Kent
    Sir Thomas Walsingham, Jr.
    Sir William Brooke
RUTLAND
    Sir Guy Palmes
    Sir William Bulstrode
Rye, Cinque Port
    Richard Tufton
    Thomas Fotherley
St. Albans, Hertfordshire
    Robert Kirkham
    Sir John Jennings
St. Germans, Cornwall
    Thomas Cotton
    Benjamin Valentine
St. Ives, Cornwall
    Francis Godolphin
    John Payne
St. Mawes, Cornwall
    Hannibal Vivian
    Thomas Cary
Salisbury, Wiltshire
    Henry Sherfield
    Bartholomew Tookie
Saltash, Cornwall
    Sir Richard Buller
    Sir Francis Cottington
Sandwich, Cinque Port
    John Philipot
    Peter Peke
Scarborough, Yorkshire

Sir William Constable
John Harrison
Shaftesbury, Dorset
    Sir John Croke
    John Thoroughgood
Shoreham, Sussex
    Robert Morley
    William Marlott
Shrewsbury, Shropshire
    Sir William Owen
    Thomas Owen
SHROPSHIRE
    Sir Richard Newport
    Sir Andrew Corbet
SOMERSET
    Sir Robert Phelips
    Sir Edward Rodney
Southampton, Hampshire
    John Mayor
    George Gollop
Southwark, Surrey
    Richard Yarwood
    William Coxe
Stafford, Staffordshire
    Matthew Cradock
    William Wingfield
STAFFORDSHIRE ,
    Sir Harvey Bagot
    Thomas Crompton
Stamford, Lincolnshire
    Sir Thomas Hatton
    Sir Edward Bashe
Steyning, Sussex
    Sir Thomas Farnefold
    Edward Alford, Sr.
Stockbridge, Hampshire
    Sir Richard Gifford
    Sir Henry Whitehead
Sudbury, Suffolk
    Sir Robert Crane
    Sir William Pooley
SUFFOLK
    Sir William Spring
    Sir Nathaniel Barnardiston
    [Sir Edward Coke]
SURREY
    Sir Ambrose Browne
    Sir Richard Onslow
SUSSEX
    Richard Lewkenor
    Sir William Goring
Tamworth, Staffordshire

Sir Thomas Puckering
Sir Walter Devereux
Taunton, Somerset
    Sir Hugh Portman
    George Browne
Tavistock, Devonshire
    Sir Francis Glanville
    John Pym
Tewkesbury, Gloucestershire
    Sir Thomas Culpeper
    Sir William Hicks; vice
    Sir Baptist Hicks
Thetford, Norfolk
    Edmund Moundeford
    Sir Henry Vane
    [Sir Henry Spiller]
Tiverton, Devonshire
    John Bluett
    Peter Ball
Totnes, Devonshire
    Sir Edward Giles
    Thomas Prestwood
Tregony, Cornwall
    John Arundel
    Francis Rous
Truro, Cornwall
    Richard Daniel
    Henry Rolle
Wallingford, Berkshire
    Sir Robert Knollys
    Edmund Dunch
Wareham, Dorset
    Sir John Miller
    Gerard Napier
Warwick, Warwickshire
    [Robert Greville]
    [Francis Lucy]
    [Sir Thomas Puckering]
WARWICKSHIRE
    Sir Thomas Lucy
    Sir Thomas Leigh
Wells, Somerset
    Sir Ralph Hopton
    John Baber
Wendover, Buckinghamshire
    John Hampden
    Ralph Hawtrey
Weobley, Herefordshire
    William Walter
    William Tomkins
West Looe, Cornwall
    Edward Thomas

John Packer
Westbury, Wiltshire
    Maximilian Petty
    Charles Thynne
Westminster, Middlesex
    Joseph Bradshaw
    Thomas Morris
WESTMORLAND
    Sir John Lowther
    John Lowther
Weymouth and Melcombe Regis, Dorset
    Hugh Pyne
    Sir Lewis Dyve
    Sir Robert Napier, Jr.
    Henry Waltham
Whitchurch, Hampshire
    Sir Thomas Jervoise
    Sir John Jephson
Wigan, Lancashire
    Sir Anthony St. John
    Edward Bridgeman
Wilton, Wiltshire
    Sir Thomas Morgan
    John Pooley
    [Sir William Herbert]
WILTSHIRE
    Sir Francis Seymour
    Sir William Button

Winchelsea, Cinque Port
    Sir William Twysden
    Sir Ralph Freeman
Winchester, Hampshire
    Sir Richard Tichborne
    Robert Mason
Woodstock, Oxfordshire
    Sir Miles Fleetwood
    Edmund Taverner
Wootton Bassett, Wiltshire
    Sir John Franklin
    Anthony Rous
Worcester, Worcestershire
    John Cowcher
    John Haselocke
WORCESTERSHIRE
    Thomas Coventry
    Sir Thomas Bromley
Yarmouth (Isle of Wight), Hampshire
    Sir Edward Denys
    Sir John Oglander
York, Yorkshire
    Sir Arthur Ingram, Sr.
    Thomas Hoyle
    [Sir Thomas Savile]
YORKSHIRE
    Henry Belasyse
    Sir Thomas Wentworth

Officials Mentioned in Commons Debates 1628

The following lists are arranged alphabetically, one by title of office and the other by name. The list by title of office is divided into five broad categories: parliament, central administration, judiciary, church, and London. This is not intended to serve as a complete list of office holders. Only major offices held either by 1628 M.P.s or by other men referred to in the text of *Commons Debates 1628* are listed. Most offices outside of the London area are not included.

OFFICES

I. Parliament
Clerk of the House of Commons
John Wright
Clerk of the Parliaments
Henry Elsynge (the elder)
Gentleman Usher of the Black Rod
James Maxwell
Serjeant at Arms of the House of Commons
Edward Grimston
Speaker of the House of Commons
Sir John Finch, M.P.

II. Central Administration
Attorney General
Sir Robert Heath
Attorney General to the Queen
Sir John Finch, M.P.
Attorney of the Court of Wards
Sir Walter Pye, M.P.
Attorney of the Duchy of Lancaster
Sir Edward Moseley
Auditor of the Duchy of Cornwall
Peter Ball, M.P.
Auditor of the Duchy of Lancaster
Sir John Trevor, M.P.
Auditors in the Exchequer
Sir Francis Gofton
Sir Robert Pye, M.P.
Sir Edmund Sawyer, M.P.
Barons of the Exchequer
Sir Thomas Trevor
Sir George Vernon
Chancellor of the Duchy of Lancaster
Sir Humphrey May, M.P.
Chancellor and Under Treasurer of the
Exchequer

Sir Richard Weston
Chief Baron of the Exchequer
Sir John Walter
Clerk of the Crown in Chancery
Sir Thomas Edmondes, M.P.
Clerk to the Secretary of the Crown
Office (Mr. Keeling)
Jasper Waterhouse
Clerks of the Pipe
Sir Henry Croke, M.P.
Anthony Rous
Clerks of the Privy Council
Sir William Beecher, M.P.
Thomas Meautys, M.P.
Nathaniel Tomkins, M.P.
William Trumbull
Clerks of the Privy Council Extraordinary
Edward Nicholas, M.P.
Lawrence Whitaker, M.P.
Clerks of the Privy Seal
John Packer, M.P.
Thomas Packer
Cofferer of the Household
Sir Henry Vane, M.P.
Collector of Customs Inward, London
Abraham Dawes
Comptroller of the Household
Sir John Savile
Customs Farmers
John Harrison, M.P.
Sir John Wolstenholme
Earl Marshal
Thomas Howard, Earl of Arundel and
Surrey
Knight Marshal
Sir Edmund Verney, M.P.
Lieutenant of Dover Castle
Sir John Hippisley, M.P.
Lieutenant of the Tower
Sir Allen Apsley
Lord Admiral
George Villiers, Duke of Buckingham
Lord Chamberlain of the Household
Philip Herbert, Earl of Montgomery
Lord Chancellor, *see* Lord Keeper
Lord Chancellor of Ireland
Adam Loftus, Viscount Ely
Lord Keeper of the Great Seal
Sir Thomas Coventry
Lord President of the Privy Council
Henry Montagu, Earl of Manchester
Lord Steward of the Household

William Herbert, Earl of Pembroke
Lord Treasurer
  James Ley, Earl of Marlborough
Lord Warden of the Cinque Ports
  George Villiers, Duke of Buckingham
Master of the Household
  Sir Roger Palmer, M.P.
Master of the Jewel House
  Sir Henry Mildmay, M.P.
Master of the Mint
  Sir Robert Harley, M.P.
Master of the Rolls
  Sir Julius Caesar
Masters in Chancery
  Sir Charles Caesar
  Sir Edward Clarke
  Thomas Eden, LL.D., M.P.
  Sir Edward Leech, M.P.
  Sir Robert Rich
  Sir Edward Salter
  Sir Eubule Thelwall, M.P.
Privy Councillors
  George Abbot, Archbishop of Canterbury
  Sir Julius Caesar
  Sir John Coke, M.P.
  Edward, Lord Viscount Conway
  Sir Thomas Coventry
  Sir Thomas Edmondes, M.P.
  Philip Herbert, Earl of Montgomery
  William Herbert, Earl of Pembroke
  William Laud, Bishop of Bath and Wells
  James Ley, Earl of Marlborough
  Sir Humphrey May, M.P.
  Henry Montagu, Earl of Manchester
    (Lord President)
  Richard Neile, Bishop of Winchester
  Sir John Savile
  George Villiers, Duke of Buckingham
  Sir Richard Weston
  John Williams, Bishop of Lincoln
Receiver General and Vice Treasurer in
    Ireland
  Sir Francis Annesley, M.P.
Receiver General of the Court of Wards
  Sir Miles Fleetwood, M.P.
Receiver of Recusant Revenues in the North
  Sir John Savile
Remembrancer of the Exchequer
  Sir Thomas Fanshawe, M.P. for Hertford
Secretaries of State
  Edward, Lord Viscount Conway
  Sir John Coke, M.P.

Secretary for Irish Affairs
  Sir Henry Holcroft, M.P.
Secretary of the Council in the North
  Sir Arthur Ingram, M.P.
Secretary of the Crown Office
  ——— Keeling
Secretary to the Admiralty
  Edward Nicholas, M.P.
Solicitor General
  Sir Richard Shelton, M.P.
Surveyor General
  Sir Thomas Fanshawe, M.P. for Lancaster
Surveyor of the Court of Wards
  Sir Benjamin Rudyard, M.P.
Surveyor of the Ordnance
  Sir Thomas Bludder, M.P.
Surveyor of Victuals for the Navy
  Sir Allen Apsley
Treasurer of the Household
  Sir Thomas Edmondes, M.P.
Treasurer of the King's Chamber
  Sir William Uvedale, M.P.
Treasurer of the Navy
  Sir Sackville Crow, M.P.
Under-officers in the Exchequer
  Thomas Paramore, M.P.
  Sir Henry Spiller, M.P.
  John West
Vice Admiral of England
  Sir Robert Mansell, M.P.
Vice Chamberlain to the Queen
  Sir George Goring, M.P.
Victualler of the Fleet
  Sir James Bagg, M.P.

III. Judiciary
Admiralty
  Judge
    Sir Henry Marten, M.P.
Common Pleas
  Chief Justice
    Sir Thomas Richardson
  Justices
    Sir George Croke
    Sir Francis Harvey
    Sir Richard Hutton
    Sir Henry Yelverton
King's Bench
  Chief Justice
    Sir Nicholas Hyde
  Justices
    Sir John Doddridge

Sir William Jones
Sir James Whitelocke
Clerk of the Crown in King's Bench
Sir Thomas Fanshawe, M.P. for Lancaster
Chief Clerk for Enrolling Pleas (jointly held)
Sir Robert Heath
Sir George Paule, M.P.
Clerk of the King's Bench
——— Keeling
Prerogative Court of Canterbury
Judge
Sir Henry Marten, M.P.
Serjeants
King's Serjeants
Sir Francis Ashley
William Ayloffe
Sir Robert Berkeley
Sir Thomas Crewe
Sir Humphrey Davenport
Serjeants at Law
John Bramston
Francis Crawley
Richard Digges, M.P.
John Hoskins, M.P.
Sir Egremont Thynne

IV. Church
Archbishop of Canterbury
George Abbot
Archbishop of York
Tobias Matthew
Bishop of Bangor
Lewis Bayly
Bishop of Bath and Wells
William Laud
Bishop of Chichester
George Carleton (d. May 1628)
Richard Montagu (elected 14 June 1628)
Bishop of Exeter
Joseph Hall
Bishop of Lincoln
John Williams
Bishop of Norwich
Samuel Harsnett
Bishop of Salisbury
John Davenant
Bishop of Winchester
Richard Neile
Dean of Rochester
Walter Balcanquhall

V. London
Lord Mayor of London
Sir Cuthbert Hacket (28 October 1626 to 28 October 1627)
Hugh Hammersley (28 October 1627 to 28 October 1628)
Recorder of London
Sir Heneage Finch

NAMES OF OFFICIALS

Abbot, George
Archbishop of Canterbury;
Privy Councillor
Annesley, Sir Francis, M.P.
Receiver General and Vice Treasurer in Ireland
Apsley, Sir Allen
Lieutenant of the Tower;
Surveyor of Victuals for the Navy
Arundel and Surrey, Earl of, see Howard, Thomas
Ashley, Sir Francis
King's Serjeant
Ayloffe, William
King's Serjeant
Bagg, Sir James, M.P.
Victualler of the Fleet
Balcanquhall, Walter
Dean of Rochester
Ball, Peter, M.P.
Auditor of the Duchy of Cornwall
Bayly, Lewis
Bishop of Bangor
Beecher, Sir William, M.P.
Clerk of the Privy Council
Berkeley, Sir Robert
King's Serjeant
Bludder, Sir Thomas, M.P.
Surveyor of the Ordnance
Bramston, John
Serjeant at Law
Buckingham, Duke of, see Villiers, George
Caesar, Sir Charles
Master in Chancery
Caesar, Sir Julius
Master of the Rolls;
Privy Councillor
Carleton, George (d. May 1628)
Bishop of Chichester
Clarke, Sir Edward
Master in Chancery
Coke, Sir John, M.P.

Secretary of State;
Privy Councillor
Conway, Edward, Lord Viscount
Secretary of State;
Privy Councillor
Coventry, Sir Thomas
Lord Keeper of the Great Seal;
Privy Councillor
Crawley, Francis
Serjeant at Law
Crewe, Sir Thomas
King's Serjeant
Croke, Sir George
Justice of the Common Pleas
Croke, Sir Henry, M.P.
Clerk of the Pipe (jointly with Rous)
Crow, Sir Sackville, M.P.
Treasurer of the Navy
Davenant, John
Bishop of Salisbury
Davenport, Sir Humphrey
King's Serjeant
Dawes, Abraham
Collector of Customs Inward, London
Digges, Richard, M.P.
Serjeant at Law
Doddridge, Sir John
Justice of the King's Bench
Duke, the, see Villiers, George
Eden, Thomas, LL.D., M.P.
Master in Chancery
Edmondes, Sir Thomas, M.P.
Treasurer of the Household;
Clerk of the Crown in Chancery;
Privy Councillor
Elsynge, Henry, (the elder)
Clerk of the Parliaments
Ely, Viscount, see Loftus, Adam
Fanshawe, Sir Thomas, M.P. for Hertford
Remembrancer of the Exchequer
Fanshawe, Sir Thomas, M.P. for Lancaster
Clerk of the Crown in King's Bench;
Surveyor General
Finch, Sir Heneage
Recorder of London
Finch, Sir John, M.P.
Speaker of the House of Commons; Attorney General to the Queen
Fleetwood, Sir Miles, M.P.
Receiver General of the Court of Wards
Gofton, Sir Francis
Auditor in the Exchequer

Goring, Sir George, M.P.
Vice Chamberlain to the Queen
Grimston, Edward
Serjeant at Arms of the House of Commons
Hacket, Sir Cuthbert
Lord Mayor of London (28 October 1626 to 28 October 1627)
Hall, Joseph
Bishop of Exeter
Hammersley, Hugh
Lord Mayor of London (28 October 1627 to 28 October 1628)
Harley, Sir Robert, M.P.
Master of the Mint
Harrison, John, M.P.
Customs Farmer
Harsnett, Samuel
Bishop of Norwich
Harvey, Sir Francis
Justice of the Common Pleas
Heath, Sir Robert
Attorney General
Chief Clerk for Enrolling Pleas in the King's Bench (jointly with Paule)
Herbert, Philip, Earl of Montgomery
Lord Chamberlain of the Household;
Privy Councillor
Herbert, William, Earl of Pembroke
Lord Steward of the Household;
Privy Councillor
Hippisley, Sir John, M.P.
Lieutenant of Dover Castle
Holcroft, Sir Henry, M.P.
Secretary for Irish Affairs
Hoskins, John, M.P.
Serjeant at Law
Howard, Thomas, Earl of Arundel and Surrey
Earl Marshal
Hutton, Sir Richard
Justice of the Common Pleas
Hyde, Sir Nicholas
Chief Justice of the King's Bench
Ingram, Sir Arthur, M.P.
Secretary of the Council in the North
Jones, Sir William
Justice of the King's Bench
Keeling, ———
Clerk of the King's Bench;
Secretary of the Crown Office
Laud, William
Bishop of Bath and Wells;

Privy Councillor
Leech, Sir Edward, M.P.
  Master in Chancery
Ley, James, Earl of Marlborough
  Lord Treasurer;
  Privy Councillor
Loftus, Adam, Viscount Ely
  Lord Chancellor of Ireland
Manchester, Earl of, *see* Montagu, Henry
Mansell, Sir Robert, M.P.
  Vice Admiral of England
Marlborough, Earl of, *see* Ley, James
Marten, Sir Henry, M.P.
  Judge of the Admiralty;
  Judge of the Prerogative Court of Canter-
    bury
Matthew, Tobias
  Archbishop of York
Maxwell, James
  Gentleman Usher of the Black Rod
May, Sir Humphrey, M.P.
  Chancellor of the Duchy of Lancaster;
  Privy Councillor
Meautys, Thomas, M.P.
  Clerk of the Privy Council
Mildmay, Sir Henry, M.P.
  Master of the Jewel House
Montagu, Henry, Earl of Manchester
  Lord President of the Privy Council
Montagu, Richard
  Bishop of Chichester(elected 14 June 1628)
Montgomery, Earl of, *see* Herbert, Philip
Moseley, Sir Edward
  Attorney of the Duchy of Lancaster
Neile, Richard
  Bishop of Winchester;
  Privy Councillor
Nicholas, Edward, M.P.
  Secretary to the Admiralty;
  Clerk of the Privy Council Extraordinary
Packer, John, M.P.
  Clerk of the Privy Seal
Packer, Thomas
  Clerk of the Privy Seal
Palmer, Sir Roger, M.P.
  Master of the Household
Paramore, Thomas, M.P.
  Under-officer in the Exchequer
Paule, Sir George, M.P.
  Chief Clerk for Enrolling pleas in the
    King's Bench (jointly with Heath)
Pembroke, Earl of, *see* Herbert, William

Pye, Sir Robert, M.P.
  Auditor in the Exchequer
Pye, Sir Walter, M.P.
  Attorney of the Court of Wards
Rich, Sir Robert
  Master in Chancery
Richardson, Sir Thomas
  Chief Justice of Common Pleas
Rous, Anthony
  Clerk of the Pipe (jointly with Croke)
Rudyard, Sir Benjamin, M.P.
  Surveyor of the Court of Wards
Salter, Sir Edward
  Master in Chancery
Savile, Sir John
  Comptroller of the Household;
  Receiver of Recusant Revenues in the
    North;
  Privy Councillor
Sawyer, Sir Edmund, M.P.
  Auditor in the Exchequer
Shelton, Sir Richard, M.P.
  Solicitor General
Spiller, Sir Henry, M.P.
  Under-officer in the Exchequer
Thelwall, Sir Eubule, M.P.
  Master in Chancery
Thynne, Sir Egremont
  Serjeant at Law
Tomkins, Nathaniel, M.P.
  Clerk of the Privy Council
Trevor, Sir John, M.P.
  Auditor of the Duchy of Lancaster
Trevor, Sir Thomas
  Baron of the Exchequer
Trumbull, William
  Clerk of the Privy Council
Uvedale, Sir William, M.P.
  Treasurer of the King's Chamber
Vane, Sir Henry, M.P.
  Cofferer of the Household
Verney, Sir Edmund, M.P.
  Knight Marshal
Vernon, Sir George
  Baron of the Exchequer
Villiers, George, Duke of Buckingham
  Lord Admiral;
  Lord Warden of the Cinque Ports;
  Privy Councillor
Walter, Sir John
  Chief Baron of the Exchequer
Waterhouse, Jasper

Clerk to the Secretary of the Crown Office
   (Mr. Keeling)
West, John
   Under-officer in the Exchequer
Weston, Sir Richard
   Chancellor and Under Treasurer of the
     Exchequer;
   Privy Councillor
Whitaker, Lawrence, M.P.
   Clerk of the Privy Council Extraordinary
Whitelocke, Sir James

   Justice of the King's Bench
Williams, John
   Bishop of Lincoln;
   Privy Councillor
Wolstenholme, Sir John
   Customs Farmer
Wright, John
   Clerk of the House of Commons
Yelverton, Sir Henry
   Justice of the Common Pleas

ABBREVIATIONS AND SHORT TITLES

A.C.	*Alumni Cantabrigienses.* Cambridge, 1922–1927.
A.O.	*Alumni Oxonienses.* Oxford, 1891–1892.
A.P.C.	*Acts of the Privy Council of England.* London, 1921—.
Anderson, *Reports*	*Les Reports du treserudite Edmund Anderson Chivalier, Nadgairs, Seigniour Chief Justice del Common Bank.* London, 1664.
Appeal	Montagu, Richard, *Appello Caesarem. A just appeale from two unjust informers.* London, 1625. *S.T.C.,* no. 18030.
Archbp.	Archbishop.
Ashton, *Crown and the Money Market*	Ashton, Robert, *The Crown and the Money Market 1603–1640.* Oxford, 1960.
Ass.	*Le Livre des Assises et Pleas del' Corone, moves & dependants devant les Justices sibien en lour circuits come aylours, en temps du Roy Edward le Tiers . . . .* London: Sawbridge, Rawlins, and Roycroft, 1679.
Birch, *Court and Times of Chas. I*	Birch, Thomas, *The Court and Times of Charles the First . . . .* 2 vols., London, 1848.
Black's *Law Dict.*	Black, Henry Campbell, *Black's Law Dictionary,* 3rd ed. St. Paul, Minn., 1933.
B.M.	British Museum.
Bodin, *The Commonwealth*	Bodin, Jean, *Six Books of the Commonwealth,* trans. by M. J. Tooley. Oxford: Blackwell's Political Texts [1955?].
Bp.	Bishop.
Bracton	Bracton, Henricus de, *De Legibus et Consuetudinibus Angliae . . . ,* ed. by Sir Travers Twiss. 6 vols., London: Rolls Series, 1878.
Branch, *Maxims*	[Branch, Thomas] *Principia Legis and Aequitatis, Being an Alphabetical Collection of Maxims . . . .* London, 1753.
Brook, *Lives of the Puritans*	Brook, Benjamin, *The Lives of the Puritans.* 3 vols., London, 1813.
Brooke, *New Cases*	*Sir Robert Brooke's New Cases in the time of Henry VIII, Ed. VI, and Queen Mary . . . .* London, 1873.
Brooke, *Abridgement*	*La Graunde Abridgement, collecte et escrie per le Judge tresreuerend Sir Robert Brooke.* London: Tottell, 1576. *S.T.C.,* no. 3828.
Brownlow and Goldesborough, *Reports*	*Reports of divers choice cases in law taken by those late and most judicious Prothonotaries of the Common Pleas, Richard Brownlow and John Goldesborough . . . .* London, 1675.
c.	*capitulum.*
Cal. Chart. Rolls	*Calendar of the Charter Rolls preserved in the Public Record Office.* London, 1916—.
Cal. Close Rolls	*Calendar of the Close Rolls preserved in the Public Record Office.* London, 1892—.
Cal. Letter Books	*Calendar of Letter-Books preserved among the Archives of the Corporation of the City of London at the Guildhall.* London, 1903–1912.
Cal. Pat. Rolls	*Calendar of the Patent Rolls preserved in the Public Record Office.* London, 1893—.
Cal. S.P. Dom.	*Calendar of State Papers: Domestic Series.* London, 1857—.
Cal. S.P. Venetian	*Calendar of State Papers and Manuscripts Relating to English Affairs, Existing in the Archives and Collections of Venice and in the Other Libraries of Northern Italy.* London, 1900—.
Camden, *Annales*	[Camden, William], *Annales rerum Anglicarum et Hibernicarum regnante Elizabetha,* ed. by Thomas Hearne. [n.p.], 1717.

Camden, *Britain*   Camden, William, *Britain, or a Chorographicall Description of the most flourishing Kingdomes, England, Scotland, and Ireland . . . ,* trans. by Philemon Holland. London, 1610. *S.T.C.,* no. 4509.

Cawston, *Early Chartered Companies*   Cawston, George and A. H. Keane, *The Early Chartered Companies.* New York: reprinted for Burt Franklin, 1968.

Chamberlain, *Letters*   Chamberlain, John, *The Letters of John Chamberlain,* ed. by N. E. McClure. Philadelphia: The American Philosophical Society, 1939.

Chron. Angliae   *Chronicon Angliae . . . ,* ed. by Edward Maunde Thompson. London: Rolls Series, 1874.

C.J.   *Journals of the House of Commons.* London, 1742—.

Clode, *Merchant Taylors*   Clode, Charles Mathew, *The Early History of the Guild of Merchant Taylors . . . with Notices of the Lives of some of its Eminent Members.* London, 1888–1889.

Cobbett, *Parl. Hist.*   Cobbett, William, *The Parliamentary History of England. From the Norman Conquest, in 1066, to the year, 1803.* 36 vols., London, 1806–1820.

Coke, *First Inst.*   *The First Part of the Institutes of the Laws of England; or A Commentary upon Littleton.* 3 vols., London, 1794.

Coke, *Second Inst.*   *The Second Part of the Institutes of the Laws of England.* 2 vols., London, 1797.

Coke, *Third Inst.*   *The Third Part of the Institutes of the Laws of England.* London, 1797.

Coke, *Fourth Inst.*   *The Fourth Part of the Institutes of the Laws of England.* London, 1797.

Coke, *Reports*   *The Reports of Sir Edward Coke in Thirteen Parts.* 6 vols., London, 1826.

Commines, *Memoirs*   *The Memoirs of Philip de Commines, Lord of Argenton; containing the Histories of Louis XI and Charles VIII . . . .* 2 vols., London, 1855.

Commons Debates 1621   *Commons Debates 1621,* ed. by Wallace Notestein, Frances Helen Relf, and Hartley Simpson. 7 vols., New Haven, 1935.

Commons Debates 1625   *Debates in the House of Commons in 1625,* ed. by Samuel Rawson Gardiner. London: Camden Society, 1873.

Commons Debates 1629   *Commons Debates for 1629,* ed. by Wallace Notestein and Frances Helen Relf. Minneapolis, 1921.

Conference, 1642   *A Conference Desired by the Lords and had by a Committee of both Houses, Concerning the Rights and Privileges of the Subjects.* London: printed for Mathew Walbancke and Richard Best, 1642.

Cosin, *A Collection of Private Devotions*   Cosin, John, *A Collection of Private Devotions; in the Practice of the Ancient Church, called the Hours of Prayer.* London, 1681.

Croke, *Reports*   *Reports of Sir George Croke, Knight, formerly one of the Justices of the Courts of King's-Bench and Common-Pleas . . . .* Revised and published in English by Sir Harbottle Grimston, Dublin, 1792.

Crompton, *Des Courts*   Crompton, [Richard], *L'Authoritie et Jurisdiction des courts de la Majestie de la Roygne . . . .* London, 1594. *S.T.C.,* no. 6050.

Sir John Davies, *Reports*   Davies, Sir John, *A Report of Cases and Matters in Law Resolved and Adjudged in the King's Courts in Ireland.* Dublin, 1762.

Dietz, *Public Finance*   Dietz, F. C., *English Public Finance 1558–1641.* New York, 1932.

D.N.B.   *The Dictionary of National Biography Founded in 1882 by George Smith,* ed. by Sir Leslie Stephen and Sir Sidney Lee. New York, 1885–1904.

Doctor and Student	[Saint German, Christopher], *Doctor and Student or Dialogue between a Doctor of Divinity and a Student in the Laws of England* . . . . Dublin, 1792.
Dugdale, *Origines Juridiciales*	Dugdale, William, *Origines Juridiciales, or Historical Memorials of the English Laws, Courts of Justice* . . . . London, 1666.
D.W.B.	*Dictionary of Welsh Biography down to 1940.* London, 1959.
Dyer, *Reports*	*Reports of Cases in the Reigns of Hen. VIII, Edw. VI, Q. Mary, and Q. Eliz., taken and collected by Sir James Dyer, Knt.* 3 vols., Dublin, 1794.
E.H.R.	*English Historical Review.*
Eliot, *Negotium Posterorum*	*An Apology for Socrates and Negotium Posterorum: by Sir John Eliot,* ed. by Rev. A. B. Grosart. 2 vols., London, 1881.
Elsynge, *Parliaments*	Elsynge, Henry, *The Manner of Holding Parliaments in England.* London, 1768.
E.R.	[The] *English Reports, full reprints.* London, 1907.
Fitzherbert, *Abridgement*	Fitzherbert, Sir Anthony, *La Graunde Abridgement.* London, 1577. *S.T.C.,* no. 10957.
Fitzherbert, *N.B.*	*The New Natura Brevium of the Most Reverend Judge, Mr. Anthony Fitzherbert* . . . . London, 1686.
Fleta	*Fleta seu Commentarius Juris Anglicani* . . . . London, 1647.
Forster, *Eliot*	Forster, John, *Sir John Eliot: A Biography, 1590–1632.* 2 vols., London, 1864.
Fortescue, *De Laudibus Legum Angliae*	Fortescue, Sir John, *De Laudibus Legum Angliae,* trans. into English, illustrated with the notes of Mr. Selden, and great variety of remarks with respect to the antiquities, history, and laws of England. London, 1737.
Fortescue, *De Laudibus Legum Anglie*	Fortescue, Sir John, *De Laudibus Legum Anglie,* ed. and trans. by S. B. Chrimes. Cambridge, England, 1942.
Foss, *Judges*	Foss, Edward, *The Judges of England.* 7 vols., London, 1848–1864.
Froissart, *Chronicles*	*The Chronicle of Froissart,* trans. by Sir John Bourchier and Lord Berners. London, 1901.
Fuller, *Ephemeris Parliamentaria*	Fuller, Thomas (ed.), *Ephemeris Parliamentaria.* London, 1654.
Gagg	Montagu, Richard, *A Gagg for the new Gospel? No: A New Gagg for an old Goose.* London, 1624. *S.T.C.,* no. 18038.
Gardiner, *Gunpowder Plot*	Gardiner, S. R., *What Gunpowder Plot Was.* London, 1897.
Gardiner, *History of England*	Gardiner, S. R., *History of England from the Accession of James I to the Outbreak of the Civil War 1603–1642.* 10 vols., London, 1886.
Girard, Bernard de, *L'histoire de France*	Girard, Bernard de, seigneur du Haillan, *L'histoire de France* . . . *Contenant* . . . *les choses plus memorables passes en Allemagne, Flanders, Angleterre* . . . . 2 vols. [Genève, 1577].
Gl.	Glossary of Foreign Words and Phrases.
Glanville, *Election Cases*	*Reports of Certain Cases Determined and Adjudged by the Commons in Parliament in the Twenty-first and Twenty-second Years of the Reign of King James the First. Collected by John Glanville, Esq.* . . . . London, 1775.
Grafton, *Chronicle*	Grafton's *Chronicle; or, History of England.* 2 vols., London, 1809.
Guthrie, *Hist. of Eng.*	Guthrie, William, *A General History of England* . . . . 3 vols., London, 1744–1751.
Hall, *Chronicle*	Hall's *Chronicle.* London, 1809.
Hatsell, *Precedents*	Hatsell, John, *Precedents of Proceedings in the House of Commons.* 4 vols., London, 1818 ed.

Hemingburgh, *Chronicle*	*Chronicon domini Walteri de Hemingburgh* . . . . 2 vols., London: Sumptibus Societatis, 1848.
Hil.	Hilary term.
H.L.R.O.	House of Lords Record Office, London.
H.M.C.	Historical Manuscripts Commission.
Holinshed, *Chronicles*	Holinshed's *Chronicles of England, Scotland, and Ireland.* 6 vols., London, 1807.
Homilies	*Sermons, or Homilies, appointed to be read in Churches in the time of Queen Elizabeth . . . to which are added, the Articles of Religion; the Constitutions and Canons Ecclesiastical.* London, 1817.
Howell, *S.T.*	*A Complete Collection of State Trials and Proceedings for High Treason . . . Compiled by T.B. Howell.* 21 vols., London, 1816.
H.R.O.	Hampshire Record Office.
Hughes and Larkin, *Tudor Proclamations*	Hughes, Paul L. and James F. Larkin, *Tudor Royal Proclamations.* 3 vols., New Haven, 1969.
Hulme, *Eliot*	Hulme, Harold, *The Life of Sir John Eliot, 1592–1632.* London, 1957.
Jacobs, *City Liberties*	Jacobs, Giles, *City Liberties: or the Rights and Privileges of Freemen.* London, 1732.
Jacobs, *Law Dict.*	Jacobs, Giles, *A New Law Dictionary.* London, 1732.
K.B.	Court of King's Bench.
Keeler, *L.P.*	Keeler, Mary Frear, *The Long Parliament, 1640–1641.* Philadelphia, 1954.
Keilway, *Reports*	*Keilway's Reports of Select Cases in the reign of K. Henry VII and K. Henry VIII not comprehended in the yearbooks* . . . . London, 1688 (see *E.R.*).
Kelham, *Dict.* '	Kelham, Robert, *A Dictionary of the Norman or Old French Language . . . to which are added the Laws of William the Conqueror, with notes and references.* London, 1779.
Kelham, *Domesday Book*	Kelham, Robert, *Domesday Book Illustrated.* London, 1788.
Knighton, *Chronicle*	*Chronicon Henrici Knighton,* ed. by Joseph Rawson Lumby. London: Rolls Series, 1889.
L.1a, L.2a	*Lectio prima* (first reading); *Lectio secunda* (second reading).
Lambarde	Lambarde, William, *Archaionomia sive Priscus Anglorum Legibus libri* . . . . Cambridge, England, 1643.
Lane, *Exchequer Reports*	Lane, Richard, *Reports in the Court of Exchequer, Beginning in the third and ending in the ninth year of the Raign of the late King James.* London, 1657.
Laud's *Works*	*The Works of the Most Reverend Father in God, William Laud, D.D.* Library of Anglo-Catholic Theology. Oxford, 1847.
Leg. Cit.	Legal Citations, list of.
Letters and Papers H. VIII	*Calendar of Letters and Papers, Foreign and Domestic, of H. VIII,* ed. by J. S. Brewer, J. Gairdner, and J. Gairdner, LL.D., and R. H. Brodie. 21 vols., London: Rolls Series, 1870—.
Lib.	Book.
Lib. Int.	*Intrationum liber omnibus legum Anglie studiosis apprime necessarius* . . . . London, 1546. *S.T.C.,* no. 14117.
Liber Albus	*Liber Albus: The White Book of the City of London,* trans. by Henry Thomas Riley. London, 1862.
Littleton, *Tenures*	[Sir Thomas] Littleton's *Tenures in English* . . . . London: printed for the Company of Stationers, 1612. *S.T.C.,* no. 15780.
L.J.	*Journals of the House of Lords.* London, 1767—.

Liv. Ass.	see *Ass.*
m. (mbs.)	membrane(s).
McGrath, *Papists and Puritans*	McGrath, Patrick, *Papists and Puritans under Elizabeth I.* London, 1967.
Mary Queen of Scots and the Babington Plot	*Mary Queen of Scots and the Babington Plot,* ed. from the original documents in the Public Record Office, the Yelverton MSS. and elsewhere, by John Hungerford Pollen. Edinburgh, 1922.
Matthew Paris, *Chronica*	Matthaei Parisiensis, *Chronica Majora,* ed. by Henry Richards Luard. London: Rolls Series, 1872–1880.
McIlwain, *Political Works of James I*	*The Political Works of James I,* ed. by Charles Howard McIlwain. Cambridge, Mass.: Harvard Political Classics, 1918.
Mich.	Michaelmas term.
Monstrelet, *Chronicles*	*The Chronicles of Enguerrand de Monstrelet . . . .* 2 vols., London, 1840.
Moody, *Londonderry*	Moody, T. W., *The Londonderry Plantation, 1609–1641.* Belfast, 1939.
M.P.	Member of Parliament.
MS., MSS.	manuscript, manuscripts.
MS. Cal. Pat. Rolls	Manuscript calendars of the patent rolls, preserved in the Public Record Office, London. (Unprinted.)
Munford, *Domesday Book of Norfolk*	Munford, George, *An Analysis of the Domesday Book of the County of Norfolk.* London, 1858.
Notestein, *1604–1610*	Notestein, Wallace, *The House of Commons, 1604–1610.* New Haven, 1971.
O.B.	Orders of Business.
O.E.D.	*Oxford English Dictionary.*
Oldfield, *Hist. of the Boroughs*	Oldfield, Thomas H.B., *An Entire and Complete History, Political and Personal, of the Boroughs of Great Britain . . . .* 3 vols., London, 1792.
O.R.	*Return of the Name of Every Member of the Lower House of Parliament.* 2 vols., Accounts and Papers, Session of 1878 [London], 1878. The Official Return.
Ordericus, *Ecclesiastical History of England*	Ordericus Vitalis, *The Ecclesiastical History of England and Normandy.* 4 vols., London, 1853.
P. & D.	see Proceedings and Debates.
Pasch.	Paschae, Easter term.
Pasquier, *Recherches de la France*	*Oeuvres Choisies D'Etienne Pasquier accompagnees de notes et d'une etude sur sa vie et sur ses ouvrages . . . .* Paris, 1849.
Petyt, *Jus Parliamentarium*	Petyt, William, *Jus Parliamentarium: or The Ancient Power, Jurisdiction, Rights, Liberties, and Privileges of the most high Court of Parliament.* London, 1741.
pl.	*placita.*
Plowden, *Commentaries*	*The Commentaries or Reports of Edmund Plowden. . . .* 2 vols., Dublin, 1792.
Pollard and Redgrave, *S.T.C.*	Pollard, A. W. and G. R. Redgrave, *A Short-Title Catalogue of Books printed in England, Scotland, and Ireland and of English Books printed Abroad, 1475–1640.* London, 1926.
Polydore Vergil, *Anglica Historia*	*The Anglica Historia of Polydore Vergil,* ed. by Denys Hay. London: Camden Society, 1950.
Porter, *Reformation and Reaction*	Porter, H.C., *Reformation and Reaction in Tudor Cambridge.* Cambridge, England, 1958.
P.R.O.	Public Record Office, London.

Proceedings and Debates	The composite narrative formed by collating Trumbull Add. MS. 50, Downshire Library, and twelve similar MSS.
Proceedings in Parliament 1610	*Proceedings in Parliament 1610*, ed. by Elizabeth Read Foster. 2 vols., New Haven, 1966.
Rastell, *Termes de la Ley*	[Rastell, John], *Les Termes de la Ley: or, certain difficult and obscure words and terms of the Common and Statute Laws of England now in use, expounded and explained.* Portland, 1812.
Red Book of the Exchequer	*Red Book of the Exchequer.* Vol. III, ed. by Hubert Hall. London: Rolls Series, 1897.
Registrum Omnium Brevium	*Registrum Omnium Brevium.* London, 1595. *S.T.C.*, no. 20838.
Reid, *Council in the North*	Reid, R. R., *The King's Council in the North.* London, 1921.
Relf, *Debates in the House of Lords, 1621–1628*	*Notes of Debates in the House of Lords, 1621–1628*, ed. by Frances Helen Relf. London: Camden Society, 1929.
Remembrancia	Overall, W. H., *Analytical Index to the Series of Records Known as the Remembrancia. Preserved among the Archives of the City of London. 1597–1664.* London, 1878.
Riley, *Memorials*	*Memorials of London and London Life in the 13th, 14th, and 15th centuries . . .* , ed. and trans. by Henry Thomas Riley. London, 1868.
rot.	roll.
rot. cont.	Controlment rolls, preserved in the Public Record Office, London. (Unprinted.)
Rot. Parl.	*Rotuli Parliamentorum ut et Petitiones, et Placita in Parliamento.* 6 vols. [n.d., n.p.].
rot. pat.	Patent rolls, preserved in the Public Record Office, London. (Unprinted.)
Rot. Scot.	*Rotuli Scotiae.* Vols. I and II, by command of his Majesty King George III [n.p.], 1814, 1819.
Ruigh, *Parliament of 1624*	Ruigh, Robert E., *The Parliament of 1624.* Cambridge, Mass., 1971.
Rushworth, *Hist. Collections*	Rushworth, John, *Historical Collections of Private Passages of State, Weighty Matters in Law, Remarkable Proceedings in Five Parliaments.* London, 1659.
Rymer, *Foedera*	Rymer, Thomas (ed.), *Foedera Conventiones, Literae, et cujuscunque generis Acta Publica inter Reges Angliae.* 10 vols. [n.p.], Joannem Neaulme, 1739–1745.
Selden Soc., *Select Cases King's Bench, E. III*	Selden Society, *Select Cases in the Court of King's Bench Under Edward III.* Vols. V and VI, ed. by G. O. Sayles. London, 1965.
Sharpe, *London*	Sharpe, Reginald R., *London and the Kingdom.* 3 vols., London, 1894.
Simon, *Wine Trade*	Simon, André L., *The History of the Wine Trade in England.* London, 1909.
Smith, *Commonwealth of England*	Smith, Sir Thomas, *The Commonwealth of England and Manner of Government Thereof.* London, 1589. *S.T.C.*, no. 22859.
S.P.	State Papers.
S.R.	*The Statutes of the Realm.* 11 vols., London, 1810–1828.
Stanford, *Plees del Coron*	*Les Plees del Coron, divisees in plusors titles & comon lieux . . . composees per le tresreuerend judge Monsieur, Guillaulme Staundforde.* London: Tottell, 1583. *S.T.C.*, no. 23223.
Stat. Rolls Ireland	*Statute Rolls of the Parliament of Ireland.* Vol. II, ed. by Henry F. Berry. Dublin, 1910.

Statutes at Large	*The Statutes at Large, from Magna Charta, to the End of the Last Parliament, 1761.* 8 vols., London, 1763.
S.T.C.	see Pollard and Redgrave, and Wing.
Stow, *Annales*	*Annales, or A General Chronicle of England begun by John Stow* . . . . London, 1631. *S.T.C.*, no. 23340.
Strype, *John Whitgift*	Strype, John, *The Life and Acts of John Whitgift, In Four Books.* Oxford, 1822.
Stubbs, *Select Charters*	Stubbs, William, *Select Charters and Other Illustrations of English Constitutional History from the Earliest Times to the Reign of Edward the First.* Oxford, 1895.
Suárez, *De Legibus*	Suárez, Francisco, *Tractatus De Legibus, ac Deo Legislatore.* Lyons, 1613.
Suppl.	Supplement
Thrupp, *Hist. of the Bakers*	Thrupp, Sylvia, *A Short History of the Worshipful Company of Bakers of London.* Croyden, 1933.
Trans. Roy. Hist. Soc.	Royal Historical Society, London. *Transactions.*
Treaty Rolls	*Treaty Rolls Preserved in the Public Record Office.* Vol. II, ed. by John Ferguson. London, 1972.
Trin.	Trinity term.
Upton, *De Studio Militari*	Upton, Nicholas. *De Studio Militari, Libri Quatuor.* London, 1654.
V.C.H.	*Victoria County History.*
Waurin, *Chronicles*	*Recueil des Croniques et Anchiennes Istories de la Grant Bretaigne, a present nomme Engleterre par Jehan de Waurin* . . . , ed. by Wm. Hardy. 5 vols., London: Rolls Series, 1868–1891.
Wilkins, *Leges Anglo-Saxonicae*	Wilkins, David, *Leges Anglo-Saxonicae Ecclesiasticae & Civiles* . . . . London, 1721.
Wing, *S.T.C.*	Wing, D.G., *Short-Title Catalogue . . . 1641–1700.* New York, 1945–51.
Y.B.	*Les Reports des Cases* . . . . 9 vols., London: Sawbridge, Rawlins, and Roycroft, 1678–1680. The Year Books.
Y.C.P.H.	Yale Center for Parliamentary History.

GLOSSARY OF FOREIGN WORDS AND PHRASES

The Glossary provides the reader with translations of foreign words and short phrases used by speakers in 1628, unless the speech in which the phrase occurs also provides a translation for it. Classical quotations, biblical quotations, legal phrases (writs, case excerpts, etc.), and remarks in Latin made by the speakers are translated in the Glossary when they are under ten words in length. Legal maxims are included in the Glossary regardless of the number of words they contain. Other foreign language passages of more than ten words are translated in footnotes.

In cases where classical authors are quoted correctly in the debates the Glossary entry gives the Latin first, followed directly by the translation, and then a reference to the source. When the Latin used in the debates is a paraphrase of a classical author, the entry in the Glossary gives (1) the Latin paraphrase as it appears in the debates, (2) a statement of the source of the paraphrase, (3) the correct translation of the original from which the paraphrase was taken. Especially since the deviation of quotations from the original may as well be the doing of the narrator or diarist as of the speaker, it appears sensible to give the translation of the original source rather than a translation of an incorrect paraphrase. In all cases citations to book and line number in the classics are from the *Loeb Classical Library*, in which the reader will be able to find the original correct Latin. In some cases the Latin in the debates is neither an accurate quotation from the original nor a paraphrase of it, but is the speaker's own vague reference in Latin to a story from the classics. In these cases the entry in the Glossary gives the Latin as it appears in the debates, followed by a translation of it, and then a reference to the classical source alluded to by the speaker.

Biblical quotations are from *The Holy Bible*, King James Version, 1611, or when the quote appears in Latin, from the *Vulgate*.

Legal writs are translated from Black's *Law Dictionary*. Following the translation is a brief explanation of the purpose of the writ as defined in Black. In cases of archaic writs (for example, *nativo habendo*, etc.) the reader will find lengthier definitions in Jacob's *Law Dictionary* (London, 1732) or in Rastell, *Les Termes de la Ley* (Portland, first American ed., 1812). Where Latin phrases are from statutes or cases, a cross-reference, following the translation, is made to the section of Legal Citations, which will give a full reference to the legal source from which the phrase is taken.

It is important to note that when several Latin phrases in the debates are joined by commas there are separate glossary entries for each phrase.

A bene divisis ad mala conjuncta (composita). Cf. Aristotle, *On Sophistical Refutations*, 4, 23–33. "The significance is not the same if one utters the words separately as it is if one combines them (compounds them)".

a circumstantia temporis. "According to the circumstance of time".

a damno et dedecore. "From injury and disgrace".

a fortiori. "With stronger reason".

a loco. "According to place".

a minore ad majus. "From the minor [premises] to the major".

a personis petentium. "According to the persons of the petitioners".

a posteriori. "Inductively".

a re ipsa. "From the matter itself".

a tacito. "From silence".

a tanto. "In part".

a tempore. "According to time".

a toto. "In whole".

a tuto. "From safety".

ab initio. "From the beginning".

ab inutili et incommodo. "From the useless and inconvenient".

ab regis honore. "From the honor of a king".

ab utili et inutili. "From the useful and the useless".

absolutam et [il]limitatam potestatem. "Absolute and unlimited power".

ac. "And", "And also".

ac etiam. "And also".

acceptum. "Received".

accordant. "Agreeing".

accumulative. "Additionally".

ad arrainandum et omnes contrarios et inobedientes incarcerandum. "To array and to incarcerate all resisters and disobedients".

ad arrestationem corporum. "For the arrest of persons".

ad audiendum judicium. "To hear the judgment".

ad audiendum, terminandum et debite puniendum. "To hear, determine, and properly to punish".

ad captandam benevolentiam. "To gain goodwill".

Ad communem totius populi salutem et non ad destructionem. "For the common welfare of the whole people, and not for its destruction".

ad conservationem generalem. "For the general preservation".

ad correctionem. "For correction".

ad debellandum et suppeditandum. "For fighting and supply".

ad debellandum inimicos domini regis. "To wage war against enemies of the lord King".

ad debellandum potestatem per arrestationem corporum. "To carry on war, power through bodily arrest".

ad debite puniendum per corpora sua capi. "Properly to punish by seizing their bodies".

ad destructionem sed ad edificationem. "For tearing down but for building up".

ad discretionem vestram. "At your discretion".

ad destruendum. "For destruction".

Ad ea quae frequentius accidunt jura adaptantur. "The laws are adapted to those cases which most frequently occur". Coke, *Second Inst.*, f. 137.

ad gubernandum secundum discretionem vestram. "For governance according to your discretion".

ad idem. "To the same point".

ad infinitum. "To infinity".

ad justitiam reddendam juxta tenorem cuiusdam schedulae annexae. "To render justice according to the tenor of a certain attached schedule".

ad locum solitarium. "To a solitary place."

ad puniendum. "To punish".

ad recipiendum quod curia considerabit (deliberabit). "To receive what the court will consider (deliberate)".

ad regendum et gubernandum secundum discretionem vestram. "For ruling and governing according to your discretion".

ad salutem. "For well-being".

ad sectam pacis. "For security of the peace".

ad subjiciendum et recipiendum. "To sumbit to and receive" whatsoever the judge or court awarding the writ shall consider in that behalf. See

habeas corpus ad subjiciendum, Black's *Law Dict.*

ad terrorem. "To frighten".

aliae causae. "Other cause".

aliis causis illos moventibus. "For other causes moving them".

aliquam gratiam. "Any grace".

Aliter scriptum est. "It is written otherwise".

alla cui monarchia nascovi mundi. "[It is] that one to whom [was given] the governance of the world". [I.e., the Pope.]

altercando amittitur veritas. Cf. Aulus Gellius, *The Attic Nights,* 17, 14, 4. " 'Mid too much wrangling truth is often lost".

alternis vicibus. "Each in turn" or "sequence".

amnestia. "Amnesty".

An non est corpus super vestimentum? "Is not the body more than raiment?" Luke 12:23.

antenati. "Born before", i.e., children born out of wedlock. See Leg. Cit., *S.R.,* 20 *H.* III, *Provisiones de Merton,* c. 9.

arcana imperii. "Secrets of state".

arcana regni. "Secrets of the crown".

arcanum. "Secret".

arrestari fac[iendum]. "[Power] to cause to be arrested".

Arthurus Rex Angliae subjugavit. "Arthur, King of England, conquered [it]".

asini calamitas. "The calamity of the ass".

assize of novel disseisin. A writ of assize for recovery of lands where the claimant had been lately disseised. See Black's *Law Dict.*

Attribuat igitur rex legi, quod lex attribuit ei. "Let the King, then, attribute to the law what the law attributes to him". Bracton, *Lib.* I, f. 5.

atturnatum domini regis. "The attorney of the lord King".

Audite ipsam biblum. "Listen to that book".

bella per Ematheos. "Wars by Macedonians".

Bellum constat fama. Cf. Quintus Curtius, *History of Alexander,* 8, 8, 15. "Wars depend upon reputation".

Bene dixit qui bene tacuit. "Well doth he speak who keeps silent".

bene esse. "Well-being".

bene positae ergo non removendi. "Well placed and all the more must not be removed".

benedictum parliamentum. "A blessed parliament".

Bis dat qui cito dat. "He gives twice who gives quickly". Alciatus, *Emblems,* 190b.

bona libertas. "Good liberty".

bona peritura. "Perishable goods".

boni [blank] curiam. "Of good [blank], the court".

bonum bene. A "good, well".

breve non est sufficiens causa. "The writ is not sufficient cause".

breve suum. "His writ".

brevia de. "Writs of".

breviter enarrare causam captionis. "[A writ] briefly
sets forth the cause of seizure".

caelum et terrae. "Heaven and earth". Cf. Hesiod,
Theogony, 125–137.

capias. "That you take". The general name for
several species of writs of attachment or arrest.
See Black's Law Dict.

capias ad respondendum. "That you take to answer".
Often shortened to capias. A writ commanding
the sheriff to take the defendant, and safely
keep him, so that he (the sheriff) may have his
body before the court on a certain day to
answer the plaintiff in the action. See Black's
Law Dict.

capias excommunicato capiendo. "That you take for
excommunication, for imprisonment". See
capias. The writ excommunicato capiendo, in
ecclesiastical law, issuing out of Chancery,
where a defendant has been excommunicated,
requiring the sheriff to arrest and imprison
him. See Black's Law Dict.

capias in withernam. "That you take by way of
reprisal". A writ which lies for one whose
goods or cattle, taken under a distress, are
removed from the county, commanding the
sheriff to seize other goods or cattle of the
distrainer of equal value. See Black's Law
Dict.

capias utlagatum. "That you take an outlaw". A
writ which lies against a person who has been
outlawed, by which the sheriff takes, and
keeps, him in custody until the day of the
return. For outlawry see Black's Law Dict.

capiatur. "Let him be taken".

capitaneus nostrae expeditionis. "Captain of our
expedition".

capitaneus Novi Castri supra Tynam. "Captain of
Newcastle upon Tyne".

Carcer ad continendos, et non puniendos haberi debeat. "A
prison ought to be kept for confinement, not
for punishment". Bracton, Lib. III, f. 105.

carcer domesticus. "Domestic prison".

carcer modicae coercionis. "Prison of moderate re-
straint".

carcer perpetuus. "Permanent prison".

Carceres non ad poenam sed ad custodiam inventi.
"Prisons were invented not for punishment
but for custody".

cardo rei. "The key to the matter".

carta clausa. "A closed charter".

carta libertatis et franchisae. "Charter of liberties and
freedoms."

castrensis jurisdictio. "Jurisdiction of the camp".

causa captionis. "Cause of arrest".

causa detentionis. "Cause of detention".

causa sine qua non. "Cause without which not", i.e.,
that without which the thing cannot be, an
indispensable requisite.

causam cum die. "Cause with the day", i.e., a return
showing the cause of imprisonment and fixing
a day for the plaintiff's appearance in court.

Caveat successibus opt[imis], quisque eventu facta notanda
putat. "Whoever thinks that deeds should be
measured by results, be wary of favorable
progress".

cessavit. "Ceased" or "stayed".

civilis mors. "Civil death".

colore cujus. "By color whereof".

columna et corona reipublicae. "The pillar and crown
of the commonwealth".

commissus Marescallo. "He was committed to the
Marshalsea".

committitur. "He is committed".

committitur marescallo praedicto, etc. "He is committed to the marshal aforesaid, etc.".

commune auxilium. "Common aid".

commune delictum. "Common offense".

commune periculum. "Common danger".

communem poenam. "Common penalty".

communibus annis. "In any given year".

compos mentis. "Sound of mind".

concessimus libertates. "The granting of liberties".

Concors discordia legibus apta. "Bringing discords into
concord is proper matter for the laws".

Consensus tollit errorem. "Consent takes away error".
Coke, First Inst., f. 126a.

consimilia. "Entirely similar".

Consuetudo est optimus legum interpres. "Custom is the
best expounder of the laws". Coke, Second Inst.,
f. 18.

Contemptum judicium vagum. "Contempt of law calls
for an uncertain judgment".

contra formam statuti. "Against the form of the
statutes".

contra legem et tenorem Magnae Cartae. "Against the
law and tenor of Magna Carta".

contra naturam. "Contrary to nature".

contra statutum. "Against the statute".

contrarios. "Resisters".

convertibilia. "Convertible" or "interchangeable".

Convicia si irascaris tua, si contempteris sua. "If you become angry at slanders they affect you, if you despise them they affect the slanderer". Cf. Tacitus, *Annals*, 4, 34; Coke, *Third Inst.*, f. 198.

cor regis inscrutabile. "The heart of king(s) is unsearchable". Prov. 25:3.

cor unum, via una. "One heart, one way".

coram domini Edᵒ. rege. "In the presence of Edward, the lord King".

coram justiciarii. "In the presence of the justices".

coram milite marescallo. "In the presence of the marshal as a knight".

coram non judice. "In presence of a person not a judge". See Black's *Law Dict.*

coram rege. "In the presence of the King", i.e., in the King's Bench.

corpus cum causa. See below, *habeas corpus*.

Corpus humanum non recipit aestimationem (de futuro). "A human body is not susceptible of appraisement (for the future)". Maxim.

Crede mihi, bene qui latuit, bene vixit. "Let me tell thee, he who hides well his life, lives well". Ovid, *Tristia*, 3, 4, 25.

crimen laesae majestatis. "The crime of high treason".

crudelis misericordia. "Cruel mercy".

cui bono. "What good".

cui, quo modo, quare, quando. "To whom, in what way, for what reason, when".

cum causa. "With cause".

cum privilegio. "With privilege".

cumulative. "Additional".

curia advisari vult. "The court will advise". A phrase signifying the resolution of the court to suspend judgment, after the argument, until they have deliberated upon the question, for example, when there is a new or difficult point involved.

curia cancellarium. "Court of Chancery".

custodes maritimi. "Maritime wardens".

custodia. "Custody".

custodia marescalli. "In the custody of the marshal".

custodiam comitatus. "In the custody of the sheriff".

custos sui. "His own keeper".

damnum sine injuria. "Damage without injury". See Black's *Law Dict.*

damus potestatem comiti prout ei viderit faciendum. "We grant power to the sheriff according as he deems appropriate".

dare leges. "To give laws".

de concubinatu episcoporum et de ebrietate episcoporum. "On the concubinage of bishops and on the drunkenness of bishops".

de die captionis. "From the day of arrest".

de die in diem. "From day to day".

de futuris contingentibus. "Of future contingencies".

de hora in horam. "From hour to hour".

de jure. "Of right".

de justiciariis assignatis. "Of assigned justices".

de legallo metallo. "Of lawful metal".

De non apparentibus, et non existentibus, eadem est ratio (sententia). "As to things not apparent and those not existing, the rule (opinion) is the same". Maxim. 5 Coke, *Reports*, f. 5b, Caudrey's case.

De non ente non fit questio. "One cannot question that which does not exist".

de novo. "Anew".

de odio et atia. A writ to the sheriff to inquire whether a man committed to prison upon suspicion of murder were committed on just cause of suspicion or only upon malice and ill will, etc. See Black's *Law Dict.*

de praeteritis. "Of past events".

de sole et vento. "Of the sun and wind".

de subellandum. "To prepare for war".

debellando et in bello. "Waging war and in time of war".

debite puniendi sicut nos presentes fuissemus. "Of appropriately punishing just as though we had been present".

decretum cancellarii. "Decretal of the Chancellor".

dedimus coronae. "We have granted to the crown".

delegatam potestatem. "Delegated power".

delicta communia. "Common offenses".

delicta levia. "Light offenses".

delictum militare. "Military offense".

detentus in prisona. "Detained in prison".

detentus per mandatum. "Detained by command".

Deum time, regem honora. "Fear God, honor the King". I Pet. 2:17.

diaboli. "Of the devil".

dies, hora, momentum sufficit. "The day, the hour, the moment is sufficient".

Digna vox majestatis regnantis. "It is a saying worthy of the majesty of one who reigns". Bracton, *Lib.* III, f. 107b.

Dilige et dic quod vis. "Love and say what you will".

disobedientes. "Disobedients", i.e., rebels.

diversorium, divertendo ex via. "An inn, from turning off the road".

divisos ab orbe Britannos. See below, *et penitus.*

doctus. "Learned".

dolosus versatur in generalibus. "A deceiver deals in general terms". 2 Coke, *Reports*, f. 34.

dominium regale politicum. "Royal sovereignty under the law".

dominus rex mandavit dilecto. "The lord King commanded the beloved".

dominus rex relaxavit mandatum. "The lord King released the command".

domus est tutissimum refugium. "A man's house is his safest refuge". Cf. 11 Coke, *Reports*, f. 82.

donec. "Until".

donec aliud inde ordinavimus. "Until we have ordained otherwise".

donec secundum legem et curiam determinetur. "Until it should be decided according to the law and the court".

ductus ad barram. "Led to the bar".

ductus ad responsionem. "Led to accountability".

ductus coram rege et recordatur. "Led before the King and a record was made".

Dum tempus habemus, bonum operemur. "While we have time, let us do some good". See Leg. Cit., *Rot. Parl.*, VI, no. 1.

durante bene placito. "During good pleasure".

durities imprisonamenti. "Duress of imprisonment". Deprivation of liberty or infliction of injury in order to force compliance. See *Duress*, Black's *Law Dict.*

dux belli. "The military commander".

e converso. "Conversely".

Eatenus ratiocinandum est donec veritas inveniatur. "Deliberation must continue until truth is found".

eius nomina. "Synonyms".

engrossetur. "Engrossed", i.e., written in a fair hand on parchment.

eodem die. "The same day".

ergo. "Therefore".

eritis sicut Dei. "Ye shall be as Gods". Gen. 3:5.

errare cum patribus. "Err with their fathers".

Errores ad sua principia referre est refellere. "To bring errors to their beginning is to see their last". Coke, *Third Inst.*, f. 15.

esse. "Being".

Est aliquid prodire tenus si non datur ultra. Cf. Horace,

Epistles, 1, 1, 32. "It is worthwhile to take some steps forward, though we may not go still further".

et eo quod non fuit. "And in that he was not".

Et nihil novum sub sole. "And there is nothing new under the sun". Eccles. 1:19.

et omnes transgressiones, etc. debite puniendi. "And all misdeeds, etc., properly to punish".

et penitus toto divisos orbe Britannos. "And the Brittons, wholly sundered from all the world . . .". Virgil, *Eclogues*, 1, 66.

et plenam potestatem puniendi prout melius viderit faciendum. "And full power to punish as he deems appropriate".

et postea immediate remittuntur. "And afterwards they are immediately remitted".

et potestas capiendi et arrestandi contrarios. "And the power to seize and arrest resisters".

et tu provincia ploras. Cf. Juvenal, *The Satires*, 1, 50. "While you, poor province, win your cause and weep".

eundo, redeundo, morando. "Going, coming, remaining".

ex altera parte. "From the other side".

ex congruo et condigno. "On fitting and worthy [grounds]".

ex gratia. "Graciously".

ex officio. "By virtue of the office". See Black's *Law Dict.*

ex pacto. "By compact".

ex parte nostri. "From our part".

ex parte regis. "From the King's part".

ex rogatu regis. "By request of the King".

ex vi termini. "From the term".

ex visceribus causae. "From the bowels of the cause".

Exceptio est de regula, et exceptio destruit regulam in casibus exceptis. "An exception is away from the rule, and an exception destroys the rule in excepted cases". Cf. 11 Coke, *Reports*, f. 41.

exceptio firmat regulam in casibus non exceptis, in casibus exceptis destruit regulam. "An exception affirms the rule in cases not excepted; in cases excepted it destroys the rule". Cf. 11 Coke, *Reports*, f. 41.

exercitibus usitatum. "Used in the armies".

Exi in vias, et sepes et compelle intrare, ut impleatur domus mea. "Go out into the highways and hedges and compel them to come in, that my house may be filled". Luke 14:23, The *Vulgate.*

exoneretur. "Let him be discharged".

Expressio eius quod tacite inest, nihil operatur. "The expressing of that which is tacitly implied is inoperative". Cf. Coke, *First Inst.*, f. 210a.

extra judicium. "Outside the law".

facere justitiam secundum formam legis militaris. "To do justice according to the form of military law".

Faciles motus mens generosa capit. "A noble spirit is capable of kindly impulses". Ovid, *Tristia*, 3, 5, 32.

factum dicitur quod perseverat. "That he had persevered is called a fact". Cf. 5 Coke, *Reports*, f. 96.

factum secundum legem Angliae. "Done according to the law of England".

felix parliamentum. "The happy parliament".

felo de se. "A felon of himself", i.e., a suicide.

feoffment. The gift or grant of any corporeal hereditament to another, etc. See Black's *Law Dict.*

Fidelem si credideris facias. "You will make a man dependable if you trust him".

filius Willielmi. "Son of William".

finis intermedius. "Mediate end".

flagrante crimine. "A fresh or recent crime". See Black's *Law Dict.*

Fortiter malum qui patitur, post potitur bonum. "The chap that endures hard knocks like a man, enjoys a soft time later on". Plautus, *The Comedy of Asses*, 2, 2, 58.

fortunam impetratam. "Attained position".

Frustanea potentia quae nunquam reducitur in actum. "Vain power which never is reduced to act". Cf. 2 Coke, *Reports*, f. 51.

Fuit resolve acc. sur antient evidence. "It was resolved in accord on ancient evidence".

furtum et adulterium. "Theft and adultery".

Futura sunt contingentia. "The future is filled with possibilities".

Genus incipit a me, tuum a te desinit. "My race begins with me, yours dies with you".

gladios cinctos. "Girded swords".

gratia curia. "By the grace of the court".

Gratior est reddita quam retenta sanitas. "Health restored is more pleasing than health retained".

gravia. "Grave".

Gravius est aeternam quam temporariam laedere majestatem. "It is more serious to commit eternal than temporal treason". Coke, *Third Inst.*, f. 43.

habeas corpus. "You have the body". The name given for a variety of writs whose object is to bring a party before a court or judge. See Black's *Law Dict.*

habeas corpus ad conservandum diem. "Habeas corpus for keeping the day". An archaic writ.

habeas corpus ad prosequendum. "*Habeas corpus* in order to prosecute". A writ that issues when it is necessary to remove a prisoner in order to prosecute in the proper jurisdiction. See Black's *Law Dict.*

habeas corpus ad standum rectum. "*Habeas corpus* for standing trial". An archaic writ.

habeas corpus cum causa. "*Habeas corpus* with the cause". Another name for the writ of *habeas corpus ad faciendum et recipiendum*, which is a writ issuing in civil actions to remove the case, as well as the body of the defendant, from an inferior court to a superior court. See Black's *Law Dict.*

Habemus optimum testem confitentem reum. "We have the best witness in an accused who confesses the charge". Maxim.

Haec via non ducit in urbem. "This road does not lead to the city".

haut et bas, sans parliament. "High and low, without parliament".

homine replegiando. A writ which lay to replevy a man out of prison. See Black's *Law Dict.*

Horresco referens. "I shudder as I tell the tale". Virgil, *Aeneid*, 2, 204.

hospitii domini regis. "Household of the lord King".

hospitii praedicti. "The aforesaid household".

humano capiti cervicem pictor equinam. Cf. Horace, *Ars Poetica*, 1. "If a painter chose to join a human head to the neck of a horse . . . ".

Humores moti et non remoti corpus destruunt (laedunt) (inficiunt). "Humors troubled and not removed destroy (injure) (weaken) the body".

Id est. "It is".

ideo tempus duellicum. "Therefore a time of war".

ignotus. "Unknown".

Ille se amari consciat. "Let him know that he is loved".

imagines patrum. "The signals of our fathers".

Imbecilliores querunt[ur] equum et justum. "The weaker parties seek that which is equal and just".

immediate. "At once".

immediate remittuntur. "They are remitted at once".

immediate remittuntur praefacto Mar. hospitii praedicti.

"Immediately the aforesaid are remitted to the aforesaid Marshal of the Household".

in medio tutissimus ibis. "In the middle is the safest path". Ovid, *Metamorphoses*, 2, 137.

impeditioris linguae sum. "I am slow of speech". Exod. 4:10, The *Vulgate.*

in abstracto. "In the abstract".

in actu. "In line of duty".

In bello qui maxime timent sunt in maximis periculis. "In war those who are especially fearful are in the greatest peril".

in capite. "In chief [importance]".

in circulo. "In a circle".

in concreto. "In the concrete".

in foro competenti. "In a suitable forum".

in foro suo. "In their own courts".

in habitu. "In appearance".

in haec verba. "In these words".

in individuo. "As an individual one".

in litera. "Behind the word".

in nullo dissimilis. "In no way dissimilar".

in omnibus. "In all respects".

in oppositio. "Inversely".

in pace. "In peace".

in partibus marchii Scotiae. "In the marches of Scotland".

in personam. "To the person".

in prisona nostras committendi. "[Power] to commit [to] our prisons".

in rem. "To the case".

In republica maxime conservanda sunt jura belli. "The laws of war are especially to be preserved in the state". Maxim.

in scriptis. "In writing".

in serie temporis. "In temporal sequence".

In statu quo. "In its present state".

In statu quo prius. "In the state that was previously".

in terminis terminantibus. "In terms of determination", i.e., in express or determinate terms.

in terrorem. "In terror", i.e., by way of threat.

In toto et qualibet parte, et qualibet syllaba. "As a whole and in every part, and in every syllable".

in verbis conceptis. "Formally".

indignum rege. "Beneath royal dignity".

individuum [et] vagum. "Individual [i.e., a single thought or concept] and vague".

inobedientes. "Disobedients".

inter alia. "Among other things".

inter brevia regis. "Among the King's writs".

inter homines in eodem exercitu. "Between men in the same army".

inter legalem et regalem authoritatem (potestatem) regis.

"Between the legal and royal authority (power) of the King".

interim sit in pace. "In the meantime let him be in peace". From the writ *libertate probanda,* see below.

inutili et incommodo. "[From] the useless and inconvenient".

ipso facto. "By the fact itself".

Jove principium. Cf. Virgil, *Eclogues*, 3, 60. "With Jove I begin".

Judicandum est legibus, non exemplis. "We must judge according to law, not by precedent". Maxim.

Judicium fuit nullum et vacuum in lege. "The judgment was null and void in law".

judicium parium. "Judgment of his peers". See Leg. Cit., Magna Carta, 9 *H.* III, c. 29.

jugum. "A yoke".

jura belli. "Rules of war".

jure divino. "By divine right".

juri suo renunciare. "Renounce his own right".

jus aequi et boni. "Law of equal and good".

jus belli. "The law of war".

jus illud non nisi in castris. "That law nowhere other than in a military camp".

jus privatum. "Private law".

jus publicum. "Public law".

jussus sedere. "[Let us have] the order to sit".

justitia prima. "A chief justice".

juxta sanam discretionem vestram gubernandi. "According to your sound discretion in governing".

juxta sanas discretiones vestras arrainari. "To be arraigned according to your sound discretion".

laicus. "A layman".

Lapis (etiamsi) male positus non est removendus. "A stone (although) poorly laid is not to be removed".

lapsus linguae. "A slip of the tongue".

lapsus pennae. "A slip of the pen".

le roi. "The King".

Le Roy l'avisera. "The King will advise upon it". The form used to express the refusal of the royal assent to public bills in parliament.

Le Roy le veult. "The King wills it". The form of the royal assent to public bills in parliament.

lectio. "Reading".

legale praeceptum. "Legal precept [order]".

legaliter. "Legally".

legem castrensem. "Law of the [military] camp".

legem potestatis. "The law of power".

Leges angliae et consuetudines are *synonymia, et consuetudo est altera natura.* "The laws and customs of England are synonymous and custom is the other nature [of law]".

leges militares. "Military laws".

leges terrae. "Laws of the land".

lento pede. "Slowly".

leproso amovendo. A writ to remove a leper who thrust himself into the company of his neighbors, etc. See Black's *Law Dict.*

les antient aides. "The ancient aids", i.e., in feudal law three aids were owed to the lord: (1) to ransom the lord's person (2) *fils chivaler*, to make the lord's eldest son a knight and (3) *file marrier*, to give a portion for the marriage of the lord's eldest daughter.

levia. "Light".

Lex caveat de futuro. "Let the law be concerned with the future".

lex et consuetudo parliamenti. "The law and custom of parliament".

lex loquens. "The law speaking".

lex sine causa. "Law without cause".

lex talionis. "Law of retaliation".

lex terrae. "Law of the land".

ley gager. "Law wager"; the giving of gage or security by a defendant that he would make or perfect his law at a certain day. See Black's *Law Dict.*

liber et legalis homo. "A free and legal man".

liber homo non imprisonetur. "A free man is not to be imprisoned".

libere licet accusare non calumniari. "It is fitting freely to accuse but not to blame unjustly".

liberi homines. "Free men".

liberos. "Freemen".

libertas. "Liberty", "Freedom".

Libertas populi est salus populi. "The liberty of the people is the same as the welfare of the people".

libertate probanda. "For proving freedom". An ancient writ directed to the sheriff that he should take security of those villeins who offered to prove themselves free before the justices of the assize.

magistrum militum. "Military commander".

magna veritas. "Great truth".

magnum in parvo. "A great [matter] in small compass".

mainprize. The delivery of a person into the custody of mainpernors (sureties for his appearance at the day to answer charges). See Black's *Law Dict.*

Maius periculum incumbet victori quam victo. "A greater danger lies upon the conqueror than upon the conquered".

mala per (in) se. "Evil of (in) themselves".

mala prohibita. "Prohibited wrongs" or "offenses".

Maledicta est expositio quae corrumpit textum. "It is a bad exposition which corrupts the text". 4 Coke, *Reports,* f. 35.

malus genius. "Evil spirit".

mandatum (domini) regis. "Command from the (lord) King".

maneat ballium. "He remains in bail".

manucaptione. A writ which lay for a man taken on suspicion of felony who could not be admitted to bail by the sheriff, etc. See Black's *Law Dict.*

mar. Short for *marrescallus*, the marshal [of the King's Bench]. See Selden's explanation of *mar.* at the conference 16 April, p. 497.

mare liberum. "[The principle of] a free sea".

marescallo remanent. "They remain with the marshal".

marrescallus. "Marshal [of the King's Bench]".

maxime conservanda sunt belli jura. "A maxim—the laws of war are to be preserved".

media. "Means".

Medio consistit virtus. "Virtue consists in moderation".

Melius est omnia mala pati quam malo consentire. "It is better to endure many wrongs than to consent to evil". Maxim. Cf. Coke, *Third Inst.,* f. 23.

Melius est petere fontem quam sectari rivulos. "It is better to go to the fountainhead than to follow the streams". Maxim.

mense. "Month".

mente obstante. "Opinion withstanding".

meum et tuum. "Mine and thine".

mihi significatum per dominos de privato consilio. "Signified to me by the lords of the Privy Council".

militaria delicta. "Military offenses".

Misera servitus est ubi jus est vagum aut (et) incognitum. "Servitude is a wretched state where the law is undefined or (and) unknown". Coke, *Fourth Inst.,* f. 246.

mittimus. "We send". In criminal practice, a writ directed to the sheriff or other officer commanding him to convey to the prison the person named therein. See Black's *Law Dict.*

Modo convenit de re nihil differt (refert) de modo. "It agrees only on the subject, nothing differs about (no reference to) the mode [of execution]".

monarcha juris. "Master [monarch] of the law".

Monarchia est imperium voluntarium et secundum legem. "A monarchy is a government consented to, and [it operates] according to law".

monstrans de droit. "Showing of right", i.e., the proceeding when the right of the party, and the crown, appears upon record and consists in putting in a claim of right grounded on facts already acknowledged and established. See Black's *Law Dict.*

mors civilis. "The death of a citizen".

Multorum consilia requiruntur in magnis. "The counsels of many are required in great things". See Leg. Cit., *Rot. Parl.*, 7 & 8 *H.* IV, no. 2.

multorum consilium et aliorum. "The counsel of many diverse men". Cf. Homer, *The Iliad*, 2, 362–363.

Multorum manibus grande levatur opus. "By the hands of many a great work is made easy". Proverb.

Munera, crede mihi, placent homines deosque. Cf. Ovid, *The Art of Love*, 3, 653. "Bribes, believe me, buy both gods and men".

nativo habendo. A writ for a lord when his villein had run away from him. It was directed to the sheriff to apprehend the villein. See Black's *Law Dict.*

ne diu detineantur in prisona. "Let [no one] be detained long in prison". See Leg. Cit., S. R., 13 *E.* I, *Statutum Westm. Sec.*, c. 29.

ne experientia docet. "Does not experience show".

ne exulemur. "That we be not exiled".

ne per diutinam macerationem. "Lest by lengthy wearing away".

ne plus ultra. "Beyond appeal".

ne verbum. "No word".

nec eum in carcerem mittimus. "Nor do we send him to prison". See 27 March, n. 51.

Necessitas non habet legem. "Necessity has no law". Plowden, *Commentaries*, f. 18.

nemine contradicente. "Without a dissenting vote".

Nemo est custos sui ipsius. "No one is his own jailer".

nemo liber. "No one free".

Nemo militat suis expendiis. "Who goeth a warfare any time at his own charges?" 1 Cor. 9:7.

nemo tenetur divinare. "No one is bound to foretell". 4 Coke, *Reports*, f. 28.

Nihil cogitat nisi de ventre et venere. "He thinks of nothing other than his belly and his loins".

nihil dicit. "He says nothing". The name of a judgment taken against a defendant who omits to plead or answer the plaintiff's declaration or complaint within the time limited. See Black's *Law Dict.*

Nihil est timor nisi (sed) proditio (perditio). "Fear is nothing else except (but) a betraying (ruin)". Cf. Wisd. of Sol. 17:12.

nihil nisi breve praedictum. "Only the aforesaid writ".

Nihil tam proprium est imperii (monarchiae) quam legibus (vivere) et sine legibus non potest esse imperium. "Nothing is so appropriate to empire (monarchy) as (to live according to) laws for without laws there can be no governance". Cf. Bracton, *Lib.* III, f. 107b.

nisi amari sentiat. "Unless he were to feel himself loved".

nisi causa pro qua captus fuerit tale judicium requireret. "Except the cause for which he was taken did require such judgment". See Leg. Cit., *S.R.*, 23 *E.* I, *Statutum de Frang. Pris.*

nisi per legale judicium parium. "But by lawful judgment of his peers". See Leg. Cit., Magna Carta, 9 *H.* III, c. 29.

nisi prius. The old name of the writ of *venire*, "to come", i.e., to appear in court. Also, *nisi prius* courts are those held for the trial of fact before a presiding judge and jury. See Black's *Law Dict.*

Nolumus mutare leges Angliae. "We do not want to change the laws of England". See Leg. Cit., *S.R.*, 20 *H.* III, *Provisiones de Merton*, c. 9.

non bene audet. "Not a good undertaking".

non bene conveniunt. "They do not go well together". Ovid, *Metamorphoses*, 2, 846.

Non bene conveniunt nec in una sede morantur et mars et judex. "War [a soldier] and justice [a judge] do not go well together, nor do they sit in the same seat". Cf. Ovid, *Metamorphoses*, 2, 846.

non bis ad idem (eundum). "Not against the same [rocks] twice", i.e., not to make the same mistake twice.

non clameum. "Nonclaim". The omission or neglect of him who ought to claim his right within the time limited by law. See Black's *Law Dict.*

Non definitur in lege. "It is not defined in law".

non est in ventus. "He is not found". The sheriff's return to process requiring him to arrest the body of the defendant, when the latter is not found within his jurisdiction. See Black's *Law Dict.*

non ibimus. "We will not go".

non in camera regis sed in curia regis. "Not in the King's chamber but in the King's court". Resolved in *Y.B.,* 2 *R.* III, Mich., *pl.* 22, see Leg. Cit.

Non intellecti nulla est curatio morbi. "There is no cure for an unknown sickness".

non obstante. "Notwithstanding". A power in the crown to dispense with the laws in any particular case. See Black's *Law Dict.*

non per regem in camera sed per judices (justiciarios) in curia. "Not by the King in chamber but by judges (justices) in court". Resolved in *Y.B.,* 2 *R.* III, Mich., *pl.* 22, see Leg. Cit.

Non refert quid notum sit judici, nisi sit notum per formam judicii. "It matters not what is known to the judge, if it be not known judicially".

non sequitur. "It does not follow".

non sic fuit ab initio. "It was not thus far from the beginning".

non sic itur ad astra. Cf. Virgil, *Aeneid,* 9, 641. "[Not] so man scales the stars".

Non vim operant naturae. "Do not effect nature".

nubecula cito transibit. "A little cloud quickly passing".

nullam et facies gratiam. "And you will do no grace".

Nullo jure humano dirimi potest. "It cannot be sundered by any human right".

nullum medicamentum omnibus horis. "No single remedy for all times".

nullum sera prise par suggestion al roy ou son counsell. "None shall be taken by suggestion to the King or his Council". See Leg. Cit., *S.R.,* 25 *E.* III, st. 5, c. 4.

nullum talliagium sera mis per nos aut haeredes. "No tallage shall be taken by us or our heirs". See Leg. Cit., *S.R.,* 25 *E.* I, *Statutum de Tallag.,* c. 1.

Nullum tempus occurrit regi. "No time runs against the King". Coke, *Second Inst.,* f. 273.

nullus imprisonetur. "No man shall be imprisoned". See Leg. Cit., Magna Carta, 9 *H.* III, c. 29.

nullus liber homo. "No free man". See Leg. Cit., Magna Carta, 9 *H.* III, c. 29.

nullus ordo. "There is no order". Cf. Job 10:22.

nunciatum per [Robertum Pecke]. "Announced by [Robert Pecke]".

nuntians A.B. "Announcing A.B.".

nuntiant. "They announce".

nuntiat. "He announces".

nuptiae et matrimonium. "The wedding ceremony and marriage".

O mihi praeteritos referat si Jupiter annos. "Oh, if Jupiter would bring me back the years that are sped". Virgil, *Aeneid,* 8, 560.

O tempora! O mores! "What an age! What morals!" Cicero, *In Catilinam,* 1, 1, 2.

occupanti conceditur. "It is conceded to the occupying power".

oculus diei. "Eye of the day", i.e., daisy.

officina justitiae. "The workshop of justice".

omnes rebelles, etc. per corpora sua capi. "All rebels, etc., by bodily seizure".

opinio subitanea. "Sudden" or "spontaneous opinion".

Oportet regem esse non tam armis decorat[um] quam legibus armatum. "It behooves the King not so much to be adorned with arms as to be armed with laws". Justinian, *Institutes,* Preface.

Optandum in legibus ut judici quam paucissima relinquuntur. "That system of law is best that confides the least possible to the judge".

opus posteriorum agimus. "We do the work of posterity".

ore tenus. "By word of mouth", i.e., orally.

ouster le main. "Out of the hand". A delivery of lands out of the King's hands by judgment given in favor of a petitioner; a delivery of the ward's lands out of the hands of the guardian when the former arrives at the proper age. See Black's *Law Dict.*

pagana delicta. "Civilian offenses".

par humeris. "Equal to the shoulders", i.e., according to ability to pay.

pardonatur. "He is pardoned".

pars prima patent. "Part one of the patent roll".

pars secundam. "Second part".

pastores populi. "Shepherd of the people".

pater patriae. "Father of his country".

pax finis belli. "Peace is the end of war".

pecus tondere non deglubere. "To shear his flock, not skin it". Suetonius, *Tiberius,* 32, 2.

peine forte et dure: fame, frigore, et pondere. "Great and heavy punishment: hunger, cold, and weight". A form of punishment for those who stood mute after being arraigned for felony. See Coke, *Second Inst.,* ff. 178–179.

per alium. "By another".

per arrestationem corporum. "By bodily arrest".

per breve de privato sigillo. "By writ of privy seal".

per breve regis. "By the King's writ".

per concilium domini regis. "By the Council of the lord King".

per consensum concilii. "By agreement of the Council".

per consensum dominorum privati concilii. "By agreement of the lords of the Privy Council".

per corpora. "Bodily".

per dominos concilii pro rebus regem tangentibus. "By the lords of the council for those things touching the King".

per duos de consilii. A misprint for d͞nos *concilio,* i.e., "by the lords of the Council". See 7 April, p. 341.

per incarcerationem corporis. "By bodily incarceration".

per indurationem corporum. "By hardening of the bodies", i.e., through imprisonment.

per ipsum regem et concilium. "By the King himself and Council".

per judicium justiciariorum. "By judgment of the justices".

per judicium parium. "By judgment of his peers".

per legale judicium parium suorum. "By lawful judgment of his peers". See Leg. Cit., Magna Carta, 9 *H.* III, c. 29.

per legem jurisdictionis, "By law of jurisdiction".

per legem terrae. "By the law of the land".

per magistrum militum. "By the military commander".

per mandatum cancellariae. "By command of the Chancellor".

per mandatum concilii. "By command of the Council".

per mandatum dominae reginae. "By command of the lady Queen".

per mandatum domini regis. "By command of the lord King".

per mandatum dominorum concilii dominae reginae. "By command of the lords of the Council of our lady Queen".

per mandatum dominorum de privato concilio reginae. "By command of the lords of the Privy Council of the Queen".

per mandatum praenobilium dominorum regis concilii. "By command of the most noble lords of the King's Council".

per mandatum privati consilii. "By command of the Privy Council".

per mandatum regis remittitur. "He is remitted by command of the King".

per mandatum regum. "By command of the King [Queen]".

per mandatum speciale. "By special command".

per molestationem corporum. "By molestation of persons".

per nomen ballivorum et burgensium. "By the name of bailiffs and burgesses".

per plevinam. "By replevin".

per preceptum justiciariorum. "By precept of the justices".

per preceptum regis. "According to the precept of the King".

per quem principes imperant et potentes decernunt justitiam. "Through whom princes rule and the mighty decree justice".

per speciale. "An exception".

per speciale mandatum domini regis. "By special command of the lord King".

per suspicionem feloniae et per mandatum regis. "For suspicion of felony and by command of the King".

per viam executionis. "By way of execution".

per viam judicii secundum judicium et legem. "By way of judgment according to the court and the law".

per vividas rationes. "Through vigorous reasons".

per warrantum diversorum concilii. "By warrant of divers of the Council".

per warrantum dominorum concilii. "By warrant of the lords of the Council".

perdit domum, familiam. "[A man] loses his home, his family".

perspicua vera non sunt probanda. "Self-evident things do not require proof". Coke, *First Inst.,* f. 16b.

perspicuus esset hic locus si nemo exposuisset. "This point would be clear even if no one exposed it".

petititio principii. In logic, begging the question.

placita coram domini rege. "Pleas in the presence of the lord King".

placita exercitus. "Pleas of the army".

placita terrae. "Pleas of the land".

plenam potestatem (exercitu puniendi) secundum consuetudinem in exercitibus (huismodi) usitatam. "Full power (in the army to punish) according to the custom used in the armies (of this kind)".

plus valet auctor quam actores. "The author is more important than the actors". Cf. 5 Coke, *Reports,* f. 99.

plus valet vulgaris consuetudo quam regalis concessio. "Common custom is better than royal grant". Coke, *Copyholder,* sect. 31.

Poena ad paucos, metus ad omnes. Cf. Cicero, *Pro Cluentio*, 46, 128. "That the warning might be felt by all, the punishment by a few".

politice. "Politically".

ponderat haec causas, percutit illa reos. "This [hand] weighs causes; that, cuts down criminals".

populus nihil consulit. "The people did not deliberate".

posse comitatus secundum discretionem. "Power over the county according to his discretion".

postea isto eodem termino traditur in ballium. "Afterward in that same term he is delivered to bail".

postea traditur in ballium. "Afterward delivered to bail".

postnati. "Born after", i.e., after the Union of Scotland and England.

potestas absoluta. "Absolute power".

potestas injuriae. "Unjust power".

potestas juris. "Power of law".

potestas juris et Dei ad salutem. "The power of right and of God is for well-being".

potestatem debite puniendi acsi nos ipsi (faceremes et) presentes essemus (fuissemus). "Power to punish properly as if we ourselves (were acting and) were (had been) present".

potestatem puniendi prout ei viderit faciendum. "Power to punish as he deems appropriate".

praeceptum regis. "Order of the King".

praecipe quod reddat. "Order that he render". A writ directing the defendant to restore the possession of land. See Black's *Law Dict.*

praemunire. An offense against the King and his government, taking its name from the ancient writ bearing that title, which placed the offender out of the King's protection. See Black's *Law Dict.*

praeter legem. "Beyond law".

praeter naturam. "Beyond nature", i.e., exceptions.

praevaluit. "Prevailed".

presidentes provinciae. "Governors of the province", i.e., lord lieutenants.

pretexere. "Allege".

pretextu cujus. "Pretext whereof".

prima facie. "On the face of it".

primae impressiones. "First impressions".

primum in intentione et postremum in executione. "First in intention and last in execution".

primum mobile. In the Ptolemaic system of astronomy, the tenth and outermost concentric sphere carrying the fixed stars in its daily revolution.

principiis obstare. Cf. Ovid, *The Remedies of Love*, 91. "Resist beginnings".

prius et posterius. "Before and after".

privilegium fori. "Right to a separate court".

pro aliis causis illos moventibus. "For other causes moving them".

pro aliis certis causis. "For certain other causes".

pro bono publico. "For the public good".

pro certis causis. "For certain causes".

pro concesso. "For granted".

pro concilio aut servitio impenso. "For council [service] or else personal service rendered".

pro confessione. "For a confession".

pro confesso. "As though".

pro contemptu. "For contempt".

pro custodia. "For custody".

pro diversis causis regem tangentibus. "For divers causes touching the King".

pro et contra. "For and against".

pro homicidio. "For homicide".

pro hominibus de exercitu et in exercitu. "For men of the army and in the army".

pro minuta transgressione. "For a small offense".

pro morte hominis. "For the death of a man".

pro pace. "For peace".

pro rata. "Proportionately", i.e., according to a certain rate, percentage, or proportion.

pro securitate pacis. "For preservation of the peace".

pro servitio suo impenso. "For his service rendered".

pro suspicione proditionis. "For suspicion of treason".

pro suspitione feloniae. "For suspicion of felony".

pro tribunali. "As a judge".

probatio major. "The major proof".

propria persona. "In one's own person".

proprio ore. "By one's own mouth".

propter bonos fines. "For good ends".

propter inobedientiam et ingratitudinem suam. "On account of his disobedience and ingratitude".

propter servicia impensa et impendenda. "On account of his past and future services".

protectio profecturis. "Protection for those setting out [for military service]".

prout ei arbitrium faciendum. "According as he deems appropriate".

prout per rotulum. "According to the roll".

Pugnant non armis modo sed precibus. "They fight not only with arms but [also] with prayers". Cf. Dio, *Roman History*, 72, 9–10.

quae ad exercitum pertinent. "Things that pertain to the army".

quae causa. "What cause".

quaedam terriculamenta. "Certain things that excite terror".

quaere. "Question".

Quando lex aliquid concedit concedere videtur et id sine quo res ipsa esse [non] potest. "When the law gives anything to anyone, it gives also all those things without which the thing itself would be unavailable". Maxim. 5 Coke, *Reports*, f. 47.

quare impedit. "Wherefore he hinders". A writ which lies for the patron of an advowson [the right of presentation to a church or ecclesiastical benefice], where he has been disturbed in his right of patronage. See Black's *Law Dict.*

quatenus. "Insofar [as they are]".

quatuor cives. "Four citizens".

quem metuerunt, oderunt. "Whom men fear, they hate". Cf. Ennius, *Incertae Fabulae*, Fragment XXXVII (XV).

questio juris (statu judiciali). "A question of law (with respect to the judicial estate)".

questio (non) facti. "A question (not) of fact".

Qui bene distinguunt, bene docent. "They teach well who make fine distinctions".

qui committitur mar. "He who is committed to the marshal [of King's Bench]".

qui committitur Mar. hospitii domini regis. "He who is committed to the Marshal of the Household of the lord King".

Qui nescit dissimulare nescit vivere (regnare). "He who knows not how to dissemble knows not how to live (to rule)".

qui nil molitur inepte. "He who makes no foolish effort". Horace, *Ars Poetica*, 140.

qui remittitur mar. prisonae praedict. "Who is remitted to the aforesaid marshal's prison".

qui remittitur marescallo, etc. "He who is remitted to the marshal, etc.".

Qui repetit separat foederatos. "He that repeateth a matter separateth very friends". Prov. 17:9.

quia curia regis aperta est. "Because the royal court was open".

quia profectus in exercitu. "Because he has gone into the army".

quid mihi dabis. "What will you give me".

quid sit justum. "What is just".

Quilibet potest renunciare juri pro se introducto. "Every man is able to renounce a right introduced for himself". Coke, *Second Inst.*, f. 183.

quo jure. "By what law?"

quo modo. "In what way?"

quo warranto. A writ which lies against any person or corporation to determine by what authority (warrant) they claim certain liberty or franchise. See Black's *Law Dict.*

quoad correctionem. "As to correction".

quoad directionem. "As to direction".

quod dubitas, ne feceris. "Where you doubt, do nothing".

quod intempestivum injucundum. "What is inconvenient is unpleasant".

Quod licet ingratum est. "What one may do freely has no charm". Ovid, *Amores*, 2, 19, 3.

quod quidem manifeste notoriosa sunt. "That they were in deed manifestly notorious".

Quodcunque aliquis ob tutelam corporis sui fecerit, jure id fecisse videtur. "Whatever anyone does in defense of his person, that he is considered to have done legally". Coke, *Second Inst.*, f. 590.

quodlibet licere. "No matter how lawful".

quorum nomina. "In the name of those who". Also an archaic writ issued in the time of H. VI to discharge tax collectors and other accountants after they made their accounts.

quousque curia advisari vult. "Until the court will advise". See *curia advisari vult*, Black's *Law Dict.*

quousque secundum legem deliberatus fuerit. "Until according to the law he shall have been delivered".

quousque secundum legem terrae deliberatur. "Until it was deliberated according to the law of the land".

ragione di stato. "Reason of state".

Ratio est anima legis, et anima rationalis est forma hominis. "Reason is the soul of the law, and the rational soul is the form of man". Aristotle, *Politics*, 7, 13.

ratio et auctoritas. "Reason and authority".

ratio una. "One reason".

ratio unica. "The only reason".

ratione. "Reason".

ratione alicuius transgressionis debet contractus non debent impressari. "By reason of someone's transgressions the contract is due, they ought not to be impressed".

rebelles in exercitu. "Rebels in the army".

rebus sic stantibus. "At this point of affairs"; "in these circumstances".

recorda regis. "Records of the King".

recte est index sui et oblique. "That is a proof of itself both directly and indirectly".

regaliter. "Royally".

rege inconsulto. "Without consulting the King".

regendum et gubernandum. "Rule and governance".

regia via. "The royal way".

regis et populi. "Of the King and of the people".

regula. "The rule".

Relatio dicitur plena cum plenam continent veritatem. "A report is called full when it contains the full truth".

Relatio plena facit plenam veritatem. "A full report carries full truth".

relaxavit mandatum domini regis. "Released the command of the lord King".

relaxavit sectam pacis. "Released the security of the peace".

rem integram. "Undetermined".

remittitur. "He is remitted", i.e., sent back, re-manded. See Selden's explanation, 7 April, pp. 343–344.

remittitur prisonae Marescalli. "He is remitted to the prison of the Marshalsea".

remittitur prisonae praedictae. "He is remitted to the aforesaid prison".

remittitur quousque secundum legem deliberatus fuerit. "He is remitted until there shall have been deliberation according to law".

remittuntur. "They are remitted".

remittuntur quousque. "They are remitted until".

replevin, personal. A species of action to replevy a man out of prison or out of the custody of any private person. It took the place of the writ *de homine replegiando.* See Black's *Law Dict.*

Rerum progressus ostendunt multa quae [in] initio praecaveri seu praevideri non possunt. "In the course of events many things arise which at the beginning could not be guarded against or foreseen". Maxim, probably from Bracton, cited 11 Coke, *Reports,* f. 69.

Res est solliciti plena timoris amor. "Love is a thing ever filled with anxious fear". Ovid, *Heroides,* 1, 12.

Res non est integra. "The matter is not undetermined".

responsio secundum legem terrae. "A response according to the law of the land".

responsum. "Response".

reticentia. "A keeping silent".

rex concedit. "The King concedes".

Rex est legalis et politicus. "The King is both legal and politic". Maxim.

Rex est lex loquens. "The King is law speaking".

rex praevaluit. "The King prevailed".

robur belli. "Oak of war", i.e., choice soldiers.

Salus populi suprema lex est. "The welfare of the people is supreme law. Maxim, 10 Coke, *Reports,* f. 139.

salvo honore Dei et ecclesiae. "Saving the honor of God and the Church".

salvo jure coronae. "Saving the right of the crown".

salvo jure suo. "Saving his right".

salvo ordine suo. "Saving his order".

salvo prerogativo regis. "Saving the prerogative of the King".

salvum custodire facias quousque aliter. "You render safe custody until otherwise".

savant le droit et seigniory. "Saving the right and lordship".

scandalum datum. "Scandal given".

scilicet manucaptor. "That is to say manucaptor", i.e., mainpernor. Mainpernor is surety for the appearance of a person under arrest who is delivered out of custody into the hands of his bail. See Black's *Law Dict.*

scire facias. A judicial writ, founded upon some record; most commonly used as a process to revive a judgment after the lapse of certain time, etc. See Black's *Law Dict.*

se defendendo. "In self-defense".

secreta regni. "Secret authority".

secundum consuetudinem in talibus (hujusmodi) exercitibus usitatam. "According to the custom used in such armies".

secundum consuetudinem legis Angliae. "According to the custom of the law of England".

secundum consuetudinem marchiarem. "According to the custom of the Marches".

secundum discretionem vestram. "According to your discretion".

secundum legem deliberatus fuerit. "According to the law he shall have been delivered".

secundum legem et consuetudinem regni. "According to the law and custom of the realm".

secundum legem (leges) et consuetudinem (consuetudines) Angliae (maresichae Scotland, marchiarum Scotiae). "According to the law(s) and custom(s) of England (the marches of Scotland)".

secundum legem marscalli. "According to the law of the Marshal".

secundum legem terrae. "According to the law of the land".

secundum leges (legem) exercitus. "According to the laws (law) of the army".

secundum quid. "In a certain respect".

secundum quod ad justitiam pertinet et consuetudinem Angliae. "According to that which pertains to the justice and custom of England".

secundum sanam discretionem gubernandi. "According to sound discretion in governing".

secundum subjectam materiam. "According to subject matter".

secundum usum coram militum marescallo. "According to usage before the Marshal of the army".

sed non secundum legem terrae. "Otherwise than in accordance with the laws of the land".

sed responderunt omnes comites et barones. "But all the earls and barons answered". See Leg. Cit., 20 *H.* III, *Provisiones de Merton,* c. 9.

sed rex (Angliae) praevaluit. "But the King (of England) prevailed".

serpens qui devorat serpentem fit draco. "A serpent who devours a serpent becomes a dragon". Proverb.

servitia militaria. "Military service".

servitia regalia. "Royal service".

Si a jure discedis vagus es et omnibus incertus. "If you depart from the law you are a wanderer and uncertain in all things". Cf. Coke, *Second Inst.,* f. 227.

si legibus uti licet. Cf. Cicero, *Post Reditum in Senatu,* 8, 19. "If legal action could be taken".

significatum per dominos de privato concilio. "Signed by the lords of the Privy Council".

silent inter arma leges. Cf. Cicero, *The Speech on Behalf of Titus Annius Milo,* 4, 11. "When arms speak, the laws are silent".

simpliciter. "Simply".

simulatio. "Simulation".

simulatio juris. "The appearance of law".

sine causa. "Without cause".

sine fide et sine sede. Cf. Cicero, *Pro Caelio,* 32, 78. "Without money or credit, without hope or home".

sine lege terrae. "Without the law of the land".

soit baile aux seigneurs. "Let it be delivered to the Lords". The form of endorsement on a bill in parliament when sent to the House of Lords.

soit c'est petition de droit baile aus seigneurs. "Let the petition of right be delivered to the Lords". See above, *soit baile aux seigneurs.*

Solum rex hoc non potest facere, quod non potest injuste agere. "Only the King cannot do this, because he cannot act unjustly". 11 Coke, *Reports,* f. 72.

Solus Deus errare non potest. "God alone cannot err".

sub modo. "Under a qualification", i.e., subject to a restriction or condition.

sub poena imprisonamenti. "Under pain of imprisonment".

summa sequar fastigia rerum. "The main heads of the story I will trace". Virgil, *Aeneid,* 1, 342.

summa totalis. "Sum total".

super totam materiam. "On the whole matter".

supersedeas. A writ containing a command to stay the proceedings at law. See Black's *Law Dict.*

supra. "Above".

suprema potestas vitae et mortis. "Supreme power of life and death".

sur les champs. "On the [battle]fields".

tabula clausa. "A closed book".

tantum. "Only".

tantum permissum quantum commissum. "Permission [to talk] is limited only to the issue at hand", i.e., a provision for a narrow scope of argumentation.

tempus belli. "Time of war".

tempus guarinum. "Time of war".

tempus pacis. "Time of peace".

tempus suum. "Its own time".

teneri faciamus (faciatis). "Let us (do you) act to be bound".

termini. "Ends", "Bounds".

terminis terminantibus. "Terms of determination". See above, *in terminis.*

terminus augens. "Increasing term".

terminus diminuens. "Decreasing term".

titulo. "Title".

tota curia. "The whole court".

toto divisos. "Wholly sundered". Virgil, *Eclogues,* 1, 66. See above, *et penitus.*

traditur in ballium. "He is delivered to bail".

traditur in ballium per consensum dominorum privati consilii. "He is delivered to bail by agreement of the lords of the Privy Council".

traditur in ballium per mandatum speciale consilii domini regis. "He is delivered to bail by special command of the Council of the lord King".

traditur in ballium virtute warranti praedicti. "He is delivered to bail by virtue of the aforesaid warrant".

transitare in Flandriam. "To go across to Flanders".

Turpius eicitur quam non admittitur hospes. "'Tis baser to thrust forth than not to receive a guest". Ovid, *Tristia,* 5, 6, 13.

Ubi de religione, ibi de vita agitur. "Where religion is in question there, too, is life (at stake)".

Ubi dolor ibi digitus, ubi amor ibi oculus. "Where the pain is, there the finger will be; where love is, there the eye will be". Proverb.

Ubi lex non distinguit, nec nos distinguere debemus. "Where the law distinguishes not, we ought not to distinguish". 7 Coke, *Reports,* f. 5b.

Ubi non est lex, ibi non est transgressio. "Where there is no law, there is no transgression". 4 Coke, *Reports,* f. 16.

Ubi non possumus respondere arridemus. "We laugh at that we cannot answer". Cf. Quintilian, *The Institutio Oratoria,* 6, 4, 10.

ultimus finis. "Ultimate end".

una domus. "A single house".

una voce. "[With] one voice".

ut dictum fuit. "As was said by".

ut supra. "As above".

valete et plangite. "Farewell and lament".

valete et plaudite. "Farewell and clap your hands". Terence, *The Eunuch,* 5, 9, 1095.

venienti occurrite morbo. "Meet the malady on its way". Persius, *The Satires,* 3, 64.

verbatim. "Word for word".

verbum regium (regis). "The King's word".

Verbum sapienti sat est. "A word to the wise is sufficient". Proverb.

vetustatis et veritatis vestigia. "The footprints of antiquity and truth".

via fausta. "An auspicious way".

via regia. "The royal way".

vicecomes Londinii. "Sheriff of London".

vide. "See", "Consult".

videlicet. "To wit", "That is to say".

Vigilantibus, et non dormientibus, jura subveniunt. "The vigilant and not the sleepy, are assisted by the laws". Maxim.

villanos. "Villeins".

villein in grosse. A villein bound to the person of the lord, and his heirs.

villein regardant. A villein bound to a manor whereof a lord was owner.

Vir sapiens est robustus. "A wise man is strong". Prov. 24:5.

viri fratres, quid faciemus. "Men and brethren, what shall we do?" Acts 2:37.

virtute cujus. "By virtue whereof".

virtute warranti a concilio praedicto. "By virtue of a warrant [issued] by the aforesaid council".

vita pejor mort. "Life worse than death".

vitae et necis (mortis) potestas. "Power of life and destruction (death)".

viva voce. "With the living voice", i.e., by word of mouth.

Volenti non fit injuria. "That to which a man consents cannot be considered an injury". Maxim.

volumus et mandamus. "We will and command".

Legal Citations

This collection of legal citations provides complete and correct citations to all legal cases referred to by name or by date in the text, to all statutes and rolls cited, and to those treatises frequently referred to in the debates. It also includes quotations or summaries of those legal sources that are central to the debates in order that they may be readily accessible to anyone attempting to follow the arguments of the members.

When in the text the references of the speakers to precedents are inaccurate, imprecise, or indirect, we have given the correct citation in a footnote, and the complete source reference for that correct citation in Legal Citations. We have not footnoted statutes and precedents cited accurately and completely in the text, nor cases cited by name, as Beckwith, Chery, etc., which can be found in the alphabetical list of cases below. Some footnotes to legal authorities, or treatises, contain not only a correct citation to the treatise but also, if it is necessary for the understanding of the debate, a summary of or a quotation from the treatise. If such information has already appeared in a previous note, then there is a cross-reference to that note.

The legal sources dealt with in Legal Citations are (a) Cases, (b) Rolls, (c) Statutes, and (d) Treatises.

Cases. Cited cases that are known by the name of either defendant or plaintiff are listed alphabetically. These are followed by a chronological list of cases from *Year Books*. Either a full reference to the source immediately follows the name of the case (as for Beckwith) or there is a cross-reference to another entry in Legal Citations, preceded by the word "See" (as in Bagg's case), which gives the source. Five kinds of sources are included under Cases: (1) *Abridgements*, (2) Controlment rolls, (3) Law reports, (4) *Year Books*, and (5) Rymer's *Foedera*.

(1) The *Abridgements* cited in the debates,

Brooke and Fitzherbert, are digests of *Year Book* cases grouped under various headings that are arranged in alphabetical order. We cite the cases by giving the heading first, then the plea number, followed by the date of the case. All of the cases in the *Abridgements* are in law French; we have translated into modern English those cases that are particularly important to the understanding of the debates. When we have found that a case in one of the *Abridgements* is cited in a report of another case, we have given the name of that report and that case; the reader should consult the case itself for the substance of the reference.

(2) The Controlment Rolls are unprinted King's Bench memoranda rolls that were compiled for the use of the King's attorney and are now in the Public Record Office. We have included the controlment roll cases here under Cases because they are proper cases in law, not commissions or appointments such as are found in the Close Rolls and Patent Rolls, nor parliamentary business as recorded in the rolls of parliament. As a group these cases constitute the precedents used by Selden in the first conference with the Lords, 7 April, to indicate the nature of imprisonment and bail. We have not summarized these cases in Legal Citations because that is adequately done by Selden in the text on pages 342–353, however they are printed in boldface. The cases are also printed in Howell, *S.T.*, III, 109–121. However, because Howell often cites roll numbers inaccurately and occasionally reports the cases incompletely, we have supplied the reader with complete correct citations. In the Legal Citations the roll number for each case is the membrane number of the document.

(3) The *Reports* of law cases vary greatly in length and coherence. Some are bare notes of facts and findings; others are long accounts of proceedings. Often they contain the view of the compiler rather than the actual decision of the judges. The lawyers in the parliament of 1628 used excerpts from these re-

ports to support points they were making in debate. For the printed law reports (e.g., Coke, Plowden, Rolle, etc.) we cite first to a foliated edition and then to the *English Reports, full reprints* (London, 1907). We have quoted the parts of those cases that were cited frequently and became focal points in the debates. Usually the cases are too long and contain too much material irrelevant to the arguments presented in Commons to be printed in more than summary. There are, however, three exceptions to this: the cases of Ruswell, Glanville, and Saltonstall. These are *habeas corpus* cases that figure predominantly in the debates of 30 and 31 March, and the Rolle *Report* of them is short enough to print in full.

(4) The *Year Books* contain accounts of the arguments in those cases that the compiler considered important enough to record. We have listed the cases chronologically and have given full citations including plea numbers (pl.) as well as page numbers.

The portions of *Year Book* cases cited by the lawyers in the parliament of 1628 were often part of one judge's opinion and did not necessarily reflect either the legal principle actually expounded in the case or the resolution of all of the judges. Members cited these portions to support specific arguments. Furthermore, the *Year Book* accounts themselves often give only partial facts about the cases, and often omit the final resolution. Because of the nature of these accounts and the way in which they were cited in 1628, we have made no attempt to reconstruct the actual cases here; we have not translated completely or noted all of the legal intricacies of the individual cases. We have selected for printing only the salient points (actions, opinions, resolutions, or principles) that relate to the material in the text.

(5) A printed collection of primary source material, Rymer's *Foedera* (Hague, 1739–1745), is the source for Beaumont's case.

Rolls. Citations to the Close, foreign, Parliament, and Patent rolls, and rolls of Scotland are to printed editions and calendars of the rolls where they exist. For the late Elizabethan and early Stuart periods the Patent rolls are for the most part unprinted. For that span of years the Public Record Office, in which the rolls are kept, has manuscript calendars of them. Also in the P.R.O. are the German and French rolls which have not yet been printed in the series of volumes entitled *Treaty Rolls Preserved in the Public Record Office* (London, 1972).

The Parliament rolls have all been printed in the *Rotuli Parliamentorum*. These contain a few of the law cases cited in debate. We have cross-referenced such cases to the accounts of them in Howell, *S.T.*, where they are made accessible, and translated into English. We have also cross-referenced to footnotes of *Commons Debates 1628* and to speeches on particular days when they contain additional information about a roll entry.

Statutes. All of the statutes referred to in debate are listed in this section. Chapters of those statutes that are important to the arguments and are frequently cited are also quoted here. When the chapters appear verbatim somewhere in the text the reader is referred by the Legal Citations' entry to the page in the text on which the quotation appears. An exception to this procedure is 3 *E. I, Statutum Westm. Prim.,* c. 15; because of its central importance to all of the debates on freedom, it is printed below as well as in Littleton's speech on 7 April, pp. 338–339. The seven crucial acts of parliament (two petitions in the Parliament rolls and five statutes) cited by Littleton at the conference, 7 April, are designated in Legal Citations by boldface type. When a chapter of a statute is peripheral rather than central to an argument we have not quoted from it but have indicated the relevant topic or, in the case of Tudor and Stuart legislation, have given the name of the act. All of the statutes are printed in full in the *Statutes of the Realm* (London, 1810–1828). A dagger (†) following a statute entry in Legal Citations indicates that there is a commentary on that statute in Coke, *Second Institute*. The translation of Magna Carta is from *Statutes at Large*, I.

Treatises. If a passage from a legal treatise, such as Stanford, is frequently discussed in the debates, we have included it in this section. Passages from treatises only rarely mentioned, or lengthy Latin quotations from treatises, are summarized and/or translated in footnotes.

Cases (Abridgements, Controlment rolls, Law reports, Rymer's *Foedera*)

Abbot, George, Archbp. of Canterbury. See Howell, *S.T.*, II.

Anderson, *Reports*, 1, (1664 ed.)

34 *Eliz.* I, Resolution of the Judges, pp. 297–298 (*E.R.*, Common Pleas I, 482–483). The Resolution reads:

"We her Majesty's justices of both benches, and Barons of the Exchequer desire your Lordships that by some good means some order may be taken, that her Highness's subjects may not be committed nor detained in prison by commandment of any nobleman or Councillor against the laws of the realm, either else to help us to have access to her Majesty to the end to become suitors to her for the same.

"For divers have been imprisoned for suing ordinary actions and suits at the common law until they have been constrained to leave the same against their wills, and put the same to order, albeit judgment and execution have been had therein to their great losses and griefs.

"For the aid of which persons, her Majesty's writs have sundry times been directed to divers persons having the custody of such persons unlawfully imprisoned, upon which writs no good or lawful cause of imprisonment hath been returned or certified: whereupon according to the laws they have been discharged from their imprisonment.

"Some of which persons so delivered have been again committed to prison in secret places, and not to any common or ordinary prisons, or lawful officer, as sheriff, or other lawfully authorized to have or keep a jail; so that upon complaint made for their delivery, the Queen's courts cannot learn to whom to direct her Majesty's writs, and by this means justice cannot be done.

"And moreover, divers officers and serjeants of London have been many times committed to prison for lawful executing of her Majesty's writs sued forth of her Majesty's court at Westminster, [p. 298] and thereby her Majesty's subjects and officers so terrified, as they dare not sue or execute her Majesty's laws, her writs, and commandments.

"And where it pleased your Lordships, to will divers of us to set down in what cases a person sent to custody by her Majesty, her Council, some one or two of them are to be detained in prison and not delivered by her Majesty's courts or judges, we think that if any person be committed by her Majesty's commandment from her person, or by order from the Council Board, or if any one or two of her Council commit one for high treason such persons so in the case before committed may not be delivered by any of her courts without due trial by the law, and judgment of acquital had.

"Nevertheless, the judges may award the Queen's writs to bring the bodies of such persons before them, and if upon return thereof the causes of their commitment be certified to the judges as it ought to be, then the judges in the cases before ought not to deliver him, but to remand the prisoner to the place from whence he came, which cannot conveniently be done unless notice of the cause in generality or else specially be given to the keeper or jailer that shall have the custody of such prisoner.

"All the judges and Barons, etc., did subscribe their names to these articles, *t[ermino] P[aschae]*, 34 *Eliz.* and deliver one to the Lord Chancellor, and one other to the Lord Treasurer, after which time there did follow more quietness than before in the causes before mentioned".

Apsley. See 1 Rolle, *Reports*.

Archbishop of Canterbury. See 2 Coke, *Reports*.

Arundel, Richard, Earl of. See *Rot. Parl.*, 4 *E. III*, no. 13.

Babington's treason. See Howell, *S.T.*, I.

Bagg, James. See 11 Coke, *Reports*.

Bartholomew, William, *et al.* Hil., 7 *H. VII*, *rot. cont.*, 13.

Bates, John. See Lane, *Exchequer Reports*.

Beamond, John. Pasch., 7 *H.* VII, *rot. cont.*, 18.

Beaumont, Henry. 18 *E.* II, Rymer, *Foedera,* II, pt. 2, 73; *S.R.*, 5 *E.* II, *Les Noveles Ordinances*, c. 22.

Beckwith, Richard. Hil., 12 *Jac.* I, *rot. cont.*, 153. For his bail letter, see 7 April, n. 103.

Berkley, Lord. See 1 Plowden, *Commentaries,* Willion vs. Berkley.

Bildeston, John de. Pasch., 18 *E.* III, *coram rege rot.*, 336, *m.* 33. The case is printed in full in Selden Soc., *Select Cases King's Bench, E. III*, VI, 31–33.

"The king sent his writ to his beloved and faithful Robert of Dalton, Constable of his Tower of London, or to his deputy, in these words: . . . We command you that you are to receive John of Bildeston, chaplain, from our sheriffs of London who will hand him over to you on our instructions at the aforesaid Tower, and have him safely guarded in our prison of the Tower until we decide to send you other instructions in the matter. Witness myself at our Tower of London on the thirtieth day of March in the sixteenth year of our reign in England and the third year of our reign in France.

"And now, that is to say, on the Morrow of the Ascension of the Lord in the eighteenth year of the present king's reign, John of Winwick, the aforesaid Constable's deputy, came before the king at Westiminister and brought before the justices here in court John of Bildeston, whom he received from the sheriffs at another time by virtue of the aforesaid writ etc. And he says that he had instructions from the king to bring and deliver John of Bildeston in person to the justices here etc. And John of Winwick was asked if he had any other reason for the detention of John of Bildeston. And he says that he had none save the aforesaid writ alone. And because it seems to the court that the aforesaid writ is not sufficient cause for detaining John of Bildeston in the prison of the king's marshalsea here etc., the said John is released by mainprise of William of wakefield [and others]. . . .

"At that Octave of Holy Trinity the aforesaid John came before the king at Westiminister by the aforesaid mainprise. And thereupon the king sent his justices here his writ close in these words:

"Edward, . . . to his beloved and faithful William Scot and his fellows, justices assigned to hold pleas before us, greeting. Whereas we have of late instructed . . . Robert of Dalton, Constable of our Tower of London, or his deputy there, to cause John of Bildeston, chaplain, who was arrested and detained in our prison of the Tower by our orders on suspicion of counterfeiting our great seal, to be brought before us on the Morrow of the Ascension of the Lord wherever we might then be in England, along with the attachments and other matters pertaining to the said arrest and detention, in order that he might be delivered there to the prison of our marshalsea of the king's bench and be kept in the same until we be more fully informed by a certain informer, to the end that, having the aforesaid information thereon, we may cause to be done further in this matter what we consider ought to be done in accordance with the law and custom of our realm of England; we, in case the said informer does not come before us to inform us more fully about the aforegoing matters and being unwilling that justice in this respect for the said John should be delayed on that account, command you that, if the aforesaid informer does not come to inform us more fully thereon at or before the Quinzaine of Holy Trinity next, then you are certainly not to await the arrival of the said informer and are to cause the fullness of justice to be done thereon to John as you think it ought to be done in accordance with the law and custom of our realm of England . . . .

"After this writ had been examined, proclamation is made that, if anyone wishes to inform the king about the aforegoing matters or to prosecute against the said John, he is to come etc. And no one came etc. And thereupon the aforesaid William of Wakefield [and others] . . . came and undertook to have John of Bildeston before the king from day to day until the aforesaid Quinzaine of Holy Trinity wherever etc.

"At that day in the eighteenth year John of Bildeston came before the king at Westminster by the aforesaid mainprise. And proclamation is made once more in the form as above etc. And no one came to inform the king etc. Therefore it is awarded that John of Bildeston is to go thence without day, saving always the king's action if any etc."

Boche, Humphrey. Hil., 9 *H.* VII, *rot. cont.,* 14.

Bohun, Humphrey de. See Keilway, *Reports.*

Bowles, Lewis. See 11 Coke, *Reports.*

Brewers. See Desmaistres.

Broket, Sir John. Trin., 1 *Jac.* I, *rot. cont.*, 30.

Brome, Lawrence. Trin., 39 *Eliz.* I, *rot. cont.*, 118.

Brooke, *Abridgement* (1576 ed.).

"Appeal", *pl.* 117, 8 *E.* III. [Cited in Hales vs. Petit, 1 Plowden, *Commentaries.*]

"Commissions", *pl.* 3, 24 *E.* III:

"Note, that the commission to certain persons for taking all that are notoriously slandered for felonies and trespass, as they were never indicted, this is against the law . . .".

"Commissions", *pl.* 15. [See 42 *Ass.*, *pl.* 5.]

"*Corone, etc.*", *pl.* 153, 10 *E.* IV, 6.

"Imprisonment", *pl.* 100, 38 *Ass.*, p. 22:

"Note, by contempt toward the King, as in the case of *corody* and *hujusmodi*, the offender will be imprisoned, and it was determined in parliament in 2 *M.* I [*sic*] that imprisonment in all cases is nothing but retention of him until he has made fine; and likewise, if he offer his fine he is able to be delivered now, and the King then, the fine tendered, may not justly retain him in prison".

"London", *pl.* 5, 2 *H.* IV, 12. [Cf. 8 Coke, *Reports*, City of London case.]

"London", *pl.* 24, 5 *E.* IV, 30. [Cf. ibid.]

"London", *pl.* 29.

"*Quinzime, disme, etc.*", *pl.* 9, Mich., 34 *H.* VIII.

"Treason and Traitors", *pl.* 32, Pasch., 4 *M.* I [*sic*]:

"Note, that if an alien born of a country that is in amity and peace with this realm, come into the realm with English traitors and levy war, it is treason in all of them, then the alien is to be killed by martial law".

"Trial", *pl.* 103, 10 *E.* IV, 6.

"Trial", *pl.* 142, 33 *H.* VIII.

Brooke's, *New Cases* (1873 ed.).

36 *H.* VIII, *pl.* 280, p. 86 (*E.R.*, K.B. II, 872):

". . . That where an alien born comes into England and brings his son with him . . . the King by his letters patent cannot make the son heir to his father . . . for he cannot alter his law by his letters patents, nor otherwise but by parliament; for he cannot disinherit the right heir, nor disappoint the lord of his escheat . . .".

37 *H.* VIII, *pl.* 310, p. 97 (*E.R.*, K.B. II, 910–911):

". . . for the King cannot make a law by his grant: and that by grant of cognizance of pleas, he shall not hold plea of an assize, nor of a certificate of an assize".

38 *H.* VIII, *pl.* 320, p. 100 (*E.R.*, K.B. II, 884).

Browning, John. Pasch., 20 *Eliz.* I, *rot. cont.*, 72.

Brownlow and Goldesborough, *Reports*, 2, (1675 ed.).

Waggoner vs. Fish, Mich., 7 *Jac.* I (1610), pp. 284–289 (*E.R.*, Common Pleas I, 944–947).

Brugge, Thomas. Mich., 7 *H.* VII, *rot. cont.*, 6.

Buckingham, Duke of. See Keilway, *Reports*, Humphrey de Bohun's case.

Burton, Christopher. Hil., 9 *H.* VII, *rot. cont.*, 14.

Bynks, John. Mich., 35 *H.* VIII, *rot. cont.*, 33.

Calvin, Robert. See 7 Coke, *Reports*.

Catesbie, Robert. *De Vacatione Hil.* We have not found the case on the roll.

Caudrey, Robert. See 5 Coke, *Reports*.

Cesar, Thomas. Mich., 8 *Jac.* I, *rot. cont.*, 99.

Chedder, Richard. See *Y.B.*, 8 *H.* IV.

Chery, Roger. Hil., 8 *H.* VII, *rot. cont.*, 12.

City of London. See 8 Coke, *Reports*.

Clark. See 5 Coke, *Reports*.

Cobham, Sir John. See *Rot. Parl.*, 21 *R.* II, no. 10.

Coke, *Reports* (1826 ed.).

2 Report

Archbishop of Canterbury's case. Trin., 38 *Eliz.* I, ff. 46a–49b (*E.R.*, K.B. V, 519–526):

(f. 46b) "But these words 'by any other means', are to be so expounded, *scil[icet]* by any other such inferior means. As it hath been adjudged, that bishops are not included within the statute of 13 *Eliz.*, cap. 10, for the statute beginneth with colleges, deans and chapters, parsons, vicars, and concludes with these words, 'and others having spiritual promotions'; these latter words do not include bishops . . .".

5 Report

Caudrey's case, of the King's Ecclesiastical Law. Hil., 33 *Eliz.* I, ff. 1a–41a (*E.R.*, K.B. VI, 1–47):

(f. 8b) ". . . England is an absolute empire and monarchy consisting of one head, which is the King, and of a body politic, compact and compounded of many . . . all which the law divideth into two several parts, that is to say, 'the clergy and the laity' . . .

"And as in temporal causes the King, by the mouth of the Judges in his courts of justice doth judge and determine the same by the temporal laws of England, so in causes ecclesiastical and spiritual . . . the same are to be determined and decided by ecclesiastical judges, according to the King's ecclesiastical laws of this realm . . .".

Clark's case. Trin., 38 *Eliz.* I, f. 64a (*E.R.*, K.B. VI, 152):

(f. 64a) ". . . King E. 6 incorporated the town of St. Albans by the name of mayor, etc., and granted to them to make ordinances . . . and that they with the assent of the plaintiff and other burgesses, did assess a sum on every inhabitant for the charges in erecting the courts there . . . and because the plaintiff being a burgess, etc., refused to pay, etc. . . . it was adjudged no plea, for this ordinance is against the statute of Magna Carta, c. 29. *Nullus liber homo imprisonetur*; which act hath been confirmed and established above thirty times . . . but it was resolved that they might have inflicted a reasonable penalty, but not imprisonment . . .".

Foster's case. Hil., 32 *Eliz.* I, f. 59a–59b (*E.R.*, K.B. VI, 145–146).

Seymayne's case. Mich., 2 *Jac.* I, ff. 91a–93a (*E.R.*, K.B. VI, 194–199):

(f. 91b) "The house of everyone is to him as his castle . . . and [if] the owner or his servants kill any of the thieves in defense of himself and his house it is not felony, and he shall lose nothing . . .".

6 *Report*

Gregory's case. Hil., 38 *Eliz.* I, ff. 19b–20a (*E.R.*, K.B. VI, 282–284):

(f. 19b) ". . . and Littleton saith, if a man speak generally of escuage, it shall be intended (*secundum excellentiam*) in common speech, of the most excellent service, and that is knights' service for the defense of the realm, and not *de servitio socae*".

Higgens's case. Mich., 3 *Jac.* I, ff. 44b–46a (*E.R.*, K.B. VI, 320–323).

7 *Report*

Calvin's case. Trin., 6 *Jac.* I, ff. 1a–28b (*E.R.*, K.B. VI, 377–411). Also printed in Howell, *S.T.*, II, 559–696:

(f. 4b) "2. For the laws: 1. That liegeance or obedience of the subject to the Sovereign is due by the law of nature: 2. That this law of nature is part of the laws of England . . .".

(f. 6b) ". . . in anno 15 H. 7, in Perkin Warbeck's case, who being an alien born in Flanders, feigned himself to be one of the sons of Edward the Fourth, and invaded this realm with great power, with an intent to take upon him the dignity royal: but being taken in the war, it was resolved by the justices that he could not be punished by the common law, but before the Constable and Marshal (who had special commission under the Great Seal to hear and determine the same according to martial law) he had sentence to be drawn, hanged, and quartered, which was executed accordingly".

8 *Report*

City of London's case. Hil., 7 *Jac.* I, ff. 121b–130a (*E.R.*, K.B. VI, 658–671).

The Prince's case. Hil., 3 *Jac.* I, ff. 1a–31b (*E.R.*, K.B. VI, 481–519):

(f. 19a) ". . . that acts of parliament do go in the form of the King's charter, we have many examples in law. 1. Magna Carta, made 9 H. 3 . . . it doth not appear in the charter itself by express words, that it was made by authority of parliament, yet because many parts of it cross and change the common law, which a charter alone cannot do, and it appears by the last chapter, that for the said grand charter, *Archiepiscopi, Episcopi, Abbates, Priores, Comites, Barones, Milites, liberi tenentes, et omnes de regno nostro dederunt nobis quintodecimam partem omnium mobilium suorum*: this clause in the conclusion of the charter proves it by implication to be an act in form of a charter. And, lastly, it hath always had the allowance of an act of parliament, and therefore ought to be so taken . . .".

9 *Report*

Lord Sanquhar's case. Trin., 10 *Jac.* I, ff. 114a–122a (*E.R.*, K.B. VI, 900–909).

Also printed in Howell, *S.T.*, II, 743–763.

> Robert Carliel, under the direction of Robert Creighton, Baron Sanquhar of Scotland, and aided by James Irweng, killed one John Turner in London, and then fled. The case presented legal problems concerning the extradition of Sanquhar and the apprehending of Carliel and Irweng. (f. 121b) ". . . but by his Majesty's command all these difficulties, with the conference and grave consideration of his principal judges, after search of cases precedent, were resolved and cleared up, and notwithstanding the impediments, difficulties, and impossibilities in legal proceeding, greater expedition was used . . . . In short, the accomplishment of the whole . . . must be attributed to the great wisdom, power, and vigilance of his Majesty . . . ".
>
> All three were convicted and hanged.

10 *Report*

The case of the Marshalsea. Mich., 10 *Jac.* I, ff. 68b–77b (*E.R.*, K.B. VI, 1027–1043):

> (f. 74a) "Then, if any against the law usurp any jurisdiction, and by color thereof arrest or imprison a man, or in any manner by color of an usurped authority oppress any man (which is a manner of destruction) against the law, he may be punished by that statute [of Magna Carta, c. 29] . . .".

11 *Report*

James Bagg's case. Trin., 13 *Jac.* I, ff. 93b–100a (*E.R.*, K.B. VI, 1271–1281):

> (f. 99a) ". . . no freeman of any corporation can be disfranchised by the corporation, unless they have authority to do it either by the express words of. the charter or by prescription . . .".

Lewis Bowles's case. Pasch., 13 *Jac.* I, ff. 79b–84a (*E.R.*, K.B. VI, 1252–1260):

> (f. 82a) "The preeminence and privilege which the law gives to houses which are for men's habitation was observed. . . . It has privilege against the King's prerogative, for it was resolved by all the judges, Mich. 4 *Jac.* . . . [See Saltpeter case, below].
>
> "He who kills a man *se defendendo*, or a thief who would rob him in the highway, by the common law shall forfeit his goods: but he who kills one that would rob and spoil him in his house shall forfeit nothing".

12 *Report*

The case of the King's prerogative in Saltpeter. 4 *Jac.* I, ff. 12–15 (*E.R.*, K.B. VI, 1294–1297):

> (f. 12) "All the justices, viz. Popham . . . resolved . . . *una voce* . . . : The ministers of the King cannot undermine, weaken, or impair any of the walls or foundation of any house . . . they cannot dig in the floor of my mansion-house which serves for the habitation of man; for this, that my house is the safest place for my refuge, safety, and comfort, and of all my family . . . .
>
> ". . . that this taking of saltpeter is a purveyance of it for the making of gunpowder for the necessary defense and safety of the realm. And for this cause . . . it is an incident inseparable to the crown and cannot be granted, demised, or transferred to an other . . . ".

Constable, Robert. Pasch., 9 *Eliz.* I, *rot. cont.*, 68.

Constable, William. See Divers gentlemen imprisoned.

Darnel case. See Howell, *S.T.*, III. Proceedings on the *habeas corpus* brought by Sir Thom. Darnel *et al.*

Davis, *Reports* (1762 ed.).
> *Le case de Tanistry.* Hil., 5 *Jac.* I, ff. 28–43 (*E.R.*, K.B. IX, 516–529).

Declaration of the Judges concerning the Darnel case. See Howell, *S.T.*, III.

Desmaistres, Jacob, and **Ed. Emerson** *et al.* (the Brewers' case). Hil., 12 *Jac.* I, *rot. cont.*, 153. See 1 Rolle, *Reports.*

Divers gentlemen imprisoned by the Queen (Wm. Constable, Robt. Vernon *et al.*). Hil., 43 *Eliz.* I, *rot. cont.*, 89; omitted in Howell. For the letter from Eliz. I to the justices concerning the case, see 7 April, n. 110.

Doughty, Thomas, and Sir Francis Drake. See 18 April, n. 44.

Duke of Buckingham. See Keilway, *Reports*, Bohun's case.

Dyer, *Reports* (1794 ed.).

1 *Report*

Anon. (sometimes referred to as Townshend's case). Mich., 32 *H.* VIII, f. 48a (*E.R.*, K.B. II, 106).

Maleverer vs. Spinke. Trin., 29 *H.* VIII, ff. 35b–37a (*E.R.*, K.B. II, 79–82):

(f. 36b) ". . . in some cases a man may justify the commission of a tort, and that is in cases where it sounds for the public good; as in time of war a man may justify making fortifications on another's land without license; also a man may justify pulling down an house on fire for the safety of the neighboring houses, for these are cases of the commonweal".

Mynours vs. Turke and Yorke, sheriffs of London. Mich., 3 *E.* VI, ff. 66a–67a (*E.R.*, K.B. II, 139–141):

(f. 66b) ". . . for it shall not be intended by the law that the prisoner was removed into another county from that in which the jail is . . . unless it be . . . that he had a special command of the King or of his Council, or of the Chancellor by his writ".

2 *Report*

Rythe, one, etc., vs. Kempe. Mich., 2 and 3 *Eliz.* I, ff. 192a and 193b (*E.R.*, K.B. II, 423 and 426).

Sherleys's case. Pasch., 3 and 4 *P.* and *M.*, ff. 144a–145a (*E.R.*, K.B. II, 315–317):

(f. 145a) ". . . in this time of peace between England and France, to levy war with other English rebels was sufficient treason; and if it were in time of war he should not be arraigned but ransomed".

Skrogges vs. Coleshil. Mich., 1 and 2 *Eliz.* I, f. 175a–175b (*E.R.*, K.B. II, 386–387):

"The office of Exigenter in London and other counties became vacant . . . Queen Mary granted the office of Exigenter to one Coleshil . . . [and] granted the office of Chief Justice to Anthony Browne . . . who refused Coleshil, and admitted to it Skrogges his nephew. And now in this term there was a great contention between them for the said office . . . .

". . . after the end of this term, having convened all the judges of the Queen's Bench, S. Catlin, Whiddon, Rastal, and Corbet, and Saunders, Chief Baron, and

Gerard, Attorney General, and also J. Caril, Attorney of the Duchy (all the judges of the Common Pleas being excluded) took a clear resolution . . . that the title of Coleshil was null, and that the gift of the said office by no means and at no time belongs or can belong to our lady the queen . . . .

"And notwithstanding the said resolution of the judges aforesaid, the Queen . . . directed her commission to the said earl of Bedford and nine others . . . giving them full authority to hear and determine the interest and title of the said office . . . and to place Coleshil in the office. . . .

"And afterwards . . . Coleshil exhibited a bill of complaint to the said commissioners against Skrogges . . . and Skrogges came and demurred upon the bill and jurisdiction of the court by the said commission, and would not make other answer; and for this contempt he was by them committed to the prison of the Fleet, and there remained for two weeks, and then request was made . . . to grant a *corpus cum causa*. And upon consideration of the Court, Ja. Dyer, A. Browne, and R. Weston, the request was held reasonable and to be granted, because he was a person in the court and a necessary member of it . . . ".

Thurland's case. Trin., 4 and 5 *P.* and *M.*, f. 162b (*E.R.*, K.B. II, 354–355).

Queen Elizabeth allowed Thurland, a prisoner in the Fleet, to be released to do military service in war "without commanding him to take bail or baston, which the statute 1 *R.* 2, c. 12, requires him to do, although he have the writ, or command of the King".

Vaux vs. Jeffern *et al.* Pasch., 2 and 3 *P.* and *M.*, ff. 114b–115a (*E.R.*, K.B. II, 251–252).

3 *Report*

Anon. Mich., 12 & 13 *Eliz.* I, f. 296b (*E.R.*, K.B. II, 666):

"But the matter of the excuse above is not sufficient, for the command of the Treasurer and Chancellor are not sufficient warrant to license one condemned in execution to go with a keeper or otherwise at large, for the Queen herself could not do that, as was holden by the opinion of all the justices of both benches in the time of Queen Mary. Thurland's [case]".

Elyott, Camel, and Richard Colgnite, William Ripby, John Coyple, Bernard Embery, Q[*illegible*] Chepham. Mich., 6 *Jac.* I, *rot. cont.*, 122.

Essex, Robert, Earl of. See Howell, *S.T.*, I.

Everard, Richard. Hil., 5 *H.* VII, *rot. cont.*, 18.

Fauconberg, Thomas. See *Y.B.*, 11 *E.* IV.

Fawkes, Guy. See Howell, *S.T.*, II.

Fitzherbert, *Abridgement* (1577 ed.).

"Assize", *pl.* 382, Trin., 18 *E.* II. Concerning the Marches of Wales.

"Corone", *pl.* 290, *Ass.*, 3 *E.* III [cited in Hales vs. Petit, 1 Plowden, *Commentaries*].

"Corone", *pl.* 303, *Ass.*, 3 *E.* III [cited in Bowles's case, 11 Coke, *Reports*].

"Corone", *pl.* 305, *Ass.*, 3 *E.* III.

"Droyt", *pl.* 67, Trin., 31 *E.* I.

"Mainprise", *pl.* 12, Hil., 33 *E.* III.

"Mainprise", *pl.* 13, Hil., 36 *E.* III.

"Monstrans de faits", *pl.* 182, Trin., 16 *H.* VI: ". . . And all the court said that if the King command me to arrest a man, because I arrest him and it is done in the presence of the King, he [the man] will have a writ of trespass or false imprisonment against me".

"Petition", *pl.* 2, Trin., 15 *E.* III.

"Protection", *pl.* 100, Mich., 7 *H.* IV.

"*Quare impedit*", *pl.* 175, Pasch., 18 *E.* II.

"*Scire facias*", *pl.* 122, Pasch., 14 *E.* III, Countess of Kent's case.

"Toll", *pl.* 5, 23 *H.* III.

"Trespass", *pl.* 253, Hil., 33 *E.* III.

Five Knights'. See Howell, *S.T.*, III, the Darnel case.

Floyde, Edward. See Howell, *S.T.*, II.

Foster. See 5 Coke, *Reports*.

Glanville. See 1 Rolle, *Reports*.

Gregory. See 6 Coke, *Reports*.

Hales vs. Petit. See 1 Plowden, *Commentaries*.

Harcorte, Edward. Hil., 40 *Eliz.* I, *rot. cont.*, 62.

Harsnett, Samuel, Bp. of Norwich. See Howell, *S.T.*, II.

Haxey, Thomas. See *Rot. Parl.*, 20 *R.* II, no. 23.

Hertford, Earl of. See Keilway, *Reports*, Bohun's case.

Heveningham, Sir John. See Howell, *S.T.*, III, the Darnel case.

Higgens. See 6 Coke, *Reports*.

Howell, *State Trials* (1816 ed.).

S.T., I

Proceedings against Sir Thomas Seymour for high treason. 2 and 3 *E.* VI, pp. 483–508.

Proceedings against Anthony Babington *et al.* for high treason. 28 *Eliz.* I, pp. 1127–1140.

Trial of Robert, Earl of Essex and Henry, Earl of Southampton. 43 *Eliz.* I, pp. 1333–1360.

S.T., II

Case of George Abbot, Archbp. of Canterbury, for refusing to license a sermon by Dr. Sibthrop. 3 *Car.* I, pp. 1449–1480.

Proceedings in parliament against Edward Floyde for scandalizing the Princess Palatine. 19 *Jac.* I, pp. 1154–1160.

Proceedings in parliament against Samuel Harsnett, Bp. of Norwich, for extortion, etc. 22 *Jac.* I, pp. 1253–1258.

Proceedings in parliament against Sir Giles Mompesson, a monopolist and patentee. 18 *Jac.* I, pp. 1119–1132.

Proceedings in parliament against Richard Montagu for publishing a seditious book. 1 *Car.* I, pp. 1257–1268.

Trials of Robert Winter, Thomas Winter, Guy Fawkes *et al.*, conspirators in the Powder Treason. 3 *Jac.* I, pp. 159–358.

S.T., III

Proceedings on the *habeas corpus* brought by Sir Thomas Darnel, Sir John Corbet, Sir Walter Erle, Sir John Heveningham, and Sir Edmund Hampden. 3 *Car.* I, pp. 1–59. The judgment against Sir John Heveningham is printed 31 March, n. 3. The Declaration of the Judges, B.M., Add. MS. 48059, ff. 281–282 reads:

"First, the judges of the King's Bench did, with one resolution, all agree, that the Great Charter of England, and the six subsequent statutes mentioned by the Commons do stand in force.

"Secondly, for the way of their proceedings in the case of the *habeas corpus*, the judges affirm that they have given no judgment at [f. 281v] all, nor done anything to the prejudice of the subject in diminution of the power the of King, or against those laws, so as therein no jealousy or fear need arise, for it was but a rule or an award of the court and no judgment, and notwithstanding anything done by them, they all agree that the next day, or the next term, a new *habeas corpus* might have been demanded by the parties, and they must have done justice.

"And whereas by a further subsequent, there was discourse of an entry *remittitur* or *remittitur quousque, etc.* The judges out of their learning, and from the experience of the clerks, assure my Lords, that the entires are all of one effect, and tend to one end, that is, to a *curia advisari vult.*

"Last of all, whereas their apprehension of some intention either of a judgment or some new fashioned entry to be made, they all protest that in the term they gave no warrant for any such thing, so immediately after the term, when the clerk attended to know their pleasure therein, they every one, man after man, commanded him not to digress from the form of entires which had been usual in all cases of that nature".

The Declaration is printed in *L.J.*, III, 738–740.

Proceedings against Roger Maynwaring, D.D., for preaching and publishing two sermons maintaining doctrines tending to the subversion of the laws and liberties of the kingdom. 4 *Car.* I, pp. 335–358.

Keilway, *Reports* (1688 ed.).

Anon., Trin., 22 *H.* VII, f. 92 (*E.R.*, K.B. I, 255).

Anon., Pasch., 7 *H.* VIII, ff. 176–177 (*E.R.*, K. B. I, 352–353):

(f. 176) ". . . and by the course of the common law of the land, which every liege man of the King has as his free inheritance . . .".

Humphrey de Bohun or the Duke of Buckingham's case. Mich., 6 *H.* VIII, ff. 170–172 (*E.R.*, K.B. I, 346–348):

Concerning the office of High Constable the King asked the judges: "What kinds of things has the Constable of England power to do by reason of his office?"

Sir John Fyneux, Chief Justice of King's Bench answered: "Sire, this point appertains to our law of arms of which we [the common law judges] have not any experience nor cognizance".

Kent, Countess of. See Fitzherbert, *Abridgement, "Scire facias".*

Lancaster, Thomas, Earl of. See *Rot. Parl.*, 1 *E.* III, no. 1.

Lane, *Exchequer Reports* (1657 ed.).

Bates's case. Mich., 4 *Jac.* I, f. 22 (*E.R.*, Exchequer I, pp. 267–274). Also printed in Howell, *S. T.*, II, 371–394.

Larke, William. See *Rot. Parl.*, 8 *H.* VI, no. 57.

Lawrence, Thomas. Mich., 9 *Eliz.* I, *rot. cont.*, 35.

London, City of. See 8 Coke, *Reports.*

Lovell, Thomas. See *Y.B.*, 1 *H.* VII.

Lyons, Richard. See *Rot. Parl.*, 50 *E.* III, nos. 17–19.

Maleverer vs. Spinke. See 1 Dyer, *Reports.*

Marshalsea. See 10 Coke, *Reports.*

Maynwaring, Roger. See Howell, *S. T.*, III.

Mompesson, Giles. See Howell, *S. T.*, II.

Montacute, Thomas. See *Rot. Parl.*, 2 *H.* V, no. 13.

Montagu, Richard. See Howell, *S. T.*, II.

Mortimer, Roger de, Earl of March. See *Rot. Parl.*, 4 *E.* III, no. 1.

Monson, Sir Thomas. Mich., 14 *Jac.* I, *rot. cont.*, 147. A record of the proceedings against Monson is printed in Howell, *S. T.*, II, 950–952.

Mynours's case. See 1 Dyer, *Reports.*

Newport, Edward. Pasch., 4 and 5 *P.* and *M.*, *rot. cont.*, 45.

Nichols vs. Nichols. See 2 Plowden, *Commentaries.*

Overton, Richard. Pasch., 2 and 3 *P.* and *M.*, *rot. cont.*, 58.

Page, Edward. Trin., 7 *H.* VIII, *rot. cont.*, 23.

Parker, John. Hil., 22 *H.* VIII, *rot. cont.*, 37.

Partridge vs. Strange and Croker. See 1 Plowden, *Commentaries.*

Percy and Bardolf. See *Rot. Parl.*, 7 and 8 *H.* IV, nos. 1–15.

Plowden, *Commentaries* (1792 ed.).

1 *Commentaries* (Plowden)

Hales vs. Petit. Mich., 4 and 5 *Eliz.* I, ff. 253–264 (*E.R.*, K.B. IV, 387–405):
> (f. 263) ". . . if a subject joins the King's enemies in battle against the King within the realm, and is killed in the field, by the ancient law of the realm he shall forfeit his goods, chattels, and lands, and his blood shall be corrupted without other judgment, for he himself is the cause why he could not be tried by the law in his lifetime".

Partridge vs. Strange and Croker. Hil., 6 and 7 *E.* VI, ff. 77–89 (*E.R.*, K.B. IV, 123–142):
> (f. 83) ". . . it appears in 7 *H.* 4 where the King demanded of Gascoigne, Justice, if he saw one in his presence kill J. S. and another that was innocent was indicted for it before him, and found guilty of the same death, what he would do in such a case? And he answered that he would respite judgment because he knew the party was innocent, and make further relation to his Majesty to grant his pardon, and the King was well pleased that the law was so . . .".

Willion vs. Berkley. Hil. and Pasch., 3 *Eliz.* I, ff. 223–387 (*E.R.*, K.B. IV, 339–387):
> (f. 236) ". . . So that there is no exception of the King either in words or in the intent of the act, [*S.R.*, 13 *E.* I, *Stat. Westm. Sec.*, c. 1, *de Donis Conditionalibus*] but he is included in the purview of the act, as others are, although he is not named by express words. And for as much as the act is made to save men's inheritances, we ought to construe it according to the consideration of the common law, and to admeasure the prerogatives of the King upon this act, which is made for the safety of the inheritances of others, in such manner as the common law admeasures them in cases that affect the inheritances of others at common law. And although by the common law the King has many prerogatives touching his person, his goods, his debts and duties, and other personal things, yet the common law has so admeasured his prerogatives that they shall not take away nor prejudice the inheritance of any. . . .
>
> "And therefore the common law so favors

the King, that a custom which binds all others to pay toll for things bought in markets or fairs . . . shall not bind the King to pay toll in such cases, but he is excepted by his prerogative. But yet a custom for toll-traverse shall bind the King . . . for toll-traverse is for crossing or going over another's soil or freehold . . .".

2 *Commentaries*

Nichols vs. Nichols. Mich., 17 and 18 *Eliz.* I, ff. 477–489 (*E.R.*, K.B. IV, 711–730):
> (f. 487) ". . . if a man has a jewel in pledge for 10 *li.*, and he that pledged it is attainted, the King shall not have the jewel unless he pays the 10 *li.*, for his prerogative shall never prejudice another".

Pole, William de la, Duke of Suffolk. See *Rot. Parl.*, 28 *H.* VI, nos. 14–51.

Poynings, Robert. See *Y.B.*, 33 *H.* VI.

Prince, (The). See 8 Coke, *Reports*.

Pryce, Ingo. Hil., 43 *Eliz.* I, *rot. cont.*, 85.

Rabaz, Stephan. See *Rot. Parl.*, 21 *E.* I, *m.* 2.

Rayner, Miles. Mich., 12 *Jac.* I, *rot. cont.*, 119. For the letter requesting his bail, see 7 April, n. 111.

Resolution of the Judges. See Anderson, *Reports*.

Rolle, *Reports*.

1 *Report*

Apsley's case. Trin., 13 *Jac.* I (*E.R.*, K.B. X, 444). *Habeas corpus sur commitment in Chancery.*

Brewers' case. Hil., 12 *Jac.* I (*E.R.*, K.B. X, 382–383).

Glanville's case. Trin., 13 *Jac.* I (*E.R.*, K.B. X, 444):
> "We have also resolved that the return for Glanville is insufficient namely, 'that Glanville was committed to prison 7 May 1615 (13 *Jac.*) by command of Thomas Ellesmere, Chancellor of England; and no cause of the commitment was returned'. And thus it is all one with a precedent in 19 Eliz., in Michell's case in the time of [William] Wray, where the return was 'that he was committed 16 Feb. by Nicholas Bacon, Keeper of the Great Seal', and he was delivered to bail, so we award in this case that the warden

of the Fleet be discharged of the prisoner and that he be committed to the Marshalsea and delivered to bail".

Ruswell's case. Trin., 13 *Jac.* I (*E.R.*, K.B. X, 445):

"Before this time Ruswell's return was amended and the substance of the decree in Chancery returned. The return was this: 'that whereas he was prosecuting certain suits, and [a suit] is pending between Everie and the said Ruswell, in Chancery, concerning the manor of Stapleton, it was decreed by the Lord Chancellor that Everie and his heirs should have the aforesaid manor without disturbance by Ruswell, and that he [Ruswell] should release all his right and make an assurance of the said manor to Everie, and that Everie pay 1,000 *li.* to Ruswell in consideration of this, within such reasonable time as the court should order, and it was after devised that the assurance should be a feoffment', which Ruswell refused to make, and for this he was committed by the court of Chancery, 19 May, 12 *Jac.*

"G. Croke [the prisoner's counsel]. It seems that this return is not good, because no good cause of commitment appears to the court. 7 *E.* IV, 14, a husband and his wife sell the land of the wife and the woman receives all the money for it, yet that could not bind the wife in Chancery. Coke 4, Beverly ['s case], a man of unsound memory will not have relief in Chancery in avoiding his own obligation because it is against a maxim of the law, so in our case this devise should not be made good [i.e., given effect] by the Chancery, being against a maxim of the law. [The purpose of the Chancery suit was to give effect to a devise of land which was invalid both by the common law and under the Statute of Wills.]

"[Sir Edward] Coke. This return in a manner that comprehends the effect of the decree because this consists of four parts: (1) it says 'certain suits', (2) 'between Ruswell and Everie', (3) 'for the manor' of Stapleton, (4) touching 'assurances' to be made of this. And in consideration of this, that Everie should pay 1,000 *li.* to Ruswell; thus we are led to consider primarily the bill, response, and

decree; and after the private conference aforesaid between the justices, Coke said in court that they had taken the case under consideration but because the return was made recently, and the case is dubious to us, we have resolved that he [the prisoner] will be remanded until the next term."

Sir Samuel Saltonstall's case. Trin., 13 *Jac.* I (*E.R.*, K.B. X, 444–445):

"Another *habeas corpus* was returned for Sir Samuel Saltonstall and another for one Allen, and one of the cause[s] for their imprisonment was returned to be 'because they were committed by the Privy Council'. And on the previous day [when the case was discussed] G. Croke said that in 40 Eliz., in Popham's time, on a *habeas corpus* for one Harcorte, the return was 'that he was committed by the command of the Council', and on this return he was bailed.

"[Sir Edward] Coke then said that the Council is able to commit a man without showing any cause, and he is not bailable when committed by the body of the Council; and so it was resolved in 34 Eliz. by all of the justices, and Stanford expounds the Statute of Westminster accordingly. And therefore, when anyone who was committed by the Council is bailed, it ought to be presumed that it was done by a warrant of the Council, *scilicet* by a letter from them or by a message sent by the Attoney [General]. And so the precedent of 40 Eliz. is to be understood to be; because within 2 terms past one was committed by the Council for the gun powder treason [see Beckwith and Rayner] and we bailed him by a letter from the Council (R.[i.e., Rolle, the reporter]: But the warrant for the commitment was without any showing of the cause).

"But now, after the said private conference on these returns Coke said that they all resolved that these prisoners should be remanded, being committed by the Privy Council".

Ruswell. See 1 Rolle, *Reports.*

Rythe vs. Kempe. See 2 Dyer, *Reports.*

St. Albans. See 5 Coke, *Reports*, Clark's case.

Saltonstall, Sir Samuel. Hil., 12 *Jac.* I.

We have not found this case on the roll. See

Selden's speech at the conference, 7 April, pp. 352–353, for an explanation of the case.

Saltonstall, Sir Samuel. See 1 Rolle, *Reports.*

Saltpeter. See 12 Coke, *Reports.*

Sanquhar, Lord. See 9 Coke, *Reports.*

Selby, David. See *Y.B.*, Mich., 31 *H.* VI.

Seymayne, Peter. See 5 Coke, *Reports.*

Seymour, Sir Thomas. See Howell, *S.T.*, I.

Sherleys, John. See 2 Dyer, *Reports.*

Skrogges vs. Coleshil. See 2 Dyer, *Reports.*

Suffolk, Duke of (Wm. de la Pole). See *Rot. Parl.*, nos. 14–51.

Tanistry. See Davis, *Reports.*

Thorpe, Thomas. See *Rot. Parl.*, 32 *H.* VI, nos. 26–29.

Thurland. See 2 Dyer, *Reports.*

Townshend. See 1 Dyer, *Reports.*

Tresilian, Robert. See *Rot. Parl.*, 11 *R.* II, *m.* 7.

Urswick, George. Pasch., 19 *H.* VII, *rot. cont.*, 23.

Vaux vs. Jefferen *et al.* See 2 Dyer, *Reports.*

Vernon, Robert. See Divers gentlemen imprisoned.

Waggoner vs. Fish. See 2 Brownlow and Goldesborough, *Reports.*

Warbeck, Perkin. Cited in Calvin's case. See 7 Coke, *Reports.*

Wenden, Thomas. Mich., 40 *Eliz.* I, *rot. cont.*, 37.

Willion vs. Berkley. See 1 Plowden, *Commentaries.*

Wilman, Benet. See *Rot. Parl.*, 5 *H.* IV, no. 39.

Yew, Thomas. Mich., 12 *H.* VII, *rot. cont.*, 8.

> Sir James Hobart, then the Attorney General, *relaxavit mandatum domini regis* (released the command of the lord King) and thereupon Yew was bailed.

Y.B., 1 *E.* III, Pasch., *pl.* 12 (p. 8):

> Coke's reference is to Loveday's case, which is cited in the principal case in the *Year Book.* Substance: The question arose in an assize whether a man was a professed Templar (i.e., a religious, and hence civilly dead). The question whether a person was a monk was in principle resolvable by certification from a bishop, but in this case no bishop could certify because the Templars were exempt from diocesan

jurisdiction. Being unable to proceed because of this roadblock, the court referred the matter to parliament where it was decided that the issue could be tried by the royal (i.e., secular) courts under the exceptional circumstances.

Y.B., 1 *E.* III, Pasch., *pl.* 45 (p. 13):

> A case of dower used by Coke to show that Gloucester is not in the Marches of Wales. Coke, *Fourth Inst.*, f. 242.

2 *Ass.*, *pl.* 3 (*Liv. Ass.*, p. 3):

> Apparent holding by Sir Geoffrey le Scrope, justice, that it is not felonious to kill an outlaw provided it is clearly established that he has not been pardoned or the outlawry reversed. Party arraigned for the homicide bailed until it is ascertained whether the victim's outlawry was pardoned or reversed.

Y.B., 6 *E.* III, Mich., *pl.* 22 (p. 41):

> Presentments in time of war. Coke, *First Inst.*, f. 249b.

Y.B., 7 *E.* III, Hil., *pl.* 19 (p. 9):

> Case of Dower, which makes the same point as 1 *E.* III, above. Coke, *Fourth Inst.*, f. 242.

Y.B., 7 *E.* III, Mich., *pl.* 24 (p. 50):

> Trespass.

Y.B., 9 *E.* III, Pasch., *pl.* 30 (p. 16):

> Writ of *Cessavit* in Northumberland because of war with the Scots.

Y.B., 21 *E.* III, Mich., *pl.* 65 (pp. 46–47):

> Custom and usage of Oxford.

22 *Ass.*, *pl.* 9 (*Liv. Ass.*, p. 87):

> *Assize of novel disseisin.*

Y.B., 24 *E.* III, Mich., *pl.* 29 (pp. 33–34):

> Corody. Coke, *Second Inst.*, f. 630.

Y.B., 24 *E.* III, Mich., *pl.* 100 (p. 76):

> One taken by the sheriff of London on a *capias utlagatum* was granted a *scire facias.*

26 *Ass.*, *pl.* 23 (*Liv. Ass.*, p. 123):

> Adjudged not a felony for one to kill a thief in self-defense.

38 *Ass.*, *pl.* 20 (*Liv. Ass.*, p. 227):

> This case is cited by Crompton to show that in the King's interest the Exchequer may assume jurisdiction where it would not ordinarily have it. The opinion of Sir William de Skipwith, justice (in response to the objection that a suit should be in a regular common law court instead of the Exchequer): "We shall take cognizance of all that touches the King and may turn to his advantage, to expedite his necessary business". Crompton, *Des Courts*, f. 105v.

Y.B., 38 *E.* III, Hil. [no *pl.* num.] (pp. 6–7):

> Flase imprisonment.

Y.B., 39 *E.* III, Hil. [no *pl.* num.] (p. 1):

Robert Thorpe [judge] gave weight to an opinion on the subject which he had just heard expressed in parliament, notwithstanding the objection that the court did not have a written record of a parliamentary decision before it.

Y.B., 39 *E.* III, Pasch. [no *pl.* num.] (pp. 11–13):

Suit brought by John, Duke of Lancaster against the Earl of Salisbury for settlement of lands in the estate of Thomas, Earl of Lancaster. See *Rot. Parl.*, 1 *E.* III, no. 1.

Y.B., 41 *E.* III, Hil., *pl.* 20 (pp. 8–9):

Villeinage.

Y.B., 41 *E.* III, Pasch., *pl.* 2 (p. 9):

Feoffment.

Y.B., 41 *E.* III, Mich., *pl.* 3 (pp. 19–20):

Annuity.

42 *Ass.*, *pl.* 5 (*Liv. Ass.*, p. 258):

Commission of oyer and terminer issued to Knivet, Thorp, and Lodel, Knights, "to hear and determine all manner of treasons, felonies, conspiracies, champerties, confederacies, ambidexters, damages, grievances, extortions, and deceits made to the King and the people. . . . And the justices said that this commission, for taking a man and his goods without indictment, or suit of a party, or other due process, is against the law". See Brooke, *Abridgement*, "Commissions", *pl.* 15.

Y.B., 43 *E.* III, Hil., *pl.* 13 (pp. 5–6):

Villeinage.

48 *Ass.*, *pl.* 5 (*Liv. Ass.*, p. 315):

Assize of novel disseisin.

49 *Ass.*, *pl.* 8 (*Liv. Ass.*, pp. 320–321):

Concerning corporations, wherein prescriptions (claims recognized by use and time) are void and good.

Y.B., 49 *E.* III, Hil., *pl.* 7 (pp. 3–5):

Prescription. This is the same case as above, 49 *Ass.*, *pl.* 8.

Y.B., 1 *H.* IV, Mich., *pl.* 5 (p. 4):

Fresh suit granted and goods returned in an appeal case in London.

Y.B., 1 *H.* IV, Mich., *pl.* 6 (p. 4):

Quo warranto brought by the King against the Abbot of B. to know by what right he claimed certain privileges. The opinion of Gascoigne, Hankeford, and Tyrwhitt that: "The King cannot grant to anyone the power to pardon a felon by any manner, because that is the King's prerogative and is not grantable over".

Y.B., 2 *H.* IV, Mich., *pl.* 51 (p. 12):

In a case of trespass in London it was held a custom in London to have a beadle (in company with the owner of the goods) enter and make search. [Cited in the City of London's case, 8 Coke, *Reports*.]

Y.B., 6 *H.* IV, Hil., *pl.* 37 (p. 9):

A *scire facias* case used by Coke to show that Shropshire is not part of the Marches of Wales. Coke, *Fourth Inst.*, f. 242.

Y.B., 7 *H.* IV, Trin., *pl.* 6 (p. 46):

Livery sued by an heir of age to obtain possession of lands in the King's hands.

The opinion of Markham: "In waging war against the King, if the one that wages the war is killed in battle, his lands are seizable; and finally, if a man, after committing treason, flees across the sea, his land will be seized".

Y.B., 8 *H.* IV., Mich., *pl.* 13 (pp. 12–14):

Case of Richard Chedder, M.P., against J. Savage for Savage's assault on Chedder during time of parliament. Savage was to appear before the court within three months after a proclamation was made in parliament [*Rot. Parl.*, 5 *H.* IV, no. 78] and a *capias* was issued returnable on a certain date.

Divers courts adjudged to have power. Gascoigne's opinion that ". . . the King has entrusted all his judicial power to divers courts, some in this place, some in another . . .". The case upholds the view that ordinance made in parliament is a judgment in law, to be upheld by judicial process. [Hatsell, *Precedents*, I, 15–16, 24–27.]

Y.B., 8 *H.* IV, Hil., *pl.* 1 (p. 17):

Abbot of St. Albans's case. Where the King grants a franchise for a jail and men are imprisoned there on suspicion, and not delivered, the King has cause to seize the franchise.

Y.B., 11 *H.* IV, Mich., *pl.* 4 (p. 2):

Fees of knights and burgesses in parliament; those from ancient boroughs pay tenths.

Y.B., 11 *H.* IV, Mich., *pl.* 27 (p. 31):

London trespass case confirming authority of the mayor in the governing of the city, etc.

Y.B., 13 *H.* IV, Mich., *pl.* 4 (pp. 1–2):

Corpus cum causa in a case of imprisonment for deceit (fraud).

Y.B., 13 *H.* IV, Mich., *pl.* 7 (pp. 2–4):

An assize case, basically about appropriate venue for trying certain issues. In the course of complex proceedings, William Thirning [judge] was asked to give his opinion for the benefit of the Chancery. He replied that he had already given it and would adhere to that opinion until corrected by parliament. Coke gives a translation of Thirning's opinion in his speech on 27 May.

Y.B., 13 *H.* IV, Mich., *pl.* 10 (pp. 4–5):

Where a liege of the King kills another liege man in Scotland, the wife of the deceased can bring suit in the court of the Constable and Marshal in England. Treatises, Stanford, *Lib.* 2, chap. 14, f. 65.

Y.B., 7 *H.* VI, Pasch., *pl.* 27 (pp. 31–33):

London's existence before the Domesday Book makes it an ancient demesne. A villein cannot be taken by a writ of *nativo habendo* if he has lived a year and a day within the City.

Y.B., 8 *H.* VI, Mich., *pl.* 21 (p. 9):

Concerning livery.

Y.B., 9 *H.* VI, Pasch., *pl.* 28 (p. 10):

What constitutes imprisonment and enables a plea of false imprisonment.

Y.B., 10 *H.* VI, Mich., *pl.* 22 (p. 7):

Leet. Newton's opinon: that the judgment will be of record because "what is judged in such a leet is a judgment of record, and the leet is the court of the King for the time . . .".

Y.B., 10 *H.* VI, Mich., *pl.* 48 (pp. 14–15):

Debt case. Custom in London to examine causes in an action pending before the sheriff of London.

Y.B., 19 *H.* VI, Pasch., *pl.* 1 (pp. 62–65):

Validity of a grant made by King and parliament. The opinion of Fray that the grant is good "because the parliament is the court of the King, and the highest court he has, and the law is the highest inheritance the King has . . .".

Y.B., 22 *H.* VI, Hil., *pl.* 34 (p. 46):

Trespass case wherein Newton gives his opinion on *supersedeas*. This opinion is printed 7 April, p. 340.

Y.B., 22 *H.* VI, Mich., *pl.* 49 (pp. 30–33):

Trespass case brought by a villein against one Robert, who took the villein by force.

Y.B., 31 *H.* VI, Mich., *pl.* 5 (p. 10). David Selby's case:

Concerning court records of acquittal and imprisonment.

Y.B., 33 *H.* VI, Mich., *pl.* 1 (pp. 28–29). Robert Poynings's case:

A writ of debt was brought against Poynings and the writ said he was committed *per duos de consilio regis, etc. pro diversis causis ipsum regem tangentibus.* . . . See 7 April p. 341 and n. 75.

Y.B., 35 *H.* VI, Mich., *pl.* 9 (p. 6):

Process of outlawry.

Y.B., 37 *H.* VI, Pasch., *pl.* 8 (pp. 19–21):

An opinion delivered by Sir John Prisot, that in time of war the appeal of a traitor cannot lie in common law but only before the Constable and Marshal by civil law.

Y.B., 38 *H.* VI, Trin., *pl.* 2 (pp. 33–38):

Case of a *quare impedit* by the King against the Abbess of Sion. Sir John Prisot, speaking for the court, gave the opinion that a parliamentary confirmation can make good a void grant.

Y.B., 39 *H.* VI, Hil., *pl.* 3 (pp. 38–40):

Concerning a *non obstante* clause in a *quare impedit.*

Y.B., 39 *H.* VI, Hil., *pl.* 16 (pp. 50–51):

Damages can be collected for words threatening imprisonment because "menace of imprisonment seems a corporal punishment as much as does menace of life and of member".

Y.B., 39 *H.* VI, Mich., *pl.* 24 (pp. 18–19):

Concerning inns. The opinion of Sir Walter Moyle, judge: that certain tradesmen, such as innkeepers, are liable to be sued in an action on the case if they refuse service to someone seeking it.

Y.B., 5 *E.* IV, Pasch., *pl.* 20 (p. 2):

A horse may be kept by a hostler until payment for lodging is made. This case makes reference to *Y.B.*, 39 *H.* VI, *pl.* 24, above.

Y.B., 8 *E.* IV, Mich., *pl.* 30 (pp. 18–19):

Trespass. Custom in Kent that all men of Kent, when they fish in the sea, are able to dig in the adjoining land, regardless of its ownership, and put in stakes on which to suspend their nets to dry, because this is for the public good.

Y.B., 9 *E.* IV, Pasch., *pl.* 1 (p. 1):

Debt. Apportionment of rent service, contract. See 24 March, n. 13.

Y.B., 9 *E.* IV, Trin., *pl.* 42 (p. 28):

Battery. It was held by the judges to be legal for the owner of goods to "put hands on" and prevent one from attempting to steal those goods, and to proceed to beat him further if he does not desist.

Y.B., 11 *E.* IV, Trin., *pl.* 8 and 11 (pp. 4–5 and 6–7):

Thomas (Bastard) Fauconberg's writ of false imprisonment because he was arrested in Kent on the suspicion that he committed felony in London.

Y.B., 13 *E.* IV, Pasch., *pl.* 5 (pp. 9–10):

A case debated in Star Chamber before the King's council concerning the transporting of a merchant's goods. The Chancellor's opinion that "this, i.e., *secundum legem naturae* [according to the law of nature] is called merchant law by all, that is, universal law, by everybody . . .".

Y.B., 16 *E.* IV, Pasch., *pl.* 7 (pp. 2–3):
Concerning the authority of the sheriff.

Y.B., 16 *E.* IV, Mich., *pl.* 3 (p. 8):
Supersedeas granted for discharge of persons, not beasts.

Y.B., 18 *E.* IV, Pasch., *pl.* 18 (pp. 3–4):
Trespass.

Y.B., 19 *E.* IV, Hil., *pl.* 12 (p. 9):
Supersedeas in a debt case.

Y.B., 21 *E.* IV, Mich., *pl.* 50 (p. 67):
Debt case in London. Catesby's opinion that: "The customs of London are broad, and confirmed by the parliament".

Y.B., 21 *E.* IV, Hil., *pl.* 10 (p. 16):
Replevin.

Y.B., 21 *E.* IV, Hil., *pl.* 12 (pp. 16–17):
Replevin.

Y.B., 21 *E.* IV, Pasch., *pl.* 24 (pp. 28–30):
Contract and debt. See 24 March, n. 14.

Y.B., 21 *E.* IV (p. 10):
De termino trinitatis nihil, quia non tenuit, propter guerram versus Scotiam. Trinity term not held because of war with Scotland.

Y.B., 22 *E.* IV, Hil., *pl.* 4 (p. 43):
Prescription that the mayor can imprison for three days a man who is convicted of felony is not good because he (the man) would be irreplevisable during those three days, which is against common right.

Y.B., 22 *E.* IV, Trin., *pl.* 47 (p. 20):
Prohibition to the ecclesiastical court, and where this lies.

Y.B., 2 *R.* III, Mich., *pl.* 22 (pp. 9–11):
A case of felony for erasure of court records, used to support the maxim that cases should be heard *non in camera regis sed in curia regis.* That is, not in the King's chamber but in the King's court, i.e., by the justices. The justices agreed they should assess fines "and not the lord King by himself in his chamber, nor otherwise before him except by his justices". And they added "and the King's will is presumed to be that the King's law and his justices are one and the same".

Y.B., 1 *H.* VII, Mich., *pl.* 5 (p. 4). Thomas Lovell's case:
Concerning procedure for the annulment of certain attainders passed by parliament. Sir William Hussey, Chief Justice, said "that Sir John Markham said to King Edward the Fourth that he [*E.* IV] was not able to arrest a man on suspicion of treason or felony, since his lieges could; because if he [*E.* IV] committed a tort the party was not able to have action [i.e., could not bring a suit against the King]".

Y.B., 4 *H.* VII, Pasch., *pl.* 2 (p. 6):
Debt case concerning rents due to the dean and chapter of St. Pauls.

Y.B., 4 *H.* VII, Mich., *pl.* 12 (p. 18):
A watchman may apprehend a nightwalker because it is for the public good.

Y.B., 6 *H.* VII, Trin., *pl.* 4 (pp. 4–5):
Concerning the King's right to grant court-leet jurisdiction over rape. What things can be inquired into and what not.

Y.B., 11 *H.* VII, Pasch., *pl.* 11 (p. 22):
The opinion of Sir William Hussey and Sir Guy Fairfax that an indictment in a leet for rape, defined by statute as felony, is void. This was not a unanimous opinion.

Y.B., 11 *H.* VII, Hil., *pl.* 6 (p. 13):
What things enfranchise a villein and what not.

Y.B., 14 *H.* VII, Pasch., *pl.* 4 (pp. 21–27):
Duties and powers of innkeepers defined in a complex case against the Bishop of Chester.

Y.B., 21 *H.* VII, Mich., *pl.* 50 (p. 39):
Concerning riots and assemblies, etc. A servant is justified, if there be no alternative, in killing a man to save the life of his master.

Y.B., 14 *H.* VIII, Hil., *pl.* 3 (p. 16):
The opinion of the majority of the court that a justice of the peace cannot make a valid warrant to arrest someone for felony unless it is someone indicted for the offense. But if a ministerial officer makes an arrest on the basis of a purported warrant from a J.P., the officer is not liable in false imprisonment. By dictum: persons suspected of felony but not indicted may be arrested, but only by those who themselves have grounds for suspicion, whether a J.P. or an ordinary subject.

Y.B., 26 *H.* VIII, Mich., *pl.* 7 (p. 8):
A king's grant of goods and/or things must be by deed, otherwise the grant is not good.

Rolls

Close Rolls

19 *E.* II, *m.* 15*d., Cal. Close Rolls, E.* III, 1323–1327, p. 539:
A petition in parliament that attachments not be made upon mere accusation without process of law. The King granted that those taken by such accusations shall have redress in Chancery and hereafter no man shall be taken contrary to the law of the land. See Selden's speech, 28 April, afternoon.

1 *E.* III, pt. 1, *m.* 21*d., Cal. Close Rolls*, E. III, 1327–1330, pp. 105–106. Thomas, Earl of Lancaster's case. See *Rot. Parl.*, 1 *E.* III, no. 1.

21 *E.* III, pt. 2, *m.* 41*d., Cal. Close Rolls*, E. III, 1346–1349, p. 356:

> Commission to Robert de Scarburgh for the collection of the subsidy in the East Riding, York. To R. de S. "to be attendant upon the collecting and levying of the subsidy of 40*s.* of all knights' fees in aid of making the King's eldest son a knight . . .".

46 *E.* III, *m.* 33*d., Cal. Close Rolls*, E. III, 1369–1374, p. 420:

> Appointment of Richard de Pembridge as King's lieutenant in Ireland. Coke, *Second Inst.*, f. 48.

Foreign Rolls

12   *E.* III, *m.* 6*d., rot. Alemanni. Treaty Rolls*, II, pp. 314–315, no. 886:

> Martial commission. See Selden's report, 25 April.

20 *E.* III, *m.* 15, *rot. Franciae*:

> Martial commission. See Selden's report, 25 April.

20 *E.* III, *m.* 23, *rot. Franciae*:

> Martial commission. See Selden's report, 25 April.

Parliament Rolls (*Rotuli Parliamentorum*)

20 *E.* I, no. 1 (*Rot. Parl.*, I, 70–77):

> Pleas between Humphrey de Bohun, Earl of Hereford and Essex, and Gilbert de Clare, Earl of Gloucester and Hertford.

21 *E.* I, *m.* 2 (*Rot. Parl.*, I, 95–96):

> Case of Stephan Rabaz, sheriff of Leicester and Warwickshire. Three charges were made against Rabaz for his releasing of three prisoners: William de Petlyng, Ralph de Cokehull, and William la Persone.
>
> The charge against Rabaz concerning Persone reads: "And similarly when William, son of Walter la Persone, was taken by the order of the Earl of Warwick, he was dismissed *per pleviam*, against the will and order of the lord King when the same lord King, by his letters under his privy seal, had ordered the same sheriff that he should not grant any favor to those taken by the Earl of Warwick, and in defiance of the aforesaid John Botetourte, who is present, and who was senior of the aforesaid judges and had the charges recorded.
>
> "The response: And as to the third [man committed], that is to say William, son of [Walter]

Persone, he [Rabaz] well knew that he [Persone] was taken by order of the aforesaid Earl of Warwick, and that he [Rabaz] dismissed him *per pleviam*. But he said that he did this at the request of certain [men] of the household and court of the lord King, etc., who had then particularly requested him by their letters. And moreover, the same sheriff, when asked by the King who requested him, and directed letters to him, and where the letters were, said Walter de Langeton requested him then by his letters.

"The judgment: And because the aforesaid justice [Botetourte] expressly recorded that himself and his colleagues, by a good and lawful inquisition of knights and other free men, made in their presence, found that the aforesaid William de Petlyng was released, *per pleviam*, a long time before the arrival of the same justices and by the aforesaid sheriff; and also as the aforesaid sheriff confirmed, the aforesaid Ralph de Cokehull was released *per pleviam* by the sheriff himself, and this he [Rabaz] said he was well able to do because he [Cokehull] was taken for a light transgression; whereas by record of the same justices it was found that he was taken for murder, which is contrary to what the aforesaid sheriff said. And similarly, which the sheriff acknowledged, he received letters of the lord King by which the King ordered him that no mercy should be shown to those taken by order of the aforesaid Earl, and the same sheriff, contrary to this order, released the aforesaid William, son of Walter, *per pleviam*, who was taken by order of the aforesaid Earl, as the same sheriff acknowledges. And so, as much for this transgression as for the aforesaid others, he stands in penalty of the statute. Judgment is that the aforesaid sheriff be committed to prison according to the form of the statute".

8 *E.* II, no. 37 (*Rot. Parl.*, I, 298):

> Petition to the King and Great Council from Isabelle, wife of Hugh Baldolf, concerning lands seized by the crown. Restitution was made.

1 *E.* III, no. 1 (*Rot. Parl.*, II, 3–5):

> The case of Thomas, Earl of Lancaster, tried for treason (15 *E.* II) and beheaded the same year. The case is printed in 1 *E.* III, pt. 1, *m.* 21*d., Cal. Close Rolls*, E. III, 1327–1330, pp. 105–106, and Howell, *S.T.*, I, pp. 39–48. Cf. also *S.R.*, 1 *E.* III, st. 1. The land settlement was reversed, 39 *E.* III, *Worcester Coram Rege, rot.* 49.

4 *E.* III, no. 1 (*Rot. Parl.*, II, 52–53):

> Articles of treason charged against Roger Mortimer, First Earl of March, executed in 1330. The case is printed in Howell, *S.T.*, I, 51–54. The judgment against him was later reversed, *Rot. Parl.*, 28 *E.* III, no. 11; *Worcester Coram Rege, rot.* 33.

4 *E*. III, no. 13 (*Rot. Parl.*, II, 55–56):
Petition to the King and parliament from Richard of Arundel [Richard Fitzalan, Third Earl of Arundel] concerning family lands, etc., lost when his father [Edmund Fitzalan, First Earl of Arundel] was executed by Queen Isabella and Mortimer. Restitution was made. See *Rot. Parl.*, 28 *E*. III, no. 13.

5 *E*. III, no. 3 (*Rot. Parl.*, II, 61):
Confirmation by King and parliament regarding armies to be sent into Ireland.

14 *E*. III, no. 18 (*Rot. Parl.*, II, 120):
Petition in parliament from merchants concerning wool.

14 *E*. III, no. 31 (*Rot. Parl.*, II, 122–125):
Petition to parliament, etc., concerning the case of Geoffrey and John Staunton. See Sir Edward Coke's speech, P. & D., 27 May.

18 *E*. III, no. 3 (*Rot. Parl.*, II, 149):
Grant by the King of a commission to raise hobblers and archers.

22 *E*. III, no. 4 (*Rot. Parl.*, II, 200–201):
The opening of parliament; concerning subsidy granted: ". . . And also that from henceforth no imposition, tallage, nor charge of tax, or other manner whatsoever, be taken by the Privy Council [of] our lord the King without their grant and assent in parliament . . .".

25 *E*. III, no. 16 (*Rot. Parl.*, II, 239):
Petition to the King from Commons "praying the Commons, that the taxes that were granted to our lord the King by divers persons of the commons, they are released; and that from henceforth no one be compelled to make such taxes against his will because this is against reason and the franchise of the land. And that restitution be made to such to whom such taxes were made".

Response: "It pleases our lord the King that it be so".

28 *E*. III, no. 11 (*Rot. Parl.*, II, 256):
Restoration of title and lands to the grandchild of Roger Mortimer, Earl of March. See *Rot. Parl.*, 4 *E*. III, no. 1.

28 *E*. III, no. 13 (*Rot. Parl.*, II, 256–257):
Petition to the King from Richard of Arundel concerning annulling the judgment against his father, Edmund. See *Rot. Parl.*, 4 *E*. III, no. 13.

36 E. III, no. 9 (*Rot. Parl.*, II, 269):
The petition to the King, with his response, is printed in Littleton's argument at the conference, 7 April, p. 336.

36 E. III, no. 20 (*Rot. Parl.*, II, 270). Ibid., see 7 April, p. 337.

36 *E*. III, no. 24 (*Rot. Parl.*, II, 271):

Petition from Commons to the King concerning the subjects' redress in Chancery.

Response: The King grants it.

37 *E*. III, no. 10 (*Rot. Parl.*, II, 276):
Confirmation of the charters.

38 *E*. III, no. 10 (*Rot. Parl.*, II, 285):
Petition to the King from Commons praying that the Grand Charter and other statutes be executed, etc.

40 *E*. III, no. 9 (*Rot. Parl.*, II, 290):
Petition to parliament from the two universities and four orders of mendicant friars concerning privileges and immunities in the universities of Oxford and Cambridge.

42 *E*. III, no. 2 (*Rot. Parl.*, II, 294):
The opening of parliament; thanks expressed by the King for victory over enemies.

42 *E*. III, no. 12 (*Rot. Parl.*, II, 295):
The petition to the King, with his response, is printed in Littleton's argument at the conference, 7 April, p. 337.

43 *E*. III, no. 19 (*Rot. Parl.*, II, 301):
Petition to the King from Commons concerning mortality in the counties.

Response: "Those [i.e., the names of those] who are grieved follow, and the King will give them grace accordingly as he sees to whom it shall be given".

45 *E*. III, no. 33 (*Rot. Parl.*, II, 307):
Petition from Commons seeking redress against Walter de Chirington for his false accusations concerning nonpayment of customs.

Response: "He who is grieved comes before the Council and shows his particular grievance, and right will be done".

46 *E*. III, no. 43 (*Rot. Parl.*, II, 314):
Petition to the King from parliament concerning court records.

47 *E*. III, no. 16 (*Rot. Parl.*, II, 318):
Petition to the King from Commons concerning ancient customs and franchises in cities, boroughs, villages, and the Cinque Ports.

Response: Show in particular what franchises were taken away, and right will be done.

50 *E*. III, nos. 17–19 (*Rot Parl.*, II, 323–324):
Case of Richard Lyons, merchant of London, accused by Commons of deceits and extortions in collecting customs and subsidies. Hatsell, *Precedents*, IV, 56–57.

50 *E*. III, no. 125 (*Rot. Parl.*, II, 342):
Declaration that no special grant for singular profit be made.

51 *E*. III, no. 19 (*Rot. Parl.*, II, 364):
Grant of a subsidy of 4*d*. on every person.

3 *R*. II, nos. 29 and 30 (*Rot. Parl.*, III, 81):
Petition to Commons from counties immediately adjoining Wales that they be not harassed by Welshmen.

4 *R*. II, nos. 10–13 (*Rot. Parl.*, III, 89–90):
Considerations between the Lords and Commons concerning the subsidy.

4 *R*. II, no. 15 (*Rot. Parl.*, III, 90):
The opening of parliament; grant of a subsidy requiring every person above fifteen years of age to pay three groats [1*s*.]. See 4 April, n. 20.

5 *R*. II, no. 11 (*Rot. Parl.*, III, 123):
Complaint to Commons by merchants suffering loss because of loans made to the King.

8 *R*. II, no. 2 (*Rot. Parl.*, III, 184):
The opening of parliament; thanks expressed by the King for victories over enemies.

9 *R*. II, no. 10 (*Rot. Parl.*, III, 204):
The opening of parliament; grant of subsidy. ". . . Item, that no other charge be put nor continued on the Commons, nor any one of them, except only this tax of *quinzieme et demi* they grant at present in this parliament . . .".

11 *R*. II, *m*. 7 (*Rot. Parl.*, III, 229–238):
Case and judgment against Alexander Neville, Archbishop of York, Robert Tresilian, Lord Chief Justice, and others brought by Thomas Woodstock, Duke of Gloucester, and other of the King's commissioners and heard by Justice Belknap *et al*. The case is printed in Howell, *S.T.*, I, 89–124.

13 *R*. II, no. 1 (*Rot. Parl.*, III, 257):
The opening of parliament; Lord Chancellor (William de Wykeham) requests subsidy for defense against France, Spain, Scotland, and Ireland.

17 *R*. II, no. 1 (*Rot. Parl.*, III, 309):
The opening of parliament; Lord Chancellor (Thomas Arundel) calls for peace within the realm and protection against enemies.

20 *R*. II, no. 23 (*Rot. Parl.*, III, 341):
A protestation by the prelates of the judgment rendered against Thomas Haxey, clerk, who was sentenced to death by parliament as a traitor. His sentence was annulled by the King following this protestation. See *Rot. Parl.*, 1 *H. IV*, nos. 90 and 104.

21 *R*. II, no. 10 (*Rot. Parl.*, III, 381–382):
Sir John Cobbam *et al*. accused and impeached in Commons for certain crimes and misdemeanors committed by him in prejudice to the King, etc. The case is printed in Howell, *S.T.*, I, 125–136; cf. also Hatsell, *Precedents*, IV, 65–66.

1 *H*. IV, nos. 1 and 7 (*Rot. Parl.*, III, 449 and 451):
Charges made in parliament against John Montacute, Third Earl of Salisbury. See *Rot. Parl.*, 2 *H*. V, no. 13.

1 *H*. IV, no. 90 (*Rot. Parl.*, III, 430):
Petition to the King and parliament from Thomas Haxey requesting that the judgment against him be annulled and that he be reinstated upon his lands, etc. The response indicates that the judgment was "reversed", "repealed", and "annulled", and that Haxey was restored to his lands, goods, offices, etc. See *Rot. Parl.*, 20 *R*. II, no. 23.

1 *H*. IV, no. 104 (*Rot. Parl.*, III, 434):
Confirmation of the restitution of Thomas Haxey by the King. See *Rot Parl.*, 20 *R*. II, no. 23.

1 *H*. IV, no. 144 (*Rot. Parl.*, III, 442):
Petition to the King from Commons requesting that any person accused or impeached by parliament have defense and response to the accusation, and trial by the law of the land.

Response: That all appeals of things done within the realm are to be tried and determined by the good laws. See *S.R.*, 1 *H*. IV, c. 10.

2 *H*. IV, no. 11 (*Rot. Parl.*, III, 456):
[Petition] to the King from Commons concerning his hearing of matters while they are being debated and before they come to resolution.

Response: ". . . that he wishes to hear no such person, nor to give him credence before such matters be shown to the King by advice and consent of all the Commons, according to the purpose of their said petition. Hatsell, *Precedents*, II, 355 n.

2 *H*. IV, no. 79 (*Rot. Parl.*, III, 473):
Petition to the King from Commons confirming the statute of 8 *R*. II, c. 5 (*S.R.*, II, 37) that pleas at common law shall not be discussed before the Marshal and Constable.

Response: The statutes must be kept.

2 *H*. IV, no. 99 (*Rot. Parl.*, III, 475):
Petition to the King from Commons confirming the statute 1 *H*. IV, c. 14 (*S.R.*, II, 116), concerning appeals of things done within and without of the realm.

Response: The statutes must be kept.

4 *H*. IV, no. 28 (*Rot. Parl.*, III, 493):
Subsidy grant.

5 *H*. IV, no. 24 (*Rot. Parl.*, III, 526–527):
Petition to the King from Commons touching the changing of some words in the commission of array.

5 *H*. IV, no. 25 (*Rot. Parl.*, III, 527):
The commission of array.

5 *H*. IV, no. 39 (*Rot. Parl.*, III, 530):

Concerning supplications to the King from Commons for Benet Wilman, who was imprisoned and brought before the Constable and Marshal against the statutes and common law of England.

5 *H*. IV, no. 71 (*Rot. Parl.*, III, 541):

Petition to the King from Commons concerning privilege. "Item, praying the Commons, that according to the custom of the realm the Lords, knights, citizens, and burgesses coming to your parliament at your command, staying there, and [later] returning to their own homes, and their men and servants with them in the said parliament, are under your special protection and defense and ought not for any debt, account, trespass, or other contract whatsoever, to be arrested or in any way imprisoned in the meantime . . .".

Response: "There is sufficient remedy in the case". Hatsell, *Precedents*, I, 13–14.

5 *H*. IV, no. 78 (*Rot. Parl.*, III, 542):

Petition to the King from Commons concerning privilege. This is the request for protection going to and returning from sessions that grew out of Richard Chedder's case (see *Y.B.*, 8 *H*. IV, Mich., *pl.* 13). Hatsell, *Precedents*, I, 15–16, 24–27.

7 and 8 *H*. IV, no. 2 (*Rot. Parl.*, III, 567):

The opening of parliament, speech by Thomas de Langley, Chancellor, where, "proceeding to the declaration of the summons of the parliament itself, he borrowed for his theme these words: *multorum consilia requiruntur in magnis*". (The counsels of many are required in great things.) Speaking on this theme, he said that ". . . for the ease and tranquillity of his lieges and inhabitants, the same who were much grieved by divers ways, and particularly by the rebels of Wales . . . our said lord the King wishes in [time of] such great need to have the advice and counsel of several and moreover, notable, persons of his realm . . .".

7 and 8 *H*. IV, no. 31 (*Rot. Parl.*, III, 572):

The opening of parliament; the Lords assign the King's Council.

7 and 8 *H*. IV, no. 32 (*Rot. Parl.*, III, 573):

The Commons's verbal request for the names of those assigned to the Council.

7 and 8 *H*. IV, nos. 1–15 (*Rot. Parl.*, III, 606–607):

Proceedings against Henry Percy and Thomas Bardolf who were convicted of treason.

9 *H*. IV, no. 36 (*Rot. Parl.*, III, 614):

Petition to the King from Commons advising that no special commissions or briefs should be granted concerning merchant aliens.

13 *H*. IV, no. 10 (*Rot. Parl.*, III, 648–649):

The opening of parliament; grant of a subsidy for defense.

13 *H*. IV, no. 43 [old no. 18] (*Rot. Parl.*, III, 664):

Petition to the King from Commons concerning subsidy (see *S.R.*, 25 *E*. I, *Statutum de Tallage*) and cloth (see *S.R.*, 27 *E*. III, st. 1, c. 4).

2 *H*. V, no. 13 (*Rot. Parl.*, IV, 35):

Petition to parliament from Thomas Montacute, son and heir of John Montacute, Third Earl of Salisbury, requesting that charges made against his father in the first parliament of *H*. IV (see *Rot. Parl.*, 1 *H*. IV, nos. 1 and 7) be annulled.

2 *H*. V, no. 22 (*Rot. Parl.*, IV, 22):

Petition to the King from Commons. ". . . Considering that the Commons of your land, the which that is and ever hath be[en] a member of your parliament, [and] been as well assenters and petitioners, that from this time forward, by complaint of the Commons of any mischief asking remedy by mouth of their Speaker for the Commons, or else by written petition: that there never be any law made thereupon and engrossed as statute and law, neither by additions, nor by diminutions, by no manner of term nor terms the which that should change the sentence, and the intent asked by the Speaker's mouth, or the petition before said, even in writing by the manner foresaid, without assent of the foresaid Commons . . .".

Response: "The King, by his special grace, granteth that from henceforth nothing be enacted to be petitions of his Commons that be contrary to their asking whereby they should be bound without their assent. Saving always to our liege lord his real prerogative to grant and deny what he list of their petitions and askings aforesaid".

2 *H*. VI, no. 9 (*Rot. Parl.*, IV, 198):

Articles presented to parliament by John Lord Talbot concerning the rebellious activities of James Butler, Earl of Ormond, in Ireland.

3 *H*. VI, no. 1 (*Rot. Parl.*, IV, 261):

The opening of parliament; speech by Henry Beaufort, Bishop of Winchester, in which he took for his theme: *Gloria et honor et pax omni operanti bonum*. Sir Edward Coke paraphrased this theme as: *Dum tempus habemus, operemur bonum*. (While we have time let us do some good.)

8 *H*. VI, no. 11 (*Rot. Parl.*, IV, 336):

The opening of parliament; grant of subsidy.

8 *H*. VI, no. 57 (*Rot. Parl.*, IV, 357–358):

Petition to the King from Commons concerning the arrest, while parliament was in session, of William

Larke, the servant of William Milrede who was an M.P. The petition requests the King ". . . to consider how the said William Larke, at the time of the said arrest, was in the service of the said William Milrede, supposing truly by the privilege of your court of parliament to be free from all arrest during your said court, except for treason, felony, or surety of the peace; to ordain by authority of your parliament itself that the said William Larke wil be able to be delivered outside of your said prison of the Fleet".

Response: "The King . . . wills and grants by authority of the said parliament that William Larke, named in the said petition, be delivered presently out of the Fleet prison. . . . And as for the rest of the petition, the King will advise". Hatsell, *Precedents*, I, 18–20; 36–38.

20 *H.* VI, no. 34 (*Rot. Parl.*, V, 61–62):
Petition to the King from Commons requesting relief from the oppressions of soldiers stationed in Suffolk, Dorest, Sussex, Kent, and other counties adjoining the seacoasts.

28 *H.* VI, nos. 14–52 (*Rot. Parl.*, V, 176–183):
Articles of treason and pronouncement of banishment against William de la Pole, Duke of Suffolk. The case is printed in Howell, *S.T.*, I, 271–276; cf. also, Hatsell, *Precedents*, IV, 66–69.

31 and 32 *H.* VI, nos. 26–29 (*Rot. Parl.*, V, 239–240):
Case of Thomas Thorpe, an M.P. who stole goods from the Duke of York. Requested by Commons to deliberate on the case, the justices determined that: ". . . if any person that is a member of this high court of parliament be arrested in such cases as be not for treason, or felony, or surety of the peace, or for a condemnation had before the parliament, it is used that all such persons should be released of such arrests and make an attorney so that they may have their freedom and liberty freely to attend upon the parliament". Hatsell, *Precedents*, I, 28–32.

38 *H.* VI, no. 7 (*Rot. Parl.*, V, 476):
Act of attainder passed against Richard, Duke of York, the Earls of Salisbury, Warwick, and others as "false traitors", and enemies against the King's person, majesty, crown, and advice. Hatsell, *Precedents*, IV, 86.

39 *H.* VI, no. 32 (*Rot. Parl.*, V, 382–383):
Martial commission to Richard, Duke of York, to suppress rebellions in Wales. See Selden's report, 7 May, afternoon.

1 *E.* IV, no. 17 (*Rot. Parl.*, V, 476):
An act passed to attaint several persons who had taken part in the civil wars between the Houses of York and Lancaster. Hatsell, *Precedents*, IV, 86.

1 *R.* III, no. 18 (*Rot. Parl.*, V, 261):
An act to free the subjects from benevolences. This is entered on the statute roll, 1 *R.* III, c. 2 (*S.R.*, II, 478).

1 *H.* VII [no num.] (*Rot. Parl.*, VI, 268–269):
Subsidy grant.

Patent Rolls

21 *H.* III, *m.* 4, *Cal. Pat. Rolls,* H. III, 1232–1247, p. 191:
Letters patent granting liberties and free customs to the men of Gascony.

27 *E.* I, *m.* 41, *Cal. Pat. Rolls,* E. I, 1292–1301, p. 387:
Appointment of Robert de Clifford as captain in the counties of Cumberland, Westmorland, Lancaster, Annandale, and the Marches. See Selden's report, 25 April.

18 *E.* II, pt. 1, *m.* 35d., *Cal. Pat. Rolls,* E. II, 1324–1327, pp. 65–66. 9 July 1324:
Commission of array to Richard Damori, Richard de Stapeldon, and Walter Stapeldon, Bp. of Exeter, to survey and array the King's passage ordered at Plymouth. See Selden's report, 25 April.

18 *E.* II, pt. 1, *m.* 35d., *Cal. Pat. Rolls,* E. II, 1324–1327, p. 65. 11 July 1324:
Commission of oyer and terminer to Richard Damori and Richard de Stapeldon, for Devon, Somerset, and Dorset. See 19 April, n. 15; and Selden's report, 25 April.

34 *E.* III, pt. 1, *m.* 11d., *Cal. Pat. Rolls,* E. III, 1358–1361, p. 419:
Commission of oyer and terminer to Henry de Motelowe, Richard de Birton, John Dabernoun, and Robert Weye, for Plymouth.

47 *E.* III, *m.* 24, *Cal. Pat. Rolls,* E. III, 1370–1374, p. 260:
Pardon to John Ullayk because he has promised to go beyond seas on the King's service.

4 *H.* IV, pt. 2, *m.* 10d., *Cal. Pat. Rolls,* H. IV, 1401–1405, p. 287:
Commission of array to Thomas Grene, for Northampton. See Seldon's report, 25 April. The commission was in accordance with *Rot. Parl.*, 5 *H.* IV, no. 25. See Selden's report, 7 May, afternoon.

6 *H.* IV, pt. 2, *m.* 15d., *Cal. Pat. Rolls,* H. IV, 1405–1408, p. 61:
Commission to Thomas de Berkeley to lead and govern men of the counties of Gloucester and Somerset against Welsh rebels. See Selden's report, 25 April.

6 *H.* IV, pt. 2, *m.* 15*d., Cal. Pat. Rolls,* H. IV, 1405–1408, p. 61:

Commission of array to Reginald de Cobham *et al.,* for Kent, for defense against the French. See Selden's report, 7 May, afternoon.

7 *H.* IV, pt. 2, *m.* 31*d., Cal. Pat. Rolls,* H. IV, 1405–1408, p. 231:

Commission of array to Michael de la Pole *et al.,* for Suffolk, for defense against the French. See Selden's report, 7 May, afternoon.

8 *H.* IV, pt. 1, *m.* 16*d., Cal. Pat. Rolls,* H. IV, 1405–1408, p. 306:

Commission of array to the Abbot of la Querre (Isle of Wight) *et al.,* for defense against the French. See Selden's report, 7 May, afternoon.

3 *H.* V, pt. 2, *m.* 36*d., Cal. Pat. Rolls.,* H. V, 1413–1416, p. 409:

Commission of array to John Louesham *et al.,* for Salisbury. See Selden's report, 7 May, afternoon.

6 *H.* V, *m.* 18*d., Cal. Pat. Rolls,* H. V, 1416–1422, p. 204:

Commission to Geoffrey Louther, [blank] Stratton, and John Hexham to supervise a muster. See Selden's report, 7 May, afternoon.

13 *H.* VI, *m.* 10*d., Cal. Pat. Rolls,* H. VI, 1429–1436, p. 474:

Commission of array to Humphrey Stafford *et al.,* for Dorest. See Selden's report, 7 May, afternoon.

14 *H.* VI, pt. 1, *m.* 20*d., Cal. Pat. Rolls,* H. VI, 1429–1436, p. 519:

Commissions of array for Kent, Devon, Cornwall, Somerset, and twenty-seven other areas. See Selden's report, 7 May, afternoon.

21 *H.* VI, pt. 2, *m.* 40*d., Cal. Pat. Rolls,* H. VI, 1441–1446, pp. 199–200:

Commission of array to Thomas Kyryell *et al.,* for Kent, etc. See Selden's report, 7 May, afternoon.

28 *H.* VI, pt. 2, *m.* 13*d., Cal. Pat. Rolls,* H. VI, 1446–1452, pp. 389–390:

Commission of array to John, Earl of Oxford, *et al.,* for Norfolk. See Selden's report, 7 May, afternoon.

29 *H.* VI, pt. 2, *m.* 6*d., Cal. Pat. Rolls,* H. VI, 1446–1452, p. 480:

Commission of array to John Colsill, Kt., John Nanfan, Esq., and John Petit for Cornwall. See Selden's report, 7 May, afternoon.

32 *H.* VI, *m.* 15*d., Cal. Pat. Rolls,* H. VI, 1452–1461, p. 171:

Commissions of array for York, Devon, and Cornwall. See Selden's report, 7 May, afternoon.

36 *H.* VI, pt. 1, *m.* 2*d., Cal. Pat. Rolls,* H. VI, 1452–1461, p. 411:

Commission of array to the abbot of the monastery of St. Augustine by Canterbury in Kent. See Selden's report, 7 May, afternoon.

37 *H.* VI, pt. 1, *m.* 6*d., Cal. Pat. Rolls,* H. VI, 1452–1461, pp. 494–495:

Commission of array for twelve areas. See Selden's report, 7 May, afternoon.

39 *H.* VI, *m.* 11*d., Cal. Pat. Rolls,* H. VI, 1452–1461, p. 656:

Commission of array to William Calthrop *et al.,* for Norfolk. See Selden's report, 7 May, afternoon.

49 *H.* VI, *m.* 12*d., Cal. Pat. Rolls,* E. IV, H. VI, 1467–1477, p. 251:

Commission of array to John Marquis of Montague, for Nottingham, Northumberland, Cumberland, and Westmorland. See Selden's report, 7 May, afternoon.

1 *E.* IV, pt. 1, *m.* 8*d., Cal. Pat. Rolls,* E. IV, 1461–1467, p. 36:

Commission of array to Walter Devereux, Kt., William Herbert, Kt., and James Baskervile, for Hereford, Gloucester, and Salop. See Selden's report, 7 May, afternoon.

1 *E.* IV, pt. 4, *m.* 18*d., Cal. Pat. Rolls,* E. IV, 1461–1467, p. 132:

Commission of array to Walter Devereux, Kt., and William Herbert, Kt., for South Wales and the Marches. See Selden's report, 7 May, afternoon.

3 *E.* IV, pt. 1, *m.* 6*d., Cal. Pat. Rolls,* E. IV, 1461–1467, p. 280:

Commission of array to John Neville, John Lescrop *et al.,* for Westmorland. See Selden's report, 7 May, afternoon.

8 *E.* IV, pt. 1, *m.* 12*d., Cal. Pat. Rolls,* E. IV, H. VI, 1467–1477, p. 103:

Commission of array to William Herbert, Kt., and Walter Devereux, Kt., for Gloucester, Hereford, and Salop. See Selden's report, 7 May, afternoon.

9 *E.* IV, pt. 1, *m.* 1*d., Cal. Pat. Rolls,* E. IV, H. VI, 1467–1477, p. 172:

Commission of array to Walter Devereux, Kt., for South Wales, Gloucester, Worcester, and Hereford. See Selden's report, 7 May, afternoon.

9 *E.* IV, pt. 2, *m.* 19*d., Cal. Pat. Rolls,* E. IV, H. VI, 1467–1477, pp. 195–196:

126

Commissions of array for twenty-eight counties. See Selden's report, 7 May, afternoon.

10 *E*. IV, *m*. 12*d*., *Cal. Pat. Rolls*, E. IV, H. VI, 1467–1477, p. 218:

Commission of array to George, Duke of Clarence, *et al*., for Warwick. See Selden's report, 7 May, afternoon.

11 *E*. IV, pt. 1, *m*. 25*d*., *Cal. Pat. Rolls*, E. IV, H. VI, 1467–1477, pp. 283–285:

Commission of array to John Cobham *et al*., for Kent. See Selden's report, 7 May, afternoon.

1 *E*. V, *m*. 3*d*., *Cal. Pat. Rolls*, E. IV, E. V, R. III, 1476–1485, p. 356:

Commission of array to Henry, Duke of Buckingham, for Salop, Hereford, Somerset, Dorest, and Wilts. See Noy's report, 7 May, afternoon.

1 *R*. III, pt. 1, *m*. 8, *Cal. Pat. Rolls*, E. IV, E. V, R. III, 1476–1485, p. 363:

Grant of the office of Constable, etc., to Henry, Duke of Buckingham, with power of array in Salop and Hereford. See Noy's report, 7 May, afternoon.

8 *H*. VII, pt. 1, *m*. 18 (3), *Cal. Pat. Rolls*, H. VII, 1485–1494, p. 411:

Commission to Robert Willughby, Kt., to be marshal of the army going into France. See Noy's report, 7 May, afternoon.

8 *H*. VII, pt. 2, *m*. 3 (19), *Cal. Pat. Rolls*, H. VII, 1485–1494, p. 419:

Commission to Roger Cotton, Kt., to be captain, etc., of an army going into Ireland, with power to hear complaints, punish delinquents, etc. See Noy's report, 7 May, afternoon.

12 *H*. VII, pt. 2, *m*. 24 (4), *Cal. Pat. Rolls*, H. VII, 1494–1509, p. 115:

Commission to John Dygby, Marshal, and Robert Clifford, Kt., to execute the office of Constable and Marshal with respect to rebels who levied war in Devon, Cornwall, and other parts. See 15 April, n. 10, and Noy's report, 7 May, afternoon.

12 *H*. VII, pt. 2, *m*. 24 (4), *Cal. Pat. Rolls*, H. VII, 1494–1509, p. 115:

Commission to John Dynham, Kt., Treasurer of England, *et al*., to execute the office of Constable and Marshal concerning James Audeley and his part in the rebellion in Cornwall and Devon. See Noy's report, 7 May, afternoon.

15 *H*. VII, pt. 2, *m*. 10 (19), *Cal. Pat. Rolls*, H. VII, 1494–1509, p. 202:

Appointment of Thomas Darcy, Kt., to execute

the office of Constable and Marshal with respect to the adherents of Michael Joseph and Peter [*sic*] Warbeck.

38 *H*. VIII, *m*. 15, *Letters and Papers H. VIII*, XXI, pt. 2, p. 233, no. 476, sect. 40:

Commission of oyer and terminer to Anthony St. Leger. See Noy's report, 7 May, afternoon.

1 *E*. VI, pt. 4, *m*. 33*d*., *Cal. Pat. Rolls*, E. VI, 1547–1548, p. 133:

Commission of oyer and terminer to Anthony St. Leger, for Ireland. See Noy's report, 7 May, afternoon.

4 *E*. VI, pt. 5, *m*. 6, *Cal. Pat. Rolls*, E. VI, 1549–1551, p. 294:

Appointment for life of Thomas Eynns as secretary of the court of the Council of York.

1 and 2 *P*. and *M*., pt. 3, *mbs*. 31–36, *Cal. Pat. Rolls*, P. and *M*., 1554–1555, pp. 55–59:

The Muscovy Co., patent for Greenland.

3 and 4 *P*. and *M*., pt. 12, *m*. 19*d*., *Cal. Pat. Rolls*, P. and *M*., 1555–1557, p. 554:

Commission of array to Henry, Earl of Sussex, for Norfolk, Suffolk, and the county of the City of Norwich. See Noy's report, 7 May, afternoon.

3 and 4 *P*. and *M*., pt. 12, *m*. 22*d*., *Cal. Pat. Rolls*, P. and *M*., 1555–1557, p. 556:

Appointment of William, Earl of Pembroke, as captain general of the army going to Calais. See Noy's report, 7 May, afternoon.

7 *Eliz*. I, pt. 5, *Cal. Pat. Rolls*, Elizabeth I, 1563–1566, p. 259:

Commission to Francis, Earl of Bedford, to be Principal Captain and Governor in the North. See Noy's report, 7 May, afternoon.

17 *Eliz*. I, pt. 1, MS. Cal. Pat. Rolls, f. 1:

License to Acerbo Velutelli for the importation of currants and oil for a term of ten years.

25 *Eliz*. I, pt. 2, MS. Cal. Pat. Rolls, f. 195:

License to Thomas Cordell for importation of currants, oil, wine, etc., for a term of six years.

30 *Eliz*. I, pt. 4, MS. Cal. Pat. Rolls, f. 344:

Commission to Francis Drake, Kt., and John Norris, Kt., to levy and govern soldiers. See Noy's report, 7 May, afternoon

35 *Eliz*. I, pt. 3, MS. Cal. Pat. Rolls, f. 253:

Special commission to George Clifford, Earl of Cumberland, to levy an army by sea and by land to destroy the preparations, etc., of the King of Spain. See Noy's report, 7 May, afternoon.

37 *Eliz*. I, pt. 17, MS. Cal. Pat. Rolls, f. 356:

Special commission to Thomas Wylford, Kt., to be Provost Marshal and to exercise martial law against rebels in London, Essex, Kent, and Surrey. See Noy's report, 7 May, afternoon.

43 *Eliz.* I, pt. 4, MS. Cal. Pat. Rolls, f. 328:
Commission to the Earl of Nottingham to govern the army in the South and to prevent tumults in London. (Cf. S.P. 13/272:35.) See Noy's report, 7 May, afternoon.

2 *Jac.* I, pt. 7, MS. Cal. Pat. Rolls, f. 117:
Special license granted to John Evelyn and others for the making of saltpeter and gunpowder.

2 *Jac.* I, pt. 13, MS. Cal. Pat. Rolls, f. 126:
William Gee and John Ferne created secretaries of the court of the Council of York.

7 *Jac.* I, pt. 11, MS. Cal. Pat. Rolls, f. 85, 31 May 1609:
Patent perpetuating the 1600 charter of the East India Co.

11 *Jac.* I, pt. 15, MS. Cal. Pat. Rolls, f. 226:
The Greenland Co. charter.

15 *Jac.* I, pt. 22, MS. Cal. Pat. Rolls, f. 161:
Patent to William Levitt for collection of toll on Willow Bridge, etc., Yorkshire.

18 *Jac.* I, pt. 18, MS. Cal. Pat. Rolls, f. 139:
Grant of a fee farm to Thomas Howard, Earl of Arundel, to collect 2s. 2d. set on currants, for a term of thirty-one years.

20 *Jac.* I, pt. 9, MS. Cal. Pat. Rolls, f. 49:
Patent to John Peck for the office of the Register of sales and pawns made to retailing brokers, during life.

20 *Jac.* I, pt. 15, MS. Cal. Pat. Rolls, f. 13v:
Grant to George Calvert, First Lord of Baltimore, of lands in Newfoundland.

21 *Jac.* I, pt. 15, MS. Cal. Pat. Rolls, f. 88:
Patent to Matthew de Questor to transport foreign letters.

2 *Car.* I, pt. 12, MS. Cal. Pat. Rolls, f. 75:
Commission to Sir John Savile for collection of revenues from lands in the West Riding, York.

2 *Car.* I, pt. 15, MS. Cal. Pat. Rolls, f. 109v:
Patent for making letters, processes, bills, and declarations granted to Sir Thomas Monson for life.

2 *Car.* I, pt. 19, MS. Cal. Pat. Rolls, f. 96v:
Patent for Royal Exchanger granted to Henry Rich, Earl of Holland, for a term of thirty-one years. The patent is printed in the P. & D., 23 June.

3 *Car.* I, pt. 21, MS. Cal. Pat. Rolls, f. 27v:
Grant to George Fielding and Robert Long of the office of receiver of the King's revenue arising by the forfeiture of popish recusants.

3 *Car.* I, pt. 34, MS. Cal. Pat. Rolls, f. 36:
Patent for Royal Exchanger for any species of foreign coin granted to Henry Rich, Earl of Holland, for a term of thirty-one years.

3 *Car.* I, pt. 21, MS. Cal. Pat. Rolls, f. 43, 15 November 1627:
Patent to Lawrence Lownes and Henry Norman for the office and place of collector of the impositions and customs set on French and Spanish wines in the port of London.

4 *Car.* I, pt. 39, MS. Cal. Pat. Rolls, f. 114:
Sir George Goring created Baron Goring of Hurstpierpoint, Sussex.

4 *Car.* I, pt. 40, MS. Cal. Pat. Rolls, f. 134v:
John Mohun created Baron Mohun of Okehampton.

4 *Car.* I, pt. 39, MS. Cal. Pat. Rolls, f. 119v:
Sir Edward Howard created Baron Howard of Escrick.

Rolls of Scotland (*Rotuli Scotiae*)

2 *E.* II, m. 12 (*Rot. Scot.*, I, 60):
Gilbert, Earl of Clare, appointed captain in an expedition against the Scots. See Selden's report, 25 April.

8 *E.* II, m. 6 (*Rot. Scot.*, I, 135):
Ralph, son of William, appointed warden of Newcastle Upon Tyne and Earl of Northumberland. See Selden's report, 25 April.

1 *E.* III, m. 4 (*Rot. Scot.*, I, 214):
Commission for arming and arraying men in the East and West Ridings of York and in the county of Lancaster for protection against the Scots. See Selden's report, 25 April.

1 *E.* III, m. 4 (*Rot. Scot.*, I, 215):
Henry, Earl of Lancaster, appointed captain in defense against the Scots. See 19 April, n. 16.

10 *E.* III, m. 28 (*Rot. Scot.*, I, 414–415):
Henry of Lancaster appointed captain and leader of the forces against the Scots. See Selden's report, 25 April.

11 *E.* III, m. 10 (*Rot. Scot.*, I, 503):
Earl of Arundel (Richard Arundel) and Earl of Salisbury (William de Montacute) appointed captains and leaders in the English army in Scotland, with full powers. See 19 April, n. 17.

18 *E.* III, m. 8 (*Rot. Scot.*, I, 651):
Commission to John Darcy and Thomas Ughtred for leading the army in northern England.

9 *R.* II, m. 1 (*Rot. Scot.*, II, 81):
Appointment of Roger Clifford, Ralph, Baron of Greystoke, Ralph Neville, and Thomas Clifford

as Keepers of the Marches of England, with full powers. See Selden's report, 25 April.

Statutes (*England*)

17 *J.* I, Magna Carta.

1 *H.* III, Magna Carta.

9 *H.* III, Magna Carta†

c. 1. "First, we have granted to God, and by this our present charter have confirmed, for us and our heirs forever, that the Church of England shall be free, and shall have all her whole rights and liberties inviolable . . .".

c. 26. "Nothing from henceforth shall be given for a writ of inquisition, nor taken of him that prayeth inquisition of life, or of member, but it shall be granted freely and not denied".

c. 29. "*Nullus liber homo capiatur vel imprisonetur aut disseisiatur de libero tenemento suo vel libertatibus vel liberis consuetudinibus suis aut utlagetur aut exulet aut aliquo modo destruatur nec super eum ibimus (nec super eum in carcerem mittimus)*[1] *nisi per legale judicium parium suorum vel per legem terre. Nulli vendemus nulli negabimus aut differemus rectum vel justiciam.* [No freeman shall be taken, or imprisoned, or be disseised of his freehold, or liberties, or free customs, or be outlawed, or exiled, or any otherwise destroyed, nor will we not pass upon him (nor do we commit him to prison) but by lawful judgment of his peers, or by the law of the land. We will sell to no man, we will not deny or defer to any man either justice or right]". *Statutes at Large*, I, 1–10.

20 *H.* III, *Provisiones de Merton*†

c. 9. "To the King's writ of bastardy, whether one being born before matrimony may inherit in like manner as he that is born after matrimony, all the bishops answered that they would not, nor could not, answer to it because it was directly against the common order of the Church . . .". ". . . And all the earls and barons with one voice answered that they would not change the laws of the realm, which hitherto have been used and approved".

21 *H.* III, *Carta Confirmationis.*

37 *H.* III, *Sententia Excommunicationis Lata in Transgressores Cartarum.*

Sentence of excommunication against transgressors of the charters.

51 and 52 *H.* III, *Dictum de Kenilworth*†

c. 40. "Such as be imprisoned . . . finding sufficient and reasonable surety, shall be delivered by pledges or by other assurance . . . according to the provision of the Lord Legate and the King".

52 *H.* III, *Statutum de Marl.*†

c. 23. "It is provided also, that if bailiffs, which

ought to make account to their lords, do withdraw themselves . . . then they shall be attached by their bodies . . .".

c. 24. Inquests.

3 *E.* I, *Statutum Westminster Primer*†

c. 1. For the maintaining of the peace of the Church and the realm.

c. 9. ". . . And if the sheriff, coroner, or any other baliff, within such franchise or without, for reward or for prayer, or for fear, or for any manner of affinity, conceal, consent, or procure to conceal the felonies done in their liberties, or otherwise will not attach nor arrest such felons there, as they may, or otherwise will not do their office for favor borne to such misdoers, and be attainted thereof, they shall have one year's imprisonment, and after make a grievous fine at the King's pleasure, if they have wherewith, and if they have not whereof, they shall have imprisonment of three years".

c. 15. "And for as much as sheriffs, and other, which have taken and kept in prison persons detected of felony, and incontinent have let out by replevin such as were not replevisable, and have kept in prison such as were replevisable, because they would gain of the one party, and grieve the other: and for as much as before this time it was not determined which persons were replevisable, and which not, but only those that were taken for the death of man, or by commandment of the King, or of his justices, or for the forest; it is provided, and by the King commanded, that such prisoners as before were outlawed, and they which have abjured the realm, provors, and such as be taken with the manour [see 7 April, nn. 55 and 56], and those which have broken the King's prison, thieves openly defamed and known, and such as be appealed by provors, so long as the provors be living, if they be not of good name, and such as be taken for house-burning feloniously done, or for false money, or for counterfeiting the King's seal, or persons excommunicate, taken at the request of the bishop, or for manifest offenses, or for treason touching the King himself, shall be in no wise replevisable by the common writ, nor without writ: but such as be indicted of larceny, by inquests taken before sheriffs or bailiffs by their office, or of light supsicion, or for petty larceny that amounteth not above the value of twelve-pence. If they were not guilty of some other larceny aforetime, or guilty of receipt of felons, or of commandment, or force, or of aid in felony done; or guilty of some other trespass, for which one ought not to lose life nor member, and a man appealed by a provor after the death

[1]See 27 March, n. 51.

of the provor, if he be no common thief, nor defamed, shall from henceforth be let out by sufficient surety, whereof the sheriff will be answerable, and that without giving aught of their goods. And if the sheriff, or any other, let any go at large by surety, that is not replevisable, if he be sheriff or constable or any other bailiff of fee, which hath keeping of prisons, and thereof be attainted, he shall lose his fee and office forever. And if the undersheriff, constable, or bailiff of such as have fee for keeping of prisons, do it contrary to the will of his lord, or any other bailiff being not of fee, they shall have three years' imprisonment, and make fine at the King's pleasure. And if any withhold prisoners replevisable, after that they have offered sufficient surety, he shall pay a grievous amercement to the King; and if he take any reward for the deliverance of such, he shall pay double to the prisoner, and also shall be in the great mercy of the King".

c. 20. "It is provided also for trespassers in parks and ponds, that if any be thereof attainted . . . [he] shall have three years' imprisonment, and after shall make fine at the King's pleasure. . .".

c. 26. In cases of extortion by the King's officers punishment is to be at the King's pleasure.

c. 29. Deceits by pleaders are punishable at the King's pleasure.

c. 51. Times of taking certain assizes.

4 *E*. I, *Statutum Rageman*.

" . . . And moreover let the justices have regard to the time of war, and to the covenants made in such time, so that by occasion thereof no man shall be troubled for the aforesaid covenants".

6 *E*. I, *Statuta Gloucestre*†

c. 9. " . . . that no writ shall be granted out of the Chancery for the death of a man to inquire whether a man did kill another by misfortune or in his own defense . . . but he shall be put in prison until the coming of the justices in eyre, or justices assigned to the jail delivery . . .".

12 *E*. I, *Statuta Wallie*†

Wales. This act annexes Wales to the crown of England.

13 *E*. I, *Statutum Westminster Secundo*†

c. 1. " . . . Wherefore our lord the King, perceiving how necessary and expedient it should be to provide remedy in the aforesaid cases, hath ordained that the will of the giver, according to the form in the deed of gift . . . shall be from henceforth observed . . .".

c. 29. " . . . But lest the parties appealed or indicted be kept long in prison, they shall have a writ of *odio et atia*, like as it is declared in Magna Carta and other statutes".

13 *E*. I, *Statutum Circumspecte Agatis*†

Concerning spiritual matters. See 1 May, n.50.

23 *E*. I, *Statutum de Frangentibus Prisonam*† Frequently cited as 1 *E*. II.

"Concerning prisoners which break prison, our lord the King willeth and commandeth, that none from henceforth that breaketh prison shall have judgment of life or member for breaking of prison only; except the cause for which he was taken and imprisoned did require such judgment, if he had been convict thereupon according to the law and custom of the realm, albeit in times past it hath been used otherwise".

25 *E*. I, *Confirmatio Cartarum*†

c. 2. "And we will, that if any judgment be given from henceforth contrary to the points of the charters aforesaid by the justices, or by any other our ministers that hold plea before them against the points of the charters, it shall be undone and holden for nought".

c. 6. "Moreover we have granted for us and our heirs . . . and to all the commonality of the land, that for no business from henceforth we shall take such manner of aids, tasks, nor prizes but by the common assent of the realm, and for the common profit thereof, saving the ancient aids and prizes due and accustomed".

25 *E*. I, *Statutum de Tallagio non Concedendo*† Frequently cited as 34 *E*. I, see *S. R.*, I, 125n.

c. 1. "No tallage or aid shall be taken or levied by us or our heirs in our realm, without the goodwill and assent of Archbishops, bishops, earls, barons, knights, burgesses, and other free men of the land".

c. 2. "No officer of ours, or of our heirs, shall take corn, leather, cattle, or any other goods of any manner of person without the goodwill and assent of the party to whom the goods belonged".

c. 6. "And for the more assurance of this thing we will and grant that all Archbishops and bishops forever shall read this present charter in their cathedral churches twice in the year, and upon the reading thereof in every of their parish churches shall openly denounce accursed all those that willingly do procure to be done anything contrary to the tenor, force, and effect of this present charter in any point and article . . .".

25 *E*. I, *Sententia lata Super Confirmatione Cartarum*. The sentence of the clergy given on the confirmation of the charters.

27 *E*. I, *Statutum de Finibus*.

c. 3. " . . . We . . . have provided and ordained

that justices assigned to take assizes in every county where they do take assizes, as they be appointed, incontinent after the assizes taken in the shires shall remain both together if they be lay; and if one of them be a clerk then one of the most discreet knights of the shire, being associate to him, that is a layman, by our writ shall deliver the jails of the shires. . . . And the same justices shall inquire then if sheriffs or any other have let out by replevin prisoners not replevisable or have offended in anything contrary to the form of the foresaid statute lately made at Westminster [3 *E.* I, *Stat. Westm. Prim.,* c. 15]; and whom they shall find guilty they shall chasten and punish in all things according to the form of the statue aforesaid".

28 *E.* I, *Articuli Super Cartas*†

c. 1. Confirmation of the Great Charter and the Charter of the Forest. ". . . And for these two charters to be firmly observed in every point and article . . . there shall be chosen in every shire . . . three substantial men . . . to hear and determine . . . such plaints as shall be made upon all those that commit or offend against any point contained in the foresaid charters. . .".

c. 2. "For as much as there is a great grievance in this realm, and damage without measure for that the King and the ministers of his house do make great prizes . . . and take the goods . . . of lay people without paying . . . . It is ordained that from henceforth none do take any such prizes within the realm, but only the King's takers and the purveyors for his house; and that the King's takers and purveyors of his house shall take nothing but only for his house. . . . Nevertheless the King and his Council do not intend, by reason of this estatute, to diminish the King's right, for the ancient prizes due and accustomed, as of wines and others goods, but that his right shall be saved unto him whole in all points".

c. 8. Election of sheriffs.

c. 12. Distresses for the King's debt.

c. 19. Return of issues where land is seised by the King without cause.

c. 20. "It is ordained that no goldsmith of England . . . make, or cause to be made, any manner of vessel, jewel, or any other thing of gold or silver except it be of good and true alloy. . . . And notwithstanding all these things before mentioned . . . both the King and his Council . . . will and intend that the right and prerogative of his crown shall be saved to him in all things".

34 *E.* I. See 25 *E.* I, *Statutum de Tallag.*

1 *E.* II. See 23 *E.* I, *Statutum de Frang. Pris.*

5 *E.* II, *Les Noveles Ordenances.*

c. 10. All prizes except those anciently due and accustomed shall cease. (This roll was called the *Rot. Ordinationum.*)

c. 11. Abolishing new customs and evil tolls.

7 *E.* II, *Statutum super Aportam' to Armor.*

A statute forbidding bearing of armour.

1 *E.* III, st. 1.

c. 8. Proceedings against offenders in forests, etc.

1 *E.* III, st. 2.

c. 5. ". . . that no man be compelled to go out of his shire but where necessity requireth, and sudden coming of strange enemies into the realm . . .". See *S.R.,* 4 *H.* IV, c. 13.

c. 7. Charges in the conveyance of soldiers.

2 *E.* III, *Statutum Northampton.*

c. 2. ". . . Wherefore it is enacted . . . that the assizes, attaints, and certifications be taken before the justices commonly assigned . . . and that the oyers and terminers shall not be granted but before justices of the one bench or the other, or the justices errants, and that for great hurt or horrible trespasses, and of the King's special grace, after the form of the statute thereof ordained in time of the said grandfather [27 *E.* I, c. 3], and none otherwise".

c. 10. Pardon of fines for writs in Chancery.

5 *E.* III.

c. 8. Of the custody of prisoners by the marshals of the King's Bench, etc.

c. 9. This chapter is printed in Littleton's speech at the conference, 7 April, p. 336.

14 *E.* III, st. 1.

c. 21. A subsidy granted to the King on wool, etc.

14 *E.* III, st. 2.

c. 1. ". . . We, willing to provide for the indemnity of the said prelates, earls, barons, and other of the commonality . . . will and grant for us and our heirs . . . that the same grant which is so chargeable shall not another time be had in example, nor fall to their prejudice in time to come; nor that they be from henceforth charged nor grieved to make any aid, or to sustain charge, if it be not by the common assent of the prelates, earls, barons, and other great men and Commons of our said realm of England, and that in the parliament; and that all the profits rising of the said aid . . . shall be put and spent upon the maintenance and the safeguard of our said realm of England, and of our wars in Scotland, France, and Gascoigne, and in no places elsewhere during the said wars".

c. 2. Safe conduct for alien merchants, etc.

15 *E.* III, st. 1.

c. 1. Confirmation of the charters.

18 *E.* III, st. 2.

c. 1. ". . . And the said Commons do grant to him, for the same cause upon a certain form . . . so that the money levied of the same, be dispended in the business showed to them in this parliament by the advice of the great men thereto assigned, and that the aids beyond Trent be put in defense of the North.

". . . that the commissions of the new enquiries shall cease and be wholly annulled, and that writs be thereupon made of the justices to surcease; saving the indictments of felonies and trespasses done against the peace . . .".

c. 7. Pay of soldiers, etc.

25 *E.* III, st. 2.

". . . It was ordained by our lord the King, and by assent of the prelates, earls, barons, and other of his Council . . .".

25 E. III, st. 5.

c. 4. This chapter is printed in Littleton's speech at the conference, 7 April, p. 336.

c. 8. "Item, it is accorded and assented that no man shall be constrained to find men of arms, hobblers, nor archers other than those which hold by such services, if it be not by common assent and grant made in parliament".

c. 13. Gold and silver coin.

c. 17. ". . . that such process shall be made in a writ of debt . . . by writ of *capias*, and by process of exigent [a writ commanding the sheriff to summon the defendant to appear upon pain of outlawry]".

27 *E.* III, st. 1.

c. 4. Subsidy granted to the King from cloth.

28 E. III.

c. 3. This chapter is printed in Littleton's speech at the conference, 7 April, p. 336.

c. 9. ". . . It is accorded and established, for to eschew all such evils and mischiefs, that all such commissions and writs before this time made, shall be utterly repealed, and that from henceforth no such commissions nor writs shall be granted". See Treatises, Stanford, *Lib.* 2, chap. 18, f. 77v, G.

34 *E.* III.

c. 1. "First, that in every county of England shall be assigned for the keeping of the peace one lord, and with him three or four of the most worthy in the county . . . and they shall have power to restrain the offenders . . . and to cause them to be imprisoned and duly punished according to the law and customs of the realm . . . and also inquire of all those that have been pillors and robbers in the parts beyond the sea . . . and to take and arrest all those that they may find by indictment, or by suspicion, and to put them in prison . . . that the

people be not by such rioters or rebels troubled nor endamaged, nor merchants nor other passing by the highways of the realm disturbed. . . . And the King will that all general inquiries before this time granted within any seigniories, for the mischiefs and oppressions which have been done to the people by such inquiries, shall cease utterly and be repealed: and that fines, which are to be made before justices for a trespass done by any person, be reasonable and just . . .".

c. 12. Seizure of lands on surmise of treason in dead persons.

36 *E.* III, st. 1.

c. 1. Confirmation of the Great Charters.

c. 9. Remedy in Chancery for breaches of statutes.

c. 10. "Item, for maintenance of the said articles and statutes, and redress of divers mischiefs and grievances which daily happen, a parliament shall be holden every year, as another time [4 *E.* III, c. 14] was ordained by statute".

36 *E.* III, st. 2.

c. 1. ". . . that the Great Charter and the Charter of the Forest, and all other statutes before this time made, be firmly kept and holden in all points of all things which be to fall, or which shall happen hereafter, as well for the King's profit, as for the quietness of his people".

37 E. III.

c. 18. This chapter is printed in Littleton's speech at the conference, 7 April, p. 337.

38 *E.* III, st. 1.

c. 9. Amends 37 *E.* III, c. 18.

42 E. III.

c. 1. Confirmation of the charters. ". . . that the Great Charter and the Charter of the Forest be holden and kept in all points; and if any statute be made to the contrary that shall be holden for none".

c. 3. This chapter is printed in Littleton's speech at the conference, 7 April, p. 337.

1 *R.* II.

c. 12. ". . . that from henceforth no Warden of the Fleet shall suffer any prisoner, there being by judgment at the suit of the party, to go out of prison by mainprize, bail, nor by baston . . . unless it be by writ or other commandment of the King . . .".

5 *R.* II, st. 1.

c. 10. Payment for military service, etc.

7 *R.* II.

c. 2. Confirmation of charters and statutes.

9 *R.* II.

c. 1. Confirmation of statutes.

12 *R.* II.

c. 1. Confirmation of liberties.

13 *R*. II, st. 1.

  c. 2. ". . . To the Constable it pertaineth to have
  cognizance of contracts touching deeds of arms and
  of war out of the realm, and also of things that
  touch war within the realm which cannot be determined nor discussed by the common law, with other
  usages and customs to the same matters pertaining,
  which other Constables heretofore have duly and
  reasonably used in their time. . . . And if any will
  complain, that any plea be commenced before the
  Constable and Marshal, that might be tried by the
  common law of the land, the same plaintiff shall
  have a privy seal of the King without difficulty,
  directed to the said Constable and Marshal to surcease in that plea until it be discussed by the King's
  Council, if that matter ought of right to pertain to
  that court, or otherwise to be tried by the common
  law of the realm of England, and also that they
  surcease in the meantime".

15 *R*. II.

  c. 1. Confirmation of the statutes.

16 *R*. II.

  c. 2. Confirms 15 *R*. II, c. 12, on private courts.

  c. 5. Praemunire, etc.

21 *R*. II.

  c. 2. Commission of the Duke of Gloucester and the
  Earl of Arundel. Repeals 10 *R*. II, treasons, etc.

1 *H*. IV.

  c. 1. Confirmation of liberties, charters, and statutes; annuls parliament of 21 *R*. II.

  c. 10. ". . . It is accorded and assented by the
  King, the Lords, and Commons aforesaid, that in
  no time to come any treason be judged otherwise
  than it was ordained by the statute in the time of
  his noble grandfather, King Edward the Third
  [25 *E*. III, st. 5, c. 2] . . .".

  c. 14. ". . . It is ordained and established from
  henceforth, that all the appeals to be made of things
  done within the realm, shall be tried and determined by the good laws of the realm . . . and that
  all the appeals to be made of things done out of the
  realm shall be tried and determined before the Constable and Marshal of England for the time being.
  And moreover it is accorded and assented, that no
  appeals be from henceforth made or any wise pur-
  sued in parliament in any time to come".

2 *H*. IV.

  c. 1. Confirmation of liberties, etc.

4 *H*. IV.

  c. 13. Military service. Confirms 1 *E*. III, st. 2, c. 5.

5 *H*. IV.

  c. 6. Assaulting servants of knights of parliament.
  Passed as a result of Richard Chedder's case, see
  Y.B., 8 *H*. IV, Mich., *pl.* 13.

7 *H*. IV.

  c. 15. The manner of election of knights of the shire
  for parliament. ". . . the names of the persons so
  chosen . . . shall be written in an indenture under
  the seals of all them that did choose them, and
  tacked to the same writ of the parliament . . .".

9 *H*. IV.

  c. 1. "First, that Holy Church have all her liberties
  and franchises; and that all the Lords spiritual and
  temporal, and other the King's liege people, having
  liberties and franchises, and all cities and boroughs
  of the realm, have and enjoy their liberties and
  franchises . . . except the franchise now late
  granted to the scholars of the University of
  Oxford . . .".

11 *H*. IV.

  c. 6. Measure of cloth, etc. ". . . that no persons
  making such manner of cloths . . . tack and plait
  together such manner of cloths before that the
  alnager hath duly made his search . . .".

13 *H*. IV.

  c. 7. Criminal law (riot).

1 *H*. V.

  c. 1. "First, that the statutes of the election of the
  knights of the shires to come to the parliament, be
  holden and kept in all points; adjoining to the same,
  that the knights of the shires which from henceforth shall be chosen in every shire be not chosen
  unless they be resident within the shire where they
  shall be chosen, the day of the date of the writ of the
  summons of the parliament; and that the knights
  and esquires, and others which shall be choosers of
  those knights of the shires, be also resident within
  the same shires, in manner and form as is aforesaid.
  And moreover it is ordained and established, that
  the citizens and burgesses of the cities and boroughs
  be chosen men, citizens, and burgesses resident,
  dwelling and free in the same cities and boroughs,
  and no other in anywise".

4 *H*. V.

  c. 1. Confirmation of liberties, etc. " . . . and all
  the cities and boroughs of the realm, have and
  enjoy all their liberties and franchises . . . except
  always those franchises and liberties . . . that be
  repealed by the common law".

9 *H*. V, st. 2.

  c. 6. Alloy and weight of money.

2 *H*. VI.

  c. 1. Confirmation of liberties.

8 *H*. VI.

  c. 7. ". . . Our lord the King . . . hath provided,
  ordained, and established by authority of this present parliament, that the knights of the shires to be
  chosen within the same realm of England to come
  to the parliaments of our lord the King hereafter to
  be holden, shall be chosen in every county of the

realm of England, by people dwelling and resident in the same counties, whereof every one of them shall have free land or tenement to the value of forty shillings by the year at the least above all charges; and that they which shall be so chosen shall be dwelling and resident within the same counties; and such as have the greatest number of them that may expend forty shillings by year and above, as afore is said, shall be returned by the sheriffs of every county, knights for the parliament, by indentures sealed betwixt the said sheriffs and the said choosers so to be made . . .".

11 *H*. VI.

c. 11. Assaults on Lords or Commoners, etc. Enforces the provisions of 5 *H*. IV, c. 6. Hatsell, *Precedents*, I, 26–27.

18 *H*. VI.

c. 19. ". . . that every man so mustering and receiving the King's wages, which departeth from his captain within his term, in any manner aforesaid, except that [of] notorious sickness or impediment by the visitation of God, which may reasonably be known, suffer him not to go, and which he shall certify presently to his captain and shall repay his money, so that he may provide him for another soldier in his place, he shall be punished as a felon; and that the justices of peace shall have power to inquire thereof, and to hear and determine the same . . .".

20 *H*. VI.

c. 9. ". . . that such ladies [duchesses, countesses, or baronesses] so indicted, or hereafter to be indicted, of any treason or felony by them done, or hereafter to be done, whether they be married or sole, that they thereof shall be brought to answer and . . . judged before such judges and peers of the realm . . .".

23 *H*. VI.

c. 4. Welshmen indicted or outlawed, etc.

31 *H*. VI.

c. 3. Attachments by the wardens of the Marches of Scotland unduly extended into Yorkshire.

8 *E*. IV.

c. 2. Liveries, etc.

1 *R*. III.

c. 2. An act to free the subjects from benevolences. ". . . Therefore the King will[s] it be ordained by the . . . Lords spiritual and temporal and the Commons of this present parliament assembled . . . that his subjects . . . from henceforth in no wise be charged by none such charge, exaction, or imposition called benevolence, nor by such like charge".

1 *H*. VII.

c. 6. Pardons.

4 *H*. VII.

c. 4. An act that all persons serving the King beyond the sea in Brittany may have their protection of prefecture and moratur.

c. 12. An act for Justices of the Peace for the due execution of their commissions.

c. 24. Fines. [Coke, *First Inst.*, sect. 441]

7 *H*. VII.

c. 1. An act against captains for not paying their soldiers their wages, and against soldiers going from their captains without license.

11 *H*. VII.

c. 1. An act that no person going with the King to the wars shall be attaint of treason. ". . . that from henceforth no manner of person nor persons whatsoever he or they be, that attend upon the King and sovereign lord of this land for the time being in his person and do him true and faithful service of allegiance in the same, or be in other places by his commandment, in his wars within this land or without, that for the same deed and true service of allegiance he or they be in no wise convict or attaint of high treason . . .".

c. 10. Benevolences.

c. 16 Calais.

c. 18. An act that the Master of the Rolls and other officers of the Chancery shall not go to the wars. "Whereas every subject . . . is bound to serve and assist his prince and sovereign lord at all seasons when need shall require . . .". Enlarged by 19 *H*. VII, c. 1, sect. 2, Proviso for their wages during such attendance.

3 *H*. VIII.

c. 5. An act against such captains as abridge their soldiers of their pay.

4 *H*. VIII.

c. 3. Juries in London.

c. 19. Subsidy.

6 *H*. VIII.

c. 16. An act concerning burgesses of the parliament. ". . . that from henceforth none of the said knights, citizens, burgesses, and barons, nor any of them that hereafter shall be elected to come or be in any parliament do not depart from the same parliament, nor absent himself from the same till the same parliament be fully finished, ended, or prorogued, except he or they so departing have license of the Speaker and Commons in the same parliament assembled, and the same license be entered of record in the book of the clerk of the parliament appointed or to be appointed for the common house . . .".

14 and 15 *H*. VIII.

c. 16. Subsidy.

21 *H*. VIII.

c. 13. An act that no spiritual persons shall take to farm of the King or any other person any lands or tenements for time of life. . . . And for plurality of benefices; and for residence.

25 *H*. VIII.

c. 14. An act for punishment of heresy. ". . . for as much as it standeth not with the right order of justice nor good equity that any person should be convicte[d] and put to the loss of his life, good name, or goods unless it were by due accusation and witness, or by presentment, verdict, confession, or process of outlawry . . .".

27 *H*. VIII.

c. 26. An act for laws and justice to be administered in Wales in like form as it is in this realm.

31 *H*. VIII.

c. 8. An act that proclamations made by the King shall be obeyed. Repealed 1 *E*. VI, c. 12, sect. 4.

32 *H*. VIII.

c. 50. Subsidy.

34 and 35 *H*. VIII.

c. 26. An act for certain ordinances in the King's Majesty's dominion and principality of Wales. [Coke, *Fourth Inst.*, ff. 242–244.]

c. 27. Temporal subsidy.

35 *H*. VIII.

c. 3. The bill for the King's style. Repealed 1 and 2 *P*. and *M*., c. 8, sect. 4.

1 *E*. VI.

c. 12, pt. 4. Repeals 31 *H*. VIII, c. 8.

2 and 3 *E*. VI.

c. 1. An act for the uniformity of service and administration of the sacraments throughout the realm.

c. 2. An act touching the true service required in captains and soldiers. ". . . that if any soldier hereafter serving the King in his wars . . . do sell, give away, or willfully purloin or otherwise exchange, alter, or put away any horse, gelding, or mare, or any harness wherewith he shall be set forth, that then every such soldier . . . shall be imprisoned . . .".

c. 2, pt. 10. Proviso for orders at Calais, etc.

c. 18. An act for the attainder of Sir Thomas Seymour. See Howell, *S.T.*, I.

5 and 6 *E*. VI.

c. 1. An act for the uniformity of common prayer and administration of the sacraments.

c. 25. An act for keepers of alehouses to be bound by recognizance.

4 and 5 *P*. and *M*.

c. 2. An act for the having of horse, armour, and weapon. "For the better furniture and defense of this realm, be it enacted by the King and Queen's majesty, with the assent of the Lords spiritual and temporal and the Commons in this present parliament assembled, and by authority of the same, that as much of all and every act and statute, concerning only the keeping or finding of horse, horses or armour, or any of them, heretofore made or provided, and all and every forfeiture and penalty concerning only the same shall be from henceforth utterly void, repealed, and of none effect.

"And be it further enacted by the authority aforesaid, that every nobleman, gentleman, and other temporal person after the rate and proportion hereafter declared, shall have and keep in a readiness such horses, geldings, armour, and other furniture for the wars . . .". Repealed 1 *Jac*. I, c. 25.

1 *Eliz*. I.

c. 1. An act restoring to the crown the ancient jurisdiction over the state ecclesiastical and spiritual, and abolishing all foreign power repugnant to the same.

c. 2. An act for the uniformity of common prayer and divine service in the Church, and the administration of the sacraments.

c. 20. An act of a subsidy of tonnage and poundage.

5 *Eliz*. I.

c. 4. An act touching divers orders for artificers, laborers, servants of husbandry, and apprentices.

13 *Eliz*. I.

c. 1. An act whereby certain offenses be made treason.

c. 10, pt. 2. "And for that long and unreasonable leases made by colleges, dean and chapters, parsons, vicars, and other having spiritual promotions be the chiefest causes of the dilapidations and the decay of all spiritual livings . . .".

c. 12. An act to reform certain disorders touching ministers of the Church.

27 *Eliz*. I.

c. 12, pt. 2. "And be it further enacted . . . that every under-sheriff that is already chosen and appointed for the execution of the said office of under-sheriff for the year or time begun . . . shall within forty days next ensuing the session of this present parliament receive and take the oaths mentioned in this act, before such person or persons as by this act is or are limited and appointed to minister the same . . .".

35 *Eliz*. I.

c. 2. An act against popish recusants. "Be it ordained and enacted . . . that every person above the age of sixteen years, born within any the Queens Majesty's realms or dominions, or made denizen, being a popish recusant . . . shall within forty days next after the end of this session of parliament . . . repair to their place of dwelling. . . and shall not any time after pass or remove above five miles from thence . . .".

1 *Jac.* I.

c. 13. An act for new executions to be sued against any which shall hereafter be delivered out of execution by privilege of parliament. . . .

c. 33. An act of a subsidy of tonnage and poundage.

3 *Jac.* I.

c. 2. An act for the attainder of offenders in the Powder Treason. Hatsell, *Precedents*, IV, 235–236.

c. 4. An act for the better discovering and repressing of popish recusants.

c. 5. An act to prevent dangers which may grow by popish recusants.

c. 5, pt. 6. ". . . that no recusant convict shall . . . practice the common law of this realm as a counselor, clerk, attorney, or solicitor in the same, nor shall practice the civil law . . . nor practice physic, nor exercise or use the trade or art of an apothecary, nor shall be judge, minister, clerk . . . nor shall bear any office or charge as captain, lieutenant, corporal . . . and every person offending herein shall also forfeit for every such offense one hundred pounds . . .".

21 *Jac.* I.

c. 3. An act concerning monopolies and dispensations with penal laws and the forfeiture thereof.

c. 7. An act for repressing of drunkenness.

c. 33. An act for a temporal subsidy.

1 *Car.* I.

c. 6. An act for a temporal subsidy.

Statutes (*Ireland*)

8 *H.* VI.

c. 10. (*Stat. Rolls, Ireland*, II, 31). "It is agreed and established that no lord or any other bring from henceforth hobblers, kernes, or idle men, English rebels, or Irish enemies . . . to be a burden . . . on the King's subjects without their goodwill".

Treatises

Fitzherbert, *Natura Brevium* (1686 ed.).

f. 66 E, Writ *de homine replegiando*.

"In divers cases a man shall not have this writ, although he be taken and detained in prison: as if a man be apprehended for the death of a man, or be taken by the King's command, or if a man be apprehended by the command of the Chief Justice, as it appeareth by the *Register*. But the statute of Westminster I is, that he shall not be replevisable if he be taken by the command of the justices, and doth not say of the Chief Justice.

"And also if a man be taken by the command of the justices of the forest, or if a man be outlawed, or if a man abjure the realm or if a man be an approver [see 7 April, n. 55], or if a man be taken for felony with the manor [i.e., the mainour. See 7 April, n. 56], or those who break the King's prison, or those who are common and known thieves, or those who are appealed by an approver so long as the approvers live, if they be not of good fame, or for burning of houses feloniously, or those who counterfeit the King's money, or the King's seal, or those who are taken by certificate of the Bishop by a writ *de excommunicato capiendo*, or those who are apprehended for treason, or those who are convict by a writ of *redisseisin*, etc. All these persons are not bailable by this common writ *de homine replegiando*".

f. 77 A, Writ *de nativo habendo*.

"The writ *de nativo habendo* lieth for a lord who claimeth the inheritance in any villein when his villein is run from him, and is remaining within any place out of the manor unto which he is regardant, or when he departeth from his lord against the lord's will. And the writ shall be directed unto the sheriff . . .".

Fitzherbert continues, on the same folio, a discussion of *libertate probanda*, an archaic writ that lay for villeins to prove themselves freemen. It was directed to the sheriff that he should take security of them for the proving of their freedom before the justices of Assize, and that in the meantime they should be unmolested. Jacobs, *Law Dict.*

Fortescue, *De Laudibus Legum Anglie* (Chrimes ed., 1942)

chap. 8, p. 23.

"In fact you [a prince] will render judgments better through others [i.e., through justices] than by yourself, for none of the kings of England is seen to give judgment by his own lips, yet all the judgments of the realm are his, though given through others . . .".

chap. 9, p. 25.

"For the king of England is not able to change the laws of his kingdom at pleasure, for he rules his people with a government not only regal but also political".

chap. 34, p. 79.
"The laws of England do not sanction any such maxim (as 'What pleased the prince has the force of law'), since the king of that land rules his people not only regally but also politically, and so he is bound by oath at his coronation to the observance of his law".

p. 81.
". . . it is not a yoke but a liberty to rule a people politically, and the greatest security not only to the people but also to the king himself, and no small alleviation of his care".

chap. 35, p. 81.
". . . you have seen how rich in fruits are the villages and towns of the kingdom of France . . . but so burdened by the men-at-arms, and their horses, of the king of that land, that you could be entertained in scarcely any of them except the great towns. There you learned from the inhabitants that those men, though they might be quartered in one village for a month or two, paid or wished to pay absolutely nothing for the expenses of themselves and their horses, and, what is worse, they compelled the inhabitants of the villages and towns on which they descended to supply them at their own charges with wines, meats, and other things that they required . . .".

chap. 36, p. 87.
"In the realm of England, no one billets himself in another's house against its master's will, unless in public hostelries, where even so he will pay in full for all that he has expended there. . . . .

"Nor can the king there [England], by himself of by his ministers, impose tallages, subsidies, or any other burdens whatever on his subjects, nor change their laws, nor make new ones, without the concession or assent of his whole realm expressed in his parliament".

chap. 37, p. 91.
". . . the power of the king ruling regally is more troublesome in practice, and less

secure for himself and his people, so that it would be undesirable for a prudent king to change a political government for a merely regal one".

Stanford, *Plees del Coron* (1583 ed.).

Lib. 2, chap. 14, f. 65, B.
"Also, by the statute made 1 *H*. 4, c. 14, if one of the lieges of the King is killed by another of the King's lieges in any foreign realm, the wife of the one that is killed is able to have an appeal for this [privately initiated criminal action] in England before the Constable and Marshal". This is the principle expounded in *Y.B.*, 13 *H*. IV, Mich., *pl*. 10, above.

Lib. 2, chap. 18, ff. 72v-73, E.
This section is printed as part of Littleton's speech at the conference, see 7 April, p. 341.

Lib. 2, chap. 18, f. 77v, G.
"And as to releasing a man to bail upon a writ of *de odio et atia* for the death of a man, I do not have to speak of that here, since all such inquiries to be taken by the sheriff, by a writ or commission, are done away with by the statute made 28 *E*. III, c. 9. The words of which can be seen later in this book, chap. 23. But by the said writ it appears that when he should be delivered in bail those who have him in bail must not be fewer than twelve, and Bracton agrees, *Lib*. 2, among the writs for attachments on appeals".

Lib.3, chap. 1, f. 152, A.
"Item, in an indictment against one of the peers of the realm for treason or felony the trial is by his peers, a form of trial that is not grantable in an appeal. Because then this trial by his peers is the proper trial that appertains to a peer of the realm (when he has pleaded not guilty on an indictment of treason or felony), let us look at the order and process of this trial". Stanford continues by analyzing the trial of John Montacute, Third Earl of Salisbury, see *Rot. Parl.*, 1 *H*. IV, no. 1; and the case of attainder brought against Edward Stafford, Duke of Buckingham, Howell, *S.T.*, I, 287-298.